RELOCATING GENDER IN SIKH HISTORY

RELOCATING GENDER IN SIKH HISTORY
Transformation, Meaning and Identity

Doris R. Jakobsh

OXFORD
UNIVERSITY PRESS

OXFORD

UNIVERSITY PRESS

YMCA Library Building, Jai Singh Road, New Delhi 110 001

Oxford University Press is a department of the University of Oxford. It furthers the
University's objective of excellence in research, scholarship, and education
by publishing worldwide in

Oxford   New York

Auckland   Bangkok   Buenos Aires   Cape Town   Chennai
Dar es Salaam   Delhi   Hong Kong   Istanbul   Karachi   Kolkata
Kuala Lumpur   Madrid   Melbourne   Mexico City   Mumbai   Nairobi
São Paulo   Shanghai   Singapore   Taipei   Tokyo   Toronto

Oxford is a registered trade mark of Oxford University Press
in the UK and in certain other countries

Published in India
By Oxford University Press, New Delhi

© Oxford University Press, 2003

ISBN 019 566 3152

Typeset in Berkeley 10.6/12
By Comprint, New Delhi 110 029
Printed at Rajshree Photolithographers, Delhi 110 032
Published by Manzar Khan, Oxford University Press
YMCA Library Building, Jai Singh Road, New Delhi 110 001

76805

for

Kaira, Jessen,
and Paul

Contents

ACKNOWLEDGEMENTS

This work has come to fruition as a result of the vision, support and guidance of a great number of people. First, Harjot Oberoi, my doctoral supervisor at the University of British Columbia; for his rigorous analytical skills and direction I owe enduring gratitude. His warm support of my work, despite numerous interruptions, was uncompromising. Hew McLeod's meticulous scholarship, abiding assistance, and generous spirit have been inspirational. Thanks also to Gerald Barrier for his interest and comments along the way. I owe a great deal to Nikki-Guninder Kaur Singh, whose work whetted my interest in gender in Sikh Studies. I was given numerous scholarships at the University of British Columbia for which I am grateful, particularly to Asa Johal who continues to contribute so generously to students of Sikhism. Thanks to Mandakranta Bose at UBC for her support during my doctoral studies. I spent a year in India, through the support of the Shastri Indo-Canadian Institute. This book would not have been written had I not been enabled to carry out extensive research in Punjab. The administration at Punjabi University in Patiala graciously provided for my family's stay; I am especially indebted to Mohal Singh Johal, former Secretary to the Vice Chancellor, for his able assistance and humour. Library facilities and archives were made widely available to me to conduct research at the university. My thanks to the members of the departments of religious studies and linguistics at Punjabi University who took an interest in my work and furthered it considerably. I was most fortunate to be able to spend time with Harbans Singh, who remained throughout his illness the most refined of individuals. To Susan Hodges-Bryant for her editorial skills and constant affirmation, my gratitude; to Darrol Bryant I owe thanks for years of moral support and mentoring. To Jim Anderson, my thanks for the hours of proofreading efforts. To

Evelyn Kober, Patricia Willms, Allison Rennie, Patti Anderson, Nancy Dykstra the sisterhood at large and countless others, you know who you are, many thanks for your enduring embrace. I am grateful to Sylvia Roorda and my late father-in-law John Roorda for their open hearts. To my parents, Sonja and Josef Jakobsh, who have loved unconditionally and given ever generously—thank you. I am thankful to my children, Jessen and Kaira, who have graced me with their love and wisdom. Lastly, my enormous debt and gratitude goes to my rock and partner, Paul Roorda, who has provided loving support and never-ending faith in me. Without his generous spirit this book could never have been birthed.

Introduction

The Sikh tradition traces its origins to fifteenth-century Punjab in North India, the birthplace of Guru Nanak, born in 1469 CE. Guru Nanak and the subsequent nine Sikh gurus were visionaries—their message of liberation extended to all, regardless of caste, religion, and gender. During the guru period, the Sikh community expanded and its traditions developed according to both the community's needs and the characters of these ten gurus. While the earlier gurus preached a radical message of interior devotion to the divine that opposed all exterior manifestations of religiosity, Guru Gobind Singh, the tenth and last guru, envisioned a novel Sikh ideal with the inauguration of the Khalsa brotherhood. He transformed the Sikh *panth* (community) into a military brotherhood; the new ideal was now that of the warrior-saint, complete with external military signifiers. After the death of the tenth guru in 1708, the fledgling Sikh community witnessed the initial stages of the dissolution of the Mughal Empire, but not before it had experienced the repressive tactics of the later Mughals, particularly Abdus Samad Khan and his successors. Many Sikhs organized themselves into roving bands of guerillas, which by the mid-eighteenth century consolidated into Sikh *misls*—independent Sikh armies that owed their allegiance to their individual commanders. Each of these chieftains controlled specific regions of Punjab. While these misls frequently fought among themselves for land and power, on occasion they united for particular purposes; as a united front they were known as Dal Khalsa, the army of the Khalsa. But for the most part, these independent misls fought for their own vested interests. It was only with the ascendancy of Ranjit Singh, who by 1801 had brought most misls under his control, that the most notable period of Sikh rule was born. However, the kingdom of Maharajah Ranjit Singh was short-lived; by 1849 Punjab was annexed by the British, under

whose control it stayed until the Independence of India in 1947.
The colonial milieu following the annexation of Punjab is the major
focus of this study.

This volume is based on a theoretical analysis of gender construction as a variable in social organization. Gender, according to
Joan Wallach Scott (1988), is an ongoing, fluid process whereby
sexual difference acquires a socially or culturally constructed meaning.
A historical focus on gender thus goes far beyond the mere
addition of women to the pre-existing male-dominated historical
narrative—it fundamentally changes one's understanding of history.
Yet, gender history is a 'hidden' history. Particularly with regard to
Sikh tradition, historiography has by and large interrogated its
development only through the lenses of class, caste, and religion.
Sikh history in the light of the process of defining gender has been
ignored.

Gender construction as a theoretical framework is here united
with an examination of two critical phases of Sikh history. These
two pivotal historical periods were important moments in terms
of Sikh identity formation, both political and religious. The first
period examined is the guru period, tracing the theological and
ritual foundation for gender constructs during this early phase of
the development of the Sikh tradition. The time following the
annexation of Punjab by the British East India Company and the
consequent Singh Sabha reform movement, birthed under the
watchful eye of the British Raj, is the second and dominant focus
of this study. The Singh Sabha reformers were the product of the
British education system; their educational advancement allowed
them to move into positions of leadership and power, and inaugurated a professional middle class in the social hierarchy among the
Sikhs.

Within this milieu, this study focuses on gender constructs
developed during the Victorian era in Britain—constructs that
informed and moulded the British administration in Punjab. It
analyses what I have called the 'politics of similarity and difference',
based both on gender ideals and religious identity formations
between the British, the Sikhs, and the Bengalis, the last having
come under British control in the eighteenth century. The process
of active gender construction through Singh Sabha educational and
religious initiatives was based on newly articulated Sikh ideals
shaped by Victorian gender ideals, as well as a 'purified' adaptation

of Sikh ideology. The Sikh tradition was increasingly presented as having undergone a thorough process of deterioration as a result of unfaithful adherence to the pristine vision of the Sikh gurus, particularly with regard to gender ideals. The onslaught of 'un-Sikh' elements on the Sikhs was primarily seen as the result of the uneducated, uncouth condition of the Sikh masses, which were unable to discern Sikh truths from the degenerate and constantly encroaching Hindu tradition. It was thus that the reformers began demarcating and redefining a pure, uncontaminated understanding of Sikh history and religion, the latter with its myriad manifestations. This study will examine this purification process under the aegis of the Singh Sabha reform movement from the perspective of gender, focusing on the literary, political, social, and religious institutions that structured this process.

It is important to acknowledge the participation of the new Sikh elite in the manifold winds of societal change whirling about the wider Indian subcontinent during the nineteenth and twentieth centuries. The distinct minority status of the Sikhs vis-à-vis other religious communities in Punjab is of particular importance in this discussion of gender construction. The tendency to present the unparalleled position of Sikh women and Sikh men as a feature of their distinctiveness from other groups became a major aspect of this process. It was fraught with an urgency to highlight, rewrite, and in some cases create interpretations of Sikh history that were conducive to the constructs of gender amiable to the reformist world view. However, dissensions among Sikh reformers were also myriad, lending themselves to variant and often opposing understandings of the exact manifestations of these constructions. The varied factions among the Sikhs, along with numerous other reform movements in North India, were intensely vying for prestige and power in the newly developing political arena under the Raj. Reform movements in the colonial period were pivotal to the discourse surrounding the power dynamics of the period. These dynamics will also be examined through the lens of gender construction.

Chapter One introduces four principles guiding contemporary or near-contemporary writings on women and the feminine in general in Sikhism. The principles of silence, negation, accommodation, and idealization have formed the general framework within which this discourse has taken place. The pitfalls inherent in each approach are outlined and more encompassing approaches are advocated. In line with Joan Wallach Scott's insistence that a study of women must also include an analysis of the formation of the male gender, this study proposes a move beyond the unearthing of 'herstory', that is, a descriptive approach to women's history, to a wider, more encompassing understanding of gender.

Chapter Two focuses on the pivotal guru period, from the fifteenth to the early eighteenth century, to come to an understanding of gender construction within this time frame. What were the ideals of gender for the Sikh gurus? How were these ideals furthered? Sikh scripture, the *Adi Granth*, and hagiographic sources known as *janam-sakhies* are analysed from a gender perspective to come to an understanding of the discourse surrounding gender during this initial phase of the formation of Sikh tradition. The aim of this chapter is to come to an understanding of gender themes within the earliest sources, both historical and scriptural. As a disclaimer, let me point out that I am not a scripture scholar. I have heavily relied on the contributions of scripture scholars from the discipline of Sikh studies.

With a theological framework in place, Chapter Three contextualizes British ideals of religion, race, and gender in India, particularly focusing on the shift in attitude from the earliest Orientalists to the later Anglicist policy, constructed by both the Evangelical revival in Britain as well as utilitarianism in the nineteenth century. It examines the role of gender and religious identities as perceived by the colonizers and the corresponding responses of the indigenous Sikh elites that led to the Singh Sabha reform endeavour of the nineteenth and early twentieth centuries.

Chapter Four moves beyond Victorian conceptions of religion and gender to examines the antecedents to the Singh Sabha reform movement as well the movement's consequent influences within the colonial context in Punjab. These included movements that originated from within the fringes of the Sikh tradition in the nineteenth century, particularly Sikh sects such as the Namdharis and Nirankaris, associations such as the Amritsar Dharm Sabha, which was comprised of both Hindu and Sikh members intent on restructuring and improving the social order in the city of Amritsar, the Brahmo Samaj movement, and the Arya Samaj, initiated in 1877, soon after the inauguration of the Singh Sabha movement in 1873. These movements formed the backdrop to the ideals and objectives of the fledgling Singh Sabha movement, the foremost Sikh association, whose membership was by and large restricted to the educated middle class.

Chapter Five investigates the educational enterprise of the Singh Sabha reformers. The Sikh literati expounded on their ideals of education through the various mediums at their disposal; tracts and newspapers were especially utilized to spread their message. While the education-wary peasant populace had slowly acknowledged the need for the education of boys, they largely rejected female literacy programmes. It was thus towards the female population that the Singh Sabha reformers directed their attention. Education came to be intricately entwined with the upliftment of women and the ensuing understanding of Sikh nation-building. The form, content, and end of female education were not initially clear. Increasingly, however, it became apparent that arrangements were necessary to protect Sikh women from the educational advances of the Arya Samaj movement, as well as from the Christian missionaries. The 'helpmate' model, adopted from the Victorian world view but 'Sikhized' by the Singh Sabha, and the notion of service, became the two-pronged ideal of Sikh educational initiatives for women.

The sixth chapter analyses the displacement and reorganization of women's popular traditions by reformers in their efforts to promote a less 'Hinduized' female Sikh identity. This included rituals specific to women, women's identity markers, and rites pertaining to notions of sacred space and time. In particular, efforts were made to define that which represented 'Sikh' and that which constituted 'un-Sikh', or corrupted, tradition.

Chapter Seven focuses on the extension and feminization of religious identity markers and rituals heretofore specific to male Sikhs, particularly those of the Khalsa brotherhood. The justification for this expansion of Sikh identity to women can best be understood as a further attempt to conclusively separate Sikh females from their Hindu and Muslim counterparts. Transformed from an imprecise indicator of Sikh identity for women, the Khalsa rite of initiation came to be a strictly prescribed injunction. Similarly, naming injunctions that for males had long been associated with the Khalsa were broadened to include female appellations as well. Certainly, Singh Sabha initiatives intent on injecting new definitions to previously indistinct cultural practices, and even formulating ritual spaces for women where they had earlier not existed, were immensely successful. Singh Sabha leaders laboured intensely to codify their visions of reform; the current Sikh code of conduct known as the *Sikh Reht Maryada* is reflective of these efforts.

Chapter Eight concludes the volume with an examination of women's agency, both from within and outside of the Sikh reform movement. Significantly, many of these female voices stemmed precisely from the heterogeneous milieu that the Singh Sabha was attempting to purify and homogenize. While the increasingly authoritative reforms led by Sikh males in many cases diminished choices for women, some women did adopt permissible ways and means of acting within the newly organized structures put in place by the reformers; the discourse of reform provided women certain, though limited, opportunities to become active agents in the movement. Moreover, the stress on women's conceptual equality with men propounded by the Tat Khalsa reformers, provided Sikh women the leverage to claim an extension of their ritual space; in essence, doors were opened for women to become far more active in the religious establishment than ever before.

This volume is a revised version of my doctoral dissertation. As I note in Chapter One, there is a dearth of writing on women in Sikhism, but an even greater paucity of the analysis of gender within Sikh studies. My hope is ultimately that this volume will stimulate further scrutiny of and engagement with the role of gender in Sikh history.

ONE

The Construction of Women in Sikh History and Religion—Attitudes and Assumptions
*An Overview of Secondary Sources**

The status of women was not an issue in Sikhism. Equality was implicit.... Women are considered as an integral part of society who must not be excluded by any ritual or doctrinal consideration. Since rituals tend to be exclusive, they cannot be made part of a true faith. In other words, the position of women could be a touchstone for the genuineness of a faith.

(Suri 1989:112)

To know whether to take speakers seriously is difficult in a society that blurs the boundary between serious and strategic communication. When are promises or statements of intent, for instance, merely the casual talk of everyday life or strategic maneuvers in compromising situations rather than acts of serious communication?

(Fenn 1982:113)

The study of Sikh history from a feminist perspective has not been given a great deal of attention in Sikh studies. While Sikh apologetics repeatedly insist that women and men are inherently equal in the Sikh world view, in reality, historical writings contain virtually nothing about women, apart from minimal asides referring to the occasional exceptional woman who has been deemed worthy enough to have made the pages of history. These exceptional women are then typically held up as the standard by which to measure the gender-egalitarian ethos of the Sikh tradition. Clarence McMullen notes that in speaking of the religious

---

* An earlier version of this chapter was published as 'The Construction of Gender in History and Religion: The Sikh Case', in Bose 2000.

beliefs and practices of the Sikhs, that it is necessary to make a distinction between what he labels normative and what he calls operative beliefs (1989:5).

Normative beliefs and practices are those which are officially stated and prescribed or proscribed by a recognized religious authority, which can be a person, organization, or an official statement. Operative beliefs and practices, on the other hand, are those actually held by people.

While McMullen uses these distinctions in his study of the contemporary beliefs and practices of Sikhs in rural Punjab, they are also useful in analysing the role and status of women from the larger theoretical perspective of history. With regard to the inherent egalitarianism between Sikh men and women, one writer notes that the 'Sikh woman has enjoyed superior status compared with her counterparts in other communities. She has earned this by showing the ability to stand by the side of her husband in difficult times' (Kaur-Singh 1994: 152). Yet if women and men are inherently equal in Sikh tradition in terms of roles and status, why are they not given similar representation in the pages of Sikh history? It is a question that can perhaps best be explained in the light of McMullen's analysis of differentiation. Namely, what is officially touted as normative with regard to gender in history is not necessarily the same as the actual and operative aspects of the same history. Further, Harjot Oberoi (1994: 30–31) has posited that the principles of silence and negation are paramount in addressing issues that could be conceived as ambiguous within the tradition. This chapter addresses these principles of silence and negation along with those of accommodation and idealization, specifically with regard to secondary sources of Sikh history.

THE PRINCIPLE OF SILENCE

The guiding principle in Sikh history with regard to women is silence. Given the traditional assumption that significant history pertains only to the realms of politics and economics, women's history has generally been neglected. The lack of tangible evidence with regard to women's participation in the businesses of economics, war, and politics has meant that they have been viewed as having had nothing to offer in the production of historical knowledge. It must also be underscored that since women have not generally been historians or recorded their own history, historical accounts have been presented only through the viewpoint of the male gender. What was and is important to men thus becomes the focus of historical analysis. Needless to say, the overwhelming impression one receives from Sikh historiography is that Sikh women do not *have* a history. From the silences surrounding women, their experiences and lives can only be perceived as inconsequential. Yet clearly, in addition to history about 'mankind' there also exists *herstory*. By and large, however, many aspects of herstory have been wiped out so that even its most basic elements are difficult to construct.

According to some feminist historians, history has less to do with facts than with historians' perceptions of history. While historical writers have operated on the principle of objectivity—pursuing facts, stringing bits of information together, and thus presenting objective 'history', a new wave of scholarly analysis, including feminist theory, argues that the process is not nearly as objective as was once believed. There has been a gradual recognition that 'the writing of history [is] a mental activity in its own right, somewhere between natural science and the writing of fiction' (Bosch 1987: 48). The historian thus has an active, creative role in this process. The specific questions asked are of the essence. Through the issues addressed, one chooses to attend to certain aspects of history; presumably, what is presented is in the writer's estimation more important than what is left out. When looking to Sikh women's history, we are told as much about the values of the chroniclers of that history as about the actual events surrounding the women themselves. Consequently, one is faced with the painstaking task of piecing together aspects of historiography which have been either disregarded, or interpreted to fit into the dominant male world view of the time. Ultimately then, the history of the Sikh population, namely, male history, is a distorted one and only half of the story. Foremost to the study of women in Sikh history is the principle of stony silence, a mechanism used to deal with the discrepancies between Sikh ideology as egalitarian and women's exclusion from the process of making and recording history.

THE PRINCIPLE OF NEGATION

The second principle is that of negation. Harjot Oberoi points out how heterogeneous elements in Sikh history, those labelled deviant, marginal, threatening, or unimportant, are negated in order to 'generate homogeneity and represent the Sikhs as a collectivity which shared the same values and movements' (Oberoi 1994: 34). The principle of negation is particularly useful in exploring the ways in which ambiguous aspects of women's history have been presented. An obvious example of the principle of negation in full force is a volume written by M.K. Gill, *The Role and Status of Women in Sikhism*. Gill focuses primarily on what she presents as the institution of guru *mahals*, the wives of the gurus. While studying each mahal within the tradition in terms of her contributions, she also addresses the fact that these women are simply not known within or outside of the tradition. Gill maintains that the guru mahals were integral to the very development of the fledgling Sikh movement but she does not delve into the indifference of Sikh historians to the mahals. For Gill (1995: 4–5), 'it is the attitude of the Gurus towards women which becomes more important than the availability of material regarding the Guru Mahals.' She insists that the gurus unequivocally raised the status of women, despite the fact that

Guru histories are, by and large, silent about the wives of the gurus. From Guru Nanak to Guru Gobind Singh the wives have been treated as part of the historical background, not as individual in themselves.... It is the silence of respect that is accorded to womanhood in the Punjabi culture and ethos. It helps surround her with an invisible cloak of dignity.... The silence that surrounds the Guru's family is an intrinsic feature of Sikh tradition (ibid.: 52–3).

Negating the obvious, namely that women, *even* the guru mahals, have not been viewed as consequential in the history of the Sikh tradition, Gill maintains that the silence surrounding the mahals is indicative of the respect accorded to women in Sikhism. She notes that after the death of the tenth guru, Guru Gobind Singh, it was Mata Sundri, one of his three wives, who conducted the political and spiritual leadership of the Khalsa for thirty-nine or forty years. Gill acknowledges that, ironically, though Mata Sundri led the panth longer than any of the nine Gurus subsequent to Guru Nanak, the founder of the Sikh tradition, and through one of its more difficult and divisive periods, there is surprisingly little known of her leadership.[1] She notes, however, that history 'is silent on this point, but the silence of history is merely a reflection of her personality' (ibid.: 59). Again, Gill deftly avoids any serious critique or analysis of the paucity of historical knowledge about women in the Sikh panth. Instead, she is content with pithy statements about the egalitarian nature of Sikhism and women's proper attitudes (silence) within their historical tradition.

Though dealing more specifically with scriptural exegesis rather than with women in history, Nikki-Guninder Kaur Singh's contributions also tend to fit into the paradigm of negation. She notes that breaking 'all patriarchal idols and icons, the Sikh sacred literature celebrates the feminine aspect of the Transcendent and poetically affirms the various associations and images that are born from her' (Singh, N.K. 1993: 243–4). Focusing on the feminine grammatical forms and images within Sikh scripture, Singh insists that it is the feminine in its myriad forms that is predominant over the male. Yet, the grammatically feminine form of the sacred word is very much in line with Vedic sacred speech, deified as the goddess *Vac*. What is not clear is whether the male gurus in fact understood their enunciation to be feminine, or whether the representation of sacred speech in the feminine form was simply indicative of their social, cultural, and religious surroundings. To move from a grammatically feminine form of speech to the theological underpinnings of the gurus' egalitarian ethos is conceivably more a *reading into* the term *bani* (voice) than a reflection of the actual intent of the gurus. Further, Singh's proposal that the feminine is prevalent over the male is contestable, since 'the Ultimate' in Sikh scripture was most often conceived in masculine terms, as *Akal Purakh, Karta Purakh*.

Singh continues that with regard to female imagery within the Granth, 'No negative associations belittle her' (ibid.: 4). Yet, numerous passages in the scripture associate woman with *maya*, that which is sensual as opposed to spiritual:

> Attachment to progeny, wife is poison
> None of these at the end is of any avail. (*Adi Granth*, p. 41)[2]

> Maya attachment is like a loose woman,
> A bad woman, given to casting spells. (*AG*, p. 796)

Further, women are exalted when obedient and subservient as wives to their divine husbands and men are ridiculed when they are not dominant:

> Men obedient to their womenfolk
> Are impure, filthy, stupid,
> Man lustful, impure, their womenfolk counsel follow. (*AG*, p. 304)

While the subject of women in the guru tradition and the feminine within Sikh scripture will be dealt with more extensively later, suffice it now to say that Singh's assertions fit neatly into the parameters of the principle of negation outlined earlier.[3]

The Principle of Accommodation

Another principle that was particularly utilized by the Singh Sabha reformers in the late nineteenth century is that of accommodation. And here a comparison of the effects of French colonialism in Muslim Algeria with the Singh Sabha reformers and British colonizer is particularly helpful. Kay Boals notes that a reformist consciousness developed among educated Muslim males after the colonization of Algeria. Attempting to accommodate the valuable aspects of the dominant colonial culture and ground them in the tradition of Islam, a process of reinterpretation and reform vis-à-vis the religion and culture of both Islam and Algeria came into being.

This process involves a reinterpretation of that tradition to read back into its past the genesis of ideas which in fact have been absorbed from the dominant culture.... The reformists, however, must show that what they advocate has long been part of their own culture and is firmly rooted there, when in fact that is usually not the case. It is not hard to see that in such a dilemma one's desire to succeed would promote easy distortion of the tradition, distortion which is probably both conscious and unconscious (Boals 1976: 198–9).

Further, the reformers were typically educated in Islamic law, while at the same time highly exposed to Western influences. According to Boals, this type of education was characteristically open only to men. Thus, men were at the forefront of reform, including changes in attitudes to gender relations. Believing that there was implicit value in tradition, they, however, strove to purify and transform it, believing that it needed reinterpretation for modern life. These reformers were deeply concerned with male-female relations, 'not directly in themselves, but rather as they reflect the Koranic prescriptions (rightly interpreted and purified) for relationships between the sexes' (ibid.: 203).

Turning to the time and context of the Singh Sabhas in late nineteenth-century Sikh history, one is faced with a similar scenario. These new elites, having imbibed a liberal Western education, decried the undesirable aspects of the Sikh tradition; however, they were unwilling to reject that tradition outright. They tended to walk the shaky line of accommodation within the two, often opposing, world views. Ultimately, their focus was also the reformation and reinterpretation of the Sikh tradition, made possible by their ascendancy into positions of power and prestige. Oberoi maintains that it was the development of print culture in Punjab, along with their Western education, that gave the Sabha reformers the necessary tools to reinterpret the Sikh tradition. Their world view, adopted from the European enlightenment, necessitated the etching out of 'a novel cultural map for Punjab that would define their aspirations and reflect the changed environment in the province' (Oberoi 1994: 277).

As in Algeria, the role and status of women was an important platform upon which the Singh Sabhas preached their reforms. There were a number of reasons for this focus. Christian missionaries had begun an active campaign to reach both the lowest castes of society and women, both groups relegated to the bottom of the Sikh and Hindu societal hierarchies. They began going into homes, attracting women from within the very bastions of protection, in attempts to convert the populace to Christianity (Kapur 1986: 15). Alarmed by these conversions, the reformers hastened to safeguard Sikh tradition from the menacing activities of the missionaries. The emancipation of women, therefore, particularly through education, became a central issue for the Singh Sabha reformers. So too did the development of female role models in literature. The prolific writer Bhai Vir Singh wrote numerous novels with female figures in central roles. His most famous, *Sundri,* depicts a young woman who was true to the faith, devout and pure, active in battle, and elevated at times to the status of a goddess. While the story was designed to advance the cause of Sikh women, it also attempted to glorify the status of Sikh women as compared to their Hindu

and Muslim counterparts. And herein we find an important difference between the Sikh reformers and the Algerian reformers, whose
main goal had been merely to accommodate positive aspects of
colonial culture through reinterpreting those attitudes into their
own tradition. While the Sikh reformers concurred with this aim,
they had another equally important objective—namely, to show
the complete separation of Sikhism from the dominant Hindu
tradition (Nabha 1914). Thus, we have Sundri pleading with her
fellow Sikhs:

I entreat you to regard your women as equal partners and never ill-treat
them with harshness and cruelty.... In the Hindu Shastras.... the woman
is treated as Shudra—an outcast. All the Gurus have praised and commended
women. In Guru Granth Sahib, woman has been eulogized and she has
been given equal right of worship and recitation of the Holy Name (Singh,
B.V. 1988: 114).

To show this positive regard for women as integral to Sikhism,
in *contrast* to the oppressive Hindu religion and *similar* to the claims
of the Christian missionaries/colonizers, was of utmost importance
for the Singh Sabha reformers. Further, particularly in *Sundri*, the
context was that of the oppressive Muslim regime which was
directly responsible for the plight of the valiant Sikhs. Much of the
revitalization efforts must be seen in the light of anti-Hindu, anti-
Muslim, anti-Christian sentiments. The focus of this effort was Sikh
scripture, for only thus could it be proven that the elevated position
of women was a long-standing tradition within Sikhism. Given Guru
Nanak's absorption in the Sant milieu of the fifteenth century, there
was indeed evidence to support the reformers' claims. The Sant
and the larger Bhakti milieu were in essence counter traditions to
the status quo, and by and large espoused egalitarian social values
(Schomer 1987: 8). It was within this atmosphere that Guru Nanak's
vision and message was born. Thus, armed with hymns supporting
their claims, the reformers insisted that what they were advocating was very much in line with the original designs of the Sikh
gurus. Further, they increasingly presented the degradation of the
Sikh tradition as a direct result of the derogatory influence of Hinduism, upon which the blame for all ills within Sikh society was
heaped.
    It is the principle of accommodation that has characterized al-
most all subsequent engagement with regard to women and the

Sikh tradition. Passages from the Granth are interpreted to show positive regard for women and are then quoted and requoted, as are a few choice anecdotes from the lives of the gurus with regard to the condemnation of *sati*, pollution, *purdah*, and female infanticide. This interpretation of Sikh history can perhaps best be captured by Eric Hobsbawm's understanding of 'invented tradition'. He notes that 'insofar as there is such reference to a historic past, the peculiarity of "invented" traditions is that the continuity with it is largely fictitious. In short, they are responses to novel situations which take the form of reference to old situations...' (Hobsbawm 1983: 2). In the case of the Sikh reformers, historical and theological inventions with regard to the status of women must invariably be understood as innovative responses to the rapidly changing cultural and socio-economic world within which they had achieved hegemony.

Nikki-Guninder Kaur Singh is also very much in line with this principle of accommodation in her analysis of the goddess Durga in the writings of Guru Gobind Singh. She critiques the way many Sikh historians and writers have attempted to distance the guru from passages celebrating Durga, striving to show that they were not actually written by Gobind Singh but by Hindu elements within his entourage. She describes this distancing as a 'not fully conscious fear of "female power"' (Singh, N.K. 1993: 123). Instead she insists that Guru Gobind Singh's incorporation of the deity is indicative of the positive Sikh attitude towards the feminine, though these instances cannot be understood as goddess worship. Accentuating the continuity of the gurus within the Sikh tradition, Singh attempts to accommodate the writings of the tenth guru and the clear rejection by the earlier gurus of the goddess within Sikh sacred scripture, particularly with regard to the following verse:

> Whoever worships the Great Mother
> Shall though man, be incarnate as woman (*AG*, p. 874)

She maintains that Durga's great literary merit was upheld by Guru Gobind Singh who used the symbolism to 'renovate and regenerate an effete society' (ibid.: 131). Contrary to being a devotee of the great goddess, Guru Gobind Singh is posited as an insightful artist. Yet one must wonder where literary licence ends and veneration begins. In what appears to be an uncompromising tribute to Durga, the *Dasam Granth* states:

> The sovereign deity on earth
> Enwrapped in all the regal pomp
> To you be the victory,
> O you of mighty arms

(*Dasam Granth*, Akal Ustati: 44).

Historical research has indicated that remnants of the feminine, the goddess, are present in all traditions that are indubitably mono-theistic and androcentric. According to Rita Gross (1994: 355), the question that needs to be answered is, 'Why did monotheism attempt to get rid of the goddess? Could it have anything to do with androcentrism and patriarchy? Feminist studies of the Ancient Near East make it overwhelmingly obvious that such is the case.' In the Durga mythology of the *Dasam Granth*, Sikhs have the goddess in their midst. To draw an unrealistically rigid line between the recognition of Durga's literary merit and actual homage to the goddess is to miss an opportunity to explore how and why a system did away with the feminine which was so obviously and critically integrated into early Sikh society. Indeed, Singh's selective endorsement of the writings of Guru Gobind Singh adheres well to the principle of accommodation. She attempts to reinterpret aspects of the female goddess tradition to reflect its emancipatory qualities for women, while not fully exploring the implications of the Durga mythology for the Sikh tradition at large.

THE PRINCIPLE OF IDEALIZATION

The fourth principle utilized in Sikh history with regard to women is that of idealization. Similar to the principle of accommodation, idealization is an extension of it, with important differences. Namely, while the positive strains of scripture are upheld as normative and of ultimate authority, the dominant need is not so much to *reform* tradition as to *idealize* aspects of history and scripture as they pertain to women. Glorified examples are presented of Sikh women who lived exceptional lives, mainly as warrior figures, as women whose illustrious deeds are the result of the 'transformation... of Guru Nanak's philosophy in action that preaches equality among the human beings irrespective of caste, creed, or sex.'[4] (G. Singh, 1988: 43) Similarly, Gill (1995: 51–2) in her treatment of guru mahals notes with regard to a particular gurdwara bearing Mata Sundri's name:

[It] is not merely a historical monument.... It is rather, a cherished haven of refuge where the devotee finds inner peace and his sense of emptiness is washed away.... Mata Sundri has a place among the few who are immortal, ever living. For hundreds of people today it is a matter of a daily relationship with her memory.

Given that Gill remonstrates that few Sikhs are knowledgeable even about the *basic* facts of Mata Sundri's life, this effort to uplift the name and contributions of Mata Sundri must be understood in the light of the principle of idealization.

Rita Gross also maintains that in traditional historical accounts, when women *are* mentioned in the annals of history, it is only because they deviate from the norm. In other words, exceptional women are uplifted when they play a part in what is considered to be normative history.

[A]ndrocentric thinking deals with them [exceptional women] only as objects exterior to humankind, needing to be explained and fitted in somewhere, having the same epistemological and ontological status as trees, unicorns, deities, and other objects that must be discussed to make experience intelligible (Gross 1994: 333).

In the paradigms representing Sikh women's history, specifically the principle of idealization, but accommodation as well, unicorns are presented as normative and indicative of the romanticizing tendencies of the Singh Sabhas and those who unquestioningly follow in their footsteps. Further, the occasional woman of note was generally situated in the uppermost echelons of society. As wives and sisters of rajahs (kings), or of gurus for that matter, they certainly did not lead lives that were very much akin to those of their 'common' contemporaries. In many ways then, these elite few conjure up false images of the roles and status of women in Sikh society. Returning once again to McMullen's observations, there is a vast divide between that which is normative and that which is operative in traditional Sikh history as it pertains to women.

Of the examples given here, only Nikki Singh situates herself squarely within Western feminist theological traditions. And the central challenge of feminists in religious studies, as in other fields, is the delineation and critique of androcentrism. Singh has not undertake such a critique. She has not delved into the ambiguous aspects within the tradition in relation to scripture. As pointed out earlier, while there *are* women-affirming tendencies within the *Adi Granth*, there are also those which support the subordination of women. The feminist theologians that Nikki Singh pays tribute to in her volume insist that to expose androcentrism within religious traditions includes a move beyond sheer affirmation, moving, in essence, *beyond* the unearthing of female principles. It involves, ultimately, invoking a 'hermeneutic of suspicion', following the model of Paul Ricoeur. For Ricoeur, this involves a deciphering process, one grounded in a 'struggling against masks' that starts from an original position of negation, but eventually moves forward in the quest of a new affirmation (Reagan and Stewart 1978: 217). There is a profound need for the hermeneutic of suspicion within the study of religion, for there is a complex interplay between religion and social change. Institutionalized religion has been at the forefront of conserving and stabilizing societal values and world views, and transplanting them from generation to generation (Falk 1985: xv). It is only through a process of unmasking the androcentric presumptions of writers and their writings, including sacred scripture, only through a suspicious reading entailing a thorough evaluation of the *inherent* sexist attitudes and practices within religious and historical works, that one is enabled to understand the sources and symbols within the tradition which sustain the subordination of women throughout history.

Conclusion: Moving beyond Description

Much of what has been presented as the construction of women within Sikh history and religion fits largely into what feminist historians have characterized as the descriptive, or her-story approach to the history of women. This first wave of feminist history, namely, the resurrection of lost women, as well as a reassessment of activities which were traditionally deemed as unworthy of fulfilling the requirements of important or 'real' history, have been critical aspects of the rewriting of history. Yet, while her-story is fundamental to addressing the paucity of historical knowledge about women, it does not confront the issue of *how* the hierarchy of male/female, dominant/subordinate is constructed and legitimated throughout history. As historian Joan Wallach Scott insists, a more radical feminist epistemology is necessary in the study of history. She advocates a post-structuralist approach, one that can address epistemology and the status of knowledge and can link knowledge and power.

The emphasis on 'how' suggests a study of processes, not of origins, of multiple rather than single causes, of rhetoric rather than ideology or consciousness. It does not abandon attention to structures and institutions, but it does insist that we need to understand what these organizations mean in order to understand how they work (Scott 1988: 4).

In particular, Michel Foucault's analysis of the domain of the private, and by implication, the feminine, is based on an understanding of power as dispersed constellations of unequal relationships discursively constituted in social 'fields of force'. His perspective is particularly useful in coming to an understanding of how unequal relations are created and sustained (Foucault 1980: 97–8). Advocating a different perspective, Pierre Bourdieu emphasizes another source of unequal relations that he defines as 'symbolic relations of power', which 'tend to reproduce and to reinforce the power relations that constitute the structure of social space' (1989: 21). These go beyond, though they are not exclusive of, economic and political spheres, to include power located within language, religion, education, art, and ideology—areas where women's participation is more readily accessible (Göçek and Balaghi 1994: 8–9).

Ultimately, it is imperative that historical research move beyond descriptions of Sikh history as it pertains exclusively to women. Historical records have traditionally been written from within the patriarchal framework; 'man' is normative, the object of study—his habits, his contributions, his world view. 'Woman' is generally the contradiction, the outsider, the passive onlooker in the process of history. In attempting to construct a truer, more encompassing perspective of history, one inclusive of both female and male realities, feminist historians have necessarily rewritten and reinterpreted many events covered in the annals of history from the perspective of women. This process has also involved a transformation of the notions of time and space to include not only those within which women act, but also domains normatively considered exclusively 'male space', to include a new, wider range of activity. It has called for a rethinking of historiography as a whole, often necessitating a pushing against the well-established boundaries of academic/scholarly disciplines. This process has been characterized by Nita Kumar (1994: 6) as finding the 'fault-lines' in the larger patriarchal structures; the positioning of a spotlight on areas where inconsistencies or surface cleavages in gender activity occur. While highlighting inconsistencies is a necessary aspect of this study on gender in Sikh history, another equally important aspect necessitates moving beyond the unveiling of women's activity in history to understanding *how* gender is actually constructed throughout historical time, thus challenging views of gender identity as 'natural' and primordial. Scott (1988: 25) for instance, advocates that gender as constructed for *both* women and men has significant consequences.

The term 'gender' suggests that relations between the sexes are a primary aspect of social organization (rather than following from, say, economic or demographic pressures); that the terms of male and female identities are in large part culturally determined (not produced by individuals or collectivities entirely on their own); and that differences between the sexes constitute and are constituted by hierarchical social structures.[5]

This idea then requires the understanding that *each* aspect of reality is gendered and that the historical process invites a deliberate investigation into the ways and means of gender construction.

In speaking specifically about Sikh history, what is the process whereby the category of woman and the category of man are constructed? How have these categories changed over time? Were there specific instances, moments in history, when this construction process assumed a vital importance to the self-understanding of the developing Sikh community? This study attempts to pursue questions regarding the correlation between historical knowledge and gender relations on a broad scale, particularly during the era of colonization when the Singh Sabha movement came to the fore. While the main focus is on the construction of gender in the nineteenth and early twentieth century, a more substantial understanding of those events also necessitates an overview of gender formation during the initial stages of Sikh development, namely, the early and later guru periods. What were the ideals of gender for the Sikh gurus? How were these ideals constructed? Further, what role did gender constructs play in the milieu of colonialism, both on the part of the colonizers and in the corresponding responses of the indigenous elites leading the reform endeavour of the nineteenth and early twentieth century in Punjab? While touching on the roles of specific players within the colonial Sikh realm, this study will focus mainly on the political, social, and religious structures of the colonial realm, from the perspective of gender construction.

To move further from a descriptive approach in an attempt to resolve these and other questions will necessarily result in moving beyond existing histories and will engender the rewriting of history. With regard to the construction of women in Sikh history and religion, alternative approaches are more likely to scrutinize *all* aspects of the past, without the need to idealize on one hand, or relegate to silence on the other.

NOTES

1. To illustrate the lack of knowledge about the female leaders of the Khalsa, Joginder Singh depicts Mata Sahib Devan, another wife of the guru, as the leader of the Sikhs. See Singh, J. 1983: 7.
2. Unless otherwise noted, the quotations from Sikh sacred scriptures are from the English translation in Talib 1987.
3. For a more detailed exploration of some of the issues raised here, see Jakobsh 1996.
4. These include Mai Bhago, Sada Kaur, and Bibi Sahib Kaur. For an example of the principle of idealization pertaining to women in Sikhism, see Gulcharan Singh 1988: 43.
5. Ruth Behar cautiously supports an analysis of gender as opposed to 'women', but warns that with this shift in focus there is for women 'a lingering fear of betrayal'. She questions whether the focus on gender once again pushes women into the realm of the invisible. See Behar 1994: 81.

TWO

THE DEVELOPMENT OF THE EARLY SIKH TRADITION
A Gender Perspective

How does one acquire a story? The culture in which one is born already
has an image of time, of the self, of heroism, of ambition, of fulfillment.
It burns its heroes and archetypes deeply into one's psyche.

(Novak 1971: 49)

THE MILIEU

In the traditional historical accounts of the Sikhs, there is little
evidence that women were in any way active participants in the
developing community. The Sikh community was born in the
fifteenth century in northern India with the birth of Guru Nanak, a
Hindu of the Khatri caste. At the time of Guru Nanak's birth in
1469, Islam was the dominant religion, with the conquering of India
by the Mughals. Islam in fifteenth-century India had a very different
constitution than in many other parts of the world. Few Indians
could go on pilgrimage to Mecca; instead, local shrines became
the focus of pilgrimage and devotion. In Punjab, the most important
forms of Muslim life were represented by various orders within
Sufism. Sufism was chronicled in the thirteenth to the seventeenth
century as having penetrated all echelons of Indo-Muslim society.
Significantly, the Sufi world view considered that both women and
men were called into a life of mystical devotion to God (Schimmel
1975: 433–4). Alongside Muslim religious culture, and perhaps
more important in terms of numbers and religious forms,
indigenous orders of Hinduism during this Indo-Islamic time period
also flourished. These were largely regional outgrowths of the Bhakti
movement that started in Tamil in the seventh century. The three

major sects of the time were the Shaivites, the Vaishnavites, and the Shaktas. In all three, gender and caste affiliation did not stand in the way of discipleship. Furthermore, varied forms of popular religion were practised in these sects in combination with 'higher' forms of religion. For the common villager, worship of the sun, moon, rivers, godlings, and ancestors was customary; the appeasement of malevolent spirits was part of daily ritual activity (Grewal 1979: 103, 136). Given the multiplicity of religious forms during the Indo-Islamic time frame, it is hardly surprising that ideas, rituals, and practices were often adopted from the prevailing milieu, their meanings merging into one another, adding to the richness of the religious culture. More importantly for the purposes of this study, caste and gender were on the whole no longer considered to be valid obstacles to the attainment of liberation. And, significantly, this was Guru Nanak's milieu.

THE EARLY GURU PERIOD

Guru Nanak has been characterized as fitting squarely within the Sant *parampara* (tradition) and also, in a wider sense, the Bhakti milieu of North India. This tradition rejected the worship of incarnations and Hindu forms of professional asceticism, spurned the authority of the Vedas and other scriptures, and ignored the ritual barriers between low and high castes. Further, the sants stressed the use of vernacular languages in their rejection of orthodoxy. Central to their doctrines, and binding them, were their ethical ideals and the notion of interiority—rituals, pilgrimages, and idols were worthless in the quest for liberation; only loving adoration to the Ultimate mattered. The strong similarities between the various groups who lived by these ideals have been characterized by W.H. McLeod (1989: 25) as the Sant synthesis, a combination of the Vaishnava tradition and the Nath tradition, with possible elements of Sufism as well. What the sants also had in common was a stress on the necessity of devotion and practice, the repetition of the divine name, the devotion to the divine guru (*satguru*), and the need for the company of sants (*satsang*).

To understand Guru Nanak's attitude towards women and gender in general, it is useful to compare his theological underpinnings with those of Kabir, the fountainhead of the Sant synthesis. Though

Kabir lived 150 years before Guru Nanak, the similarity of their teachings is striking, and as Karine Schomer points out, it is precisely this aspect as opposed to historical connection or institutional foci that closely binds Guru Nanak and Kabir. The latter's compositions figure prominently in the sacred scriptures of the Sikhs (Schomer and McLeod 1987: 5). Yet, especially with regard to Kabir's attitude towards women, there appears to be a subtle break in the similarities between the two. Grewal (1996: 150) explains this in terms of their relative standings in the Sant tradition of northern India. It would appear that one of the strands of this synthesis, *hathyoga*, was much less important to Guru Nanak than to Kabir. For yogis, whose primary aim was the vanquishing of desire, particularly sexual desire, women were great obstacles to be conquered. Kabir's attitude towards women was similar to that of the yogis in that he too viewed women as seductive, as tempting men away from their true calling. Guru Nanak, on the other hand, criticized yogis for their solitary, ascetic, spiritual search. Contrary to the yogic apprehension of sexuality, Guru Nanak furthered the ideal of the householder. Enlightenment was not to be found within the realm of austerity. The religious community of householders, who contributed concretely to society, who offered their services to their religious community, who brought forth children and provided for them, were, for Guru Nanak, ideal devotees.

With regard to women, Guru Nanak's writings, and those of subsequent gurus, contain a range of views, from the positive to the negative as well as ambivalent attitudes, which suggest a tension between normative, negative assumptions towards women and more positive, inclusive, and emancipated attitudes (Shanker 1994: 191). Clearly, Nanak's message maintained that women and members of the lower castes were not in any way barred from attaining enlightenment, the highest purpose of human life (*Adi Granth*: 9, 223). However, procreation, the procreation of sons specifically, was central to Nanak's vision of the ideal woman. An oft-quoted verse, supposedly indicative of Guru Nanak's positive evaluation of womanhood, points to an appreciation of woman only vis-à-vis the procreative process.

We are conceived in the woman's womb and we grow in it. We are engaged to women and we wed them. Through the woman's cooperation new generations are born. If one woman dies, we seek another; without the woman there can be no bond. Why call her bad who gives birth to *rajas*? The woman herself is born of the woman, and none comes into this world without the woman; Nanak, the true one alone is independent of the woman (*Adi Granth*, quoted in Grewal 1993:5).

Guru Nanak's stance towards women as manifested in this passage was strikingly similar to that of the writer of the *Brhaspatismrti*, written in the fourth century CE, albeit from within a different context. The earlier writer questioned the inconsistencies in the inheritance rights of daughters and sons. These too were based upon the same notion later advocated by Nanak: 'A daughter is born from [the same] human bodies as does a son. Why then should the father's wealth be taken by another person' (Aiyanger 1941, cited in Bose 1996: 3). While Guru Nanak's words have been lauded as the slogan of emancipation for women in the Sikh tradition, they had more to do with the rejection of prevailing notions of ritual purity and support of the social hierarchy of the time. For women gave birth to sons, *especially* those of noble birth; how then could they be considered ritually impure? The birthing of sons was the most elevated of aspirations; sons were avenues to fulfilment and the fervent wish of any woman during Indo-Islamic times. Thus, Guru Nanak's challenge, in referring to the contemporary hierarchical order, one which placed rajahs at the top of that order, also indicated his support of the dominant social and political order of his time.

Yet, more often than not, one senses Guru Nanak's apprehension of the female. Women are often associated with maya, the feminine principle that deludes the seeker, she that acts as a barrier to the attainment of emancipation. According to the *Adi Granth*, '[t]here is pleasure in gold, pleasure in silver, pleasure in women, pleasure in scents, pleasure in horses, pleasure in the conjugal bed, pleasure in sweets, pleasure in the flesh—there are so many pleasures of the body that there is no room for the name' (*Adi Granth*: 3). While woman is only one of the various attachments specified, she is mentioned time and time again; as an attraction to the male, woman thus becomes part of maya. Further, negative images of women were frequently compounded by ambivalent messages towards outcasts of the time: 'Evil mindedness is a low woman, cruelty a butcher's wife, a slanderous heart a sweeper woman, wrath which ruineth the world a pariah woman' (*Adi Granth*, Macauliffe 1990, Vol. I: 52).

While Guru Nanak grieved the rape of women during the time of Babur, he did not censure the social order on the whole. Moreover, he firmly believed in God's omnipotence and the will of God behind such events (Grewal 1979: 162, 176). While aware of the social challenges facing the widows of his day, Nanak instead censured them for their unrestrained desires. He did not re-evaluate social institutions such as marriage and marriage practices to make them more equitable for women. Moreover his silence regarding sati is rather surprising, given that it was primarily confined to the upper echelons of society, to which he belonged. There was also no critique of female infanticide, again, a practice closely aligned to the upper castes. In the final analysis, when it came to the social status of women, Nanak seemed content to leave the prevailing system in place. In the patriarchal world view, women were indeed assigned a position of inferiority, however, that inferiority in no way detracted from their ability to attain salvation; salvation, regardless of station or gender was pronounced open to all who devoted themselves wholeheartedly to the Ultimate.

As noted earlier, Nikki Singh has pointed to Nanak's use of the feminine voice in his bani as indicative of the high regard the guru had for women. Yet, this practice was certainly not unique to Guru Nanak; many North Indian sants used the female voice. David Lorenzen in his analysis of upper-caste Bhakti saints makes note of a number of reversals—active responses towards the normative Hindu world view as represented in Manu's *Darmasastra*. For according to Manu, the female was necessarily subordinate to the male and the outcast subordinate to the upper caste. However, in the lives of the Bhakti saints, the notion that 'the last shall be first' led men to 'renounce their masculinity and to become as women; upper-caste males wish to renounce pride, privilege, and wealth, seek dishonor and self-abasement, and learn from the untouchable devotee' (Lorenzen 1995: 190–1). However, these men were only temporarily engaged in role play, be that as females or as low-caste persons, while women saints committed themselves to a permanent transformation of social status. When the psychological role playing ended, these upper-caste males could return to their original social status. According to Lorenzen, if women or low-caste devotees were to engage in similar role playing, for instance, to become 'king for the day', the consequences would be great, most likely leading to permanent social and economic ostracism and even physical danger. From this perspective, the female voice of the Sikh gurus points less to their positive stance toward womanhood as to a rejection of orthodoxy as represented by the *Darmasastra*. It is also indicative of their elevated caste position. Moreover, addressing the divine through the feminine voice allowed for the maintenance of an understanding of the primary masculine identity of God; if the bride, the guru, was overcome with desire and love for the bridegroom, the Ultimate could thus primarily be identified as male.

The Janam-Sakhis

While the sacred writings of Guru Nanak offer some information with regard to his attitudes towards women, the janam-sakhi literature of the Sikhs, written during the first half of the seventeenth century, well after Guru Nanak's time, further adds to the picture (McLeod 1996: 17). Given the nature of janam-sakhis, they cannot be understood as necessarily biographical but rather as responding to the needs of the later community within which this genre developed (McLeod 1989: 15–22). While claiming full authority on the life and works of Guru Nanak, the *Janam-sakhis* give rather meagre information regarding the female members of his family. This incongruity, however, speaks volumes about the insignificance awarded the women of his family. The *Puratan* janam-sakhi refers to Nanak's mother, his sister, and his wife, but they are not named. The *Miharban Janam-sakhi* identifies Guru Nanak's mother as Tipara but does not name his sister. The *Bala* janam-sakhi names Tripata as his mother and Nanaki as his sister. Further, Nanak's wife is called Ghumi in the *Miharban Janam-sakhi* and Sulakhani in the *Bala* janam-sakhi (McLeod 1996: 101–3). While there is evidence that these women played important roles in the fledgling Sikh community, the inconsistencies regarding their names point to an indifference indicative of the status of women during the time of the guru and the subsequent periods during which the janam-sakhis were compiled.

Moreover, while insisting that caste was no bar to enlightenment, Guru Nanak and the gurus who followed married within Khatri caste regulations. Further, though strongly espousing the status of the householder and highly critical of the ascetic, Nanak relegated the running of his household and the raising of his children to his wife and extended family. There are also nuanced implications that he perceived his conjugal relationship as a burden, an obstacle that needed to be overcome. Speculating about these recurring under-currents of discontent in popular literature, the celebrated historian of the Sikhs, Max Arthur Macauliffe, wrote in the early twentieth century: 'If Nanak had been left to his own discretion, and if his marriage had not been made for him by his parents, it is most probable that he would not have turned his attention to that part of a man's duties after entering the service of the government in Sultanpur' (Macauliffe 1990, Vol. I: 29). Sources often portrayed his spouse as unhappy with their marital situation. In the *B40 Janam-sakhi*, Guru Nanak's wife pleaded with him: 'You showed me no affection when you were with me. Once you have gone to another place you will never return....' She was chided for her insistence but Nanak promised to eventually send for her (Mcleod 1980: 18). Further, the *Bala* janam-sakhi presented Nanak's wife as regretting her marriage. The compiler, however, put the blame squarely on the woman, for she was apparently hot tempered and full of anger (Singh, K. 1969, quoted in Hans 1988: 204).

The janam-sakhis also, however, depicted the women of Guru Nanak's family as playing an important role in the acknowledgment and development of his guru status. The *Bala* janam-sakhi paints a more human, less idealized picture of the guru, particularly with regard to his family life; the sister, Nanaki, is portrayed as having played a central role in furthering his cause. But she also had the upper hand over her brother; in fact, Guru Nanak could not deny Nanaki's wishes (Singh, K. 1969, in Hans 1980: 325). While the his-torical elements of this literature must be questioned, it does point to later understandings of the guru, and indeed, of the role of women reflected in the ensuing society. Certainly, the presence of the female, though almost exclusively of the members of the guru's family, pointed to an understanding of women as active agents in the wider sphere of the later Sikh panth as well.

Guru Nanak was a visionary who lived squarely within the patriarchal framework surrounding him. His genius and his appeal lay in his assertion that salvation was open to all, regardless of gender, regardless of their station in life. There is little criticism of the society he lived in with regard to the status of women beyond his abrupt disagreement with established religion and religious mores. His was a message of interior religion, a vision of love and devotion to the Ultimate, who in grace and promise of emancipation made no distinction between men and women, or between castes.

It is to the third guru, Guru Amar Das, who succeeded Guru Angad in 1552, that both scriptural and popular sources attribute a shift towards the inclusion of women in the Sikh panth. It is to him that tradition credits a definitive criticism of society beyond that of religious ineptitude; much of this criticism is directed towards the situation of women in society. With regard to sati, the third Guru stated: 'They are not satis who are burnt alive on the pyres; Rather satis are they who die of the blow of separation [from their husbands]' (*Adi Granth*: 787). Later accounts present Guru Amar Das as having denounced the custom of purdah; he did not allow visiting queens to remain veiled in his presence (see Bhalla 1971, in Singh, F. 1979: 324). Further, *Mehma Parkash* by Sarup Das Balla, a descendent of Guru Amar Das, written in 1776, chronicled that it was through a woman that Amar Das first became acquainted with the Sikh community. Amar Das heard Bibi Amro, the daughter of Guru Angad, the second guru, reciting the *Japji*. Tradition has it that Amar Das was so moved that he insisted that she immediately introduce him to the source of the composition, namely, Guru Angad. Amar Das eventually succeeded Guru Angad as the third Guru of the Sikh community.

Female infanticide was also condemned by the gurus. Yet this practice may well have stemmed directly from the highly esteemed guru lineages. According to Punjabi lore, Dharam Chand, a grandson of Guru Nanak, was humiliated at his daughter's marriage by the groom's family. Chand was so incensed that he ordered all Bedis to henceforth kill their daughters as soon as they were born rather than bear such humiliation. Dharam Chand, the story continues, took on the burden of the crime of female infanticide; from that day on, he moved as though bearing a heavy weight upon his shoulders. According to Anshu Malhotra (2002: 55–6), the latter part of the story may well be interpreted as showing the permanent humiliation of daughters being born to the Bedi family (Browne 1857: 115–16). Guru Amar Das' condemnation of the practice may well have stemmed from a need to distance the Sikh panth under his leadership from the original guru lineage that was at the forefront of the practice of female infanticide.

It was during Guru Amar Das' time that missionaries were appointed to extend the message of the Sikh panth beyond the immediate surroundings of Goindwal, the seat of his leadership. The community had obviously expanded, and with new congregations (*sangats*) and swelling numbers, immediate contact with the guru became increasingly difficult. Thus the *manji* system was created, a word literally meaning 'string bed' and referring to the seat of authority. Manji were leaders of local gatherings who were directly accountable to the guru, and thus an extension of his influence (Singh, F. 1979: 116–29). While sources conflict with regard to the actual number of manjis as well as their gender, there is evidence that there may have been women sent out to preach the guru's message of emancipation. The appointment of manjis indicates an increasing institutionalization of the Sikh panth as well as an expansion in the actual numbers of the guru's followers. Given the esteemed place held by these emissaries, the very possibility of women being included in their numbers speaks at least to a growing concern about women, if not to an active reaching out towards them. Women missionaries would have proven most effective in the recruitment of other women into the Sikh fold.

A later source, Santokh Singh's *Suraj Prakash*, an extension of the janam-sakhi genre though inclusive of Guru Nanak's successors, was completed in the mid-nineteenth century. Santokh Singh posits the devotion of Bibi Bhani, Guru Amar Das' daughter, as the deciding factor in the nomination of her husband, Jetha, later renamed Ram Das, as the fourth guru (Singh, B.J. 1979: 298). Later writers interpreted this incident as a deliberate intervention by the ambitious Bhani to secure the succession of the guruship for posterity (Cunningham 1990: 45). Regardless of the historical accuracy of this narrative, it is clear that, thereafter, the succession of Sikh gurus continued on through the male line of the Sodhi family descending from Guru Ram Das. Further, *Suraj Prakash* noted that when Emperor Akbar in appreciation of the guru and his *langar* (public kitchen) wished to grant him lands, Guru Amar Das refused. The emperor then gave a number of villages and their surroundings to Amar Das' daughter Bhani instead. The tradition is fascinating given that Guru Amar Das had three other children, two of whom were male. Yet Bhani alone was singled out as his economic successor. Bequeathing lands and villages to a female heir would have been inconceivable in even the later social and cultural milieu of ensuing chroniclers. Clearly, even the insinuation of Bibi Bhani as a possible leader points to an imagination which, given the Guru's estimation of his daughter and the possible inclusion of females among the elite devotees, envisioned a central place of leadership for women in the Sikh world view. While Bibi Bhani was never given the status of the leader of the Sikh panth, her husband Jetha, Guru Ram Das, did benefit from his wife's intense devotion to Guru Amar Das.

The very possibility of a woman being honoured as the economic successor of the guru was dealt with by subsequent writers in fascinating ways. Hari Ram Gupta noted that upon 'learning that the Guru's son-in-law, Ram Das, was in search of some land in the heart of Majha, the Emperor granted a tract of land not far from Chubhal to Bibi Bhani. The Guru could not refuse a gift to a girl' (Gupta 1980: 122). Here, her husband was closely tied to the gift-giving, which deflected the magnitude of the entire incident. But it also made the occurrence altogether more plausible and acceptable given the consequences of a literal reading of the narrative—namely, a woman being at the helm of the panth. Popular writings focusing on this time period in Sikh history are also at a loss to explain the significant place of Bibi Bhani in the development of the early guru period. One explanation insists that Guru Amar Das did indeed pass the mantle on to his daughter, but she in turn bequeathed it to her husband, Guru Ram Das (see Singh, N. 1983: 12).

If we turn to the writings of the fourth guru, Guru Ram Das, what has generally been pointed out in Sikh historical writings is an increasingly institutionalized community of followers. This included the installation of the pilgrimage site, Goindwal. Further, while sources are obscure as to the exact time of the introduction of the institution of langar, it appears that it acquired a new force with Guru Amar Das. Surjit Hans (1980: 142) adds that there is also a noticeable increase of feminine imagery in the writings of the fourth guru. 'Lyricism in Guru Ram Das has a social counterpart. It points to the entry of women in appreciable numbers in the sangat in particular and in the community at large.... It may be reasonable to suggest that a large scale entry of women into Sikhism contributed to the lyricism of Guru Ram Das.' While earlier gurus had indeed addressed the divine in the female voice as a symbol of their submission, with Guru Ram Das the symbol takes on a more palpable reality; indeed, love of the divine came to be expressed in

utterly profane language. Further, the female perspective towards
the *body* of the guru is conspicuously emphasized; the corporeality
of Ram Das is central in these writings: 'Looking again and again at
the body of the Guru has filled me with intense joy' (ibid.). And,
'How can I meet my handsome Man? God accepts even wayward
and squat women.' According to Hans (1988: 95), the 'increased
presence of women in the sangat and their greater participation in
the Sikh panth is very much in evidence in the compositions of
Guru Ram Das.' While Hans makes note of a possible influx of
women, he does not consider the possibility of their agency in the
changing constitution of the panth.

Historians of Sikhism have repeatedly questioned the cultural
and caste-based make-up of the early Sikh panth. Clearly, the earliest followers were Khatris, as were all the gurus. At some point,
however, the composition of the community radically changed, as
a new caste grouping, the Jats, emerged into prominence. During
the later guru period and even to the present day, Jats were and are
the dominant caste group among the Sikhs. McLeod has analysed
this transformation of the caste constituency of the early Sikh
period extensively. McLeod (1976: 11) notes that the urban Khatris
commonly served as teachers to the illiterate masses and the Jats
constituted a large percentage of the peasantry. Irfan Habib (1966:
94) contemplating the inclusion of Jats into the Sikh fold, attributes
this *en masse* migration to a disparity between the Jats' economic
status and their caste status in the sixteenth century. The earliest
sources, from between the seventh and ninth centuries, refer to
the Jats as a pastoral community. By the eleventh century they had
attained *sudra* status and by the sixteenth century, had moved to
the status of *vaisya*, peasants par excellence and *zamindars*, or land
owners (Habib 1995: 175). Despite this upward mobility, the older
caste stigma as pastoral community is likely to have persisted. While
this explanation of Jat migration into the Sikh fold is entirely
plausible, it would appear that Jat women may well have been at
the forefront of the migration. The earliest sources depicting
the pastoral Jats made specific mention of a disposition of equality
between women and men. The traveller Hiuen Tsang noted in the
seventh century:

By the side of the river Sindh, along the flat marshy lowlands for some
thousand *li*, there are several hundreds of thousands (a very great many)

families settled.... They give themselves to tending cattle and from this derive their livelihood.... *They have no masters, and whether men or women, have neither rich nor poor* [italics mine].

This unnamed group claimed to be Buddhist. *Chachnama*, written in the eighth century, noted that the people were Jats. According to the chronicler, 'There were no small or great among them. They were supposed to lack marital laws. The only tribute they could pay was in the form of firewood. They owed allegiance to the Buddhist *shramanas*' (Tsang's *Chachnama*, in Habib 1996: 94–5). A northward migration of the Jats into the southern parts of Punjab took place by the eleventh century, indicating the social and economic changes that were taking place in Punjab during Indo-Islamic times. From a pastoral community with an egalitarian social structure, the Jats became, by the sixteenth century, a largely agricultural group and acquired zamindar status. Habib posits that the mechanism of Sanskritization, normatively utilized in attempts to elevate groups' social status, could not have been applied by the Jats, given their egalitarian or semi-egalitarian social structure. Thus, the fledgling Sikh community, which theoretically rejected the entire system of caste, could have been seen as an avenue for the recognition the Jats felt they deserved.

While the polemics of scholars have tended to rehash the reasons behind this transformation, perhaps it is time to move beyond these arguments and contemplate a different theory, one based on an analysis of gender composition. Undoubtedly, the early gurus lived within or near the Majha area of Punjab, a region that was and is still known for a strong Jat constituency. Given the egalitarian nature of the Jats in the early Indo-Islamic period, it is possible that it was women in particular who were attracted to the message of emancipation of the Sikh gurus and, consequently, to full participation in the developing Sikh community. A number of factors point to this development.

One, the message of the Sikh gurus with regard to salvation was accessible to both women and men; two, there are strains within sources (though typically barely audible) which point to women as having been active participants in the developing community; three, Guru Amar Das' criticism of society with regard to the situation of women; four, the plausibility of missionary activities by women also during the time of Guru Amar Das, resulting most certainly in an active outreach towards women; and five, scriptural indications of an influx of women into the Sikh panth during the time of the fourth guru.

From the perspective of traditional Sikh history, the notion of women as active agents in the changes in the Sikh panth may well appear foreign. Nonetheless, women would have had the most to gain from rejecting the restrictions placed upon them by an orthodox Brahminical system and embracing the egalitarian message of the early Sikh gurus. The third guru's criticism of the societal norms pertaining to women would conceivably have encouraged their movement into the Sikh fold.

It was during the time of the fourth guru that the manji system was transformed into the order of *masands. Dabistan-i-Mazahib*, an early seventeenth-century Persian source, noted that the masands had a dual responsibility: they were to preach the message of the gurus and collect the voluntary tribute from the followers. Thus the new order was tailored to suit both the missionary activities and the economic interests of the gurus. As with the manjis, the masands also had the authority to initiate new entrants into the Sikh panth (Singh, G. 1967: 47–71). According to all accounts, women were excluded from this new system. Significantly, the fourth guru was highly critical of women in his writings. With the influx into the young Sikh tradition of women and men with a history of egalitarianism and a lack of marital laws, the guru was prompted to write, 'Sinful men, licentious and stupid, act as their women command. Lust abounds; thus do impure men take orders from their women and act accordingly' (*Adi Granth*: 304). Linda Hess has pointed out that similar 'upside-down-language' in Kabir's thought had manifold roots, in the Hindu and Buddhist tantras and the texts of hathyoga. There are 'tangled domestic relationships (incestuous sons and mothers, conspiring in-laws, one bride who becomes a widow during the marriage ceremony, another who ties her mother-in-law to the bed)' (Hess and Singh 1986: 137). From the hathyoga perspective, woman was the supreme temptress and thus overtly circumscribed with suspicion and dread. Needless to say, this new breed of Jat constituents would have threatened the established order of the Sikh panth; it became necessary to take action to stem the tide of an unwarranted egalitarian ethos. This fact may also have accounted for the absence of women in the system of masand administrators.

The panth was being increasingly moulded to satisfy the needs of the growing numbers of followers. Pilgrimage centres were already in place, the words of the gurus were being collected for collation, and places of ritual cleansing and worship were being constructed. What Weber (1946: 297) refers to as 'the routinization of charisma', the institutionalization of an earlier strictly interior tradition, had increasingly become the order of the day. With an increase in numbers and the lack of immediate personal contact with the guru came a need for something beyond a doctrine of interiority to bind the community. It was in the adaptability to changing circumstances that the Sikh panth remained vibrant and continued to grow. Still, with the process of institutionalization, gender differences within the Sikh panth became increasingly pronounced. The viability of a religion based on interior devotion for women in sixteenth and seventeenth-century India needs little explanation. With increased institutionalization, traditionally established roles for men and women became more socially and materially feasible and were thus consolidated. As the masands were not only missionaries but also administrators who travelled far and wide to collect the guru's dues, the once open door of possibilities for women within the early panth was thus effectively fastened.

THE LATER GURU PERIOD

The move away from interiority continued with the fifth guru, Guru Arjan. Contemporary works certainly point to an augmented secularization and politicization of the Sikh panth in the late sixteenth century. The *Dabistan* points to a leader who was increasingly viewed as not only a religious, but also a political leader. Impressive buildings were built at Amritsar; the guru 'wore rich clothes, kept fine horses procured from Central Asia and some elephants and maintained retainers as bodyguards in attendance.' He became known as *sachcha padishah*, the true king, who 'led human souls to salvation as opposed to worldly kings who controlled people's mundane deeds' (Fani 1904, in Gupta 1980: 133). Given Guru Arjan's elevated visibility as a regal leader, the Sikhs came to be perceived as a separate state within the Mughal dominion. According to Sikh traditional sources, this culminated in Emperor Jahangir's orders to kill Guru Arjan in 1606, while was in custody in Lahore. McLeod has questioned the element of martyrdom that has been attached to Arjan's death, given its obscurity within available sources. According to McLeod, all that is known for certain is that Guru Arjan died while imprisoned by the Mughals. He also points to Mughal mistrust of the growing power of the guru as being not entirely unfounded. 'The increasing influence of the Jats within the Sikh *panth* suggests that Jahangir and his subordinates may well have had good reason for their fears, and that these fears would not have related exclusively, nor even primarily, to the *religious* influence of the Guru'. (McLeod 1976: 12). What is important to this study is the question of gender construction during this time period. With the heightened politicization of the panth, women would increasingly have been relegated to positions more in line with traditional female roles. The expanded milieu of business and politics could only have been restrictive towards women's participation in the leadership of the community.

It was Guru Hargobind who brought this development to a more readily recognizable political and theological level. Alarmed at the increased meddling of the government into Sikh affairs, and particularly with the death of his father while in custody, Guru Hargobind styled his guruship as a combination of the religious and political; not only did he represent the religious concerns of the Sikh panth, he also wore arms, a symbol of his temporal power. The now almost complete transformation of caste constituency, from Khatri to Jat dominance, would also have been pivotal to this change. The Jats were known for their resistance to authority and would not have been averse to armed resistance. Intrusion from the government would have exacerbated a militant reaction from the Jats. Guru Hargobind's military stance is likely to have originated with the armed Jat constituency, as opposed to the religious ideology of the young guru (McLeod 1989: 40). Regardless of the actual origin of the politicization of the Sikh leadership, sources indicate that the new direction taken by the young guru was not without its critics. The beloved scribe Bhai Gurdas (cited in Macauliffe 1990, Vol. IV: 76–7) questions Hargobind's directives:

People say the former Gurus used to sit in the temple; the present Guru remaineth not in any one place.... The former Gurus sitting on their thrones used to console the Sikhs; the present Guru keepeth dogs and hunteth. The former Gurus used to compose hymns, listen to them, and sing them; the present Guru composeth not hymns, or listeneth to them, or singeth them. He keepeth not his Sikh followers with him, but taketh enemies of his faith and wicked persons as his guides and familiars. I say, the truth within him cannot possibly be concealed; the true Sikhs like bumble-bees are enamoured of his lotus feet. He supporteth a burden intolerable to others and asserteth not himself.

While Bhai Gurdas was ultimately firm in his support for Guru Hargobind, his apprehension was undeniable. Needless to say, a new phase of Sikh history had begun.

On the question of gender construction, the new developments augmented by Guru Hargobind's identity as both religious and political leader would most certainly have had a dramatic effect on the role and status of both women and men within the panth. Though women would still have been a part of the wider Sikh community, they would not have been part of the military retinue that was part of the young guru's vision and understanding of his mission. More precisely, given the role of women in the seventeenth century, they would most certainly not have accompanied the guru into his skirmishes with the Mughals. The Sikh male thus also took on a new identity sanctioned by the order put in place by Guru Hargobind—protector of the faith, armed, and ready for battle. This role, however, was denied to women, who by a process of elimination would have been relegated to a secondary position, possibly even viewed as impediments to the true calling of the Sikh community. The demotion of women in military environments was certainly not confined to this period of Sikh history. During the later Vedic Age in Punjab, a time when militarism had become an established world view for the exalted Kshatriya caste group, Vig (1966: 44) notes that the 'corresponding fall in the position of the women in Punjab were indications of gradual withdrawal by the society of the concessions from the physically inferior class of women who either could not actively participate in war and were considered unnecessary impediments for a Kshatriya.'

GENDER AND THE THEOLOGY OF DIFFERENCE

The development of militancy among the Sikhs peaked with the ascendancy of the tenth and last guru, Gobind Rai, to the seat of

Sikh authority. It was during the Baisakhi festival of 1699 that the tenth guru established the institution of the Khalsa, inviting all to follow his ordinances and leave the now clearly established authority of the masands. The term 'Sikh', meaning disciple, was replaced by 'Khalsa', which in the seventeenth century reflected its usage by the Mughals for revenue collection on lands that were directly supervised by the government (Grewal and Bal 1967: 113–15). This change was also made in order to consolidate the guru's own position in the increasingly crowded milieu of those of the guru lineage who had, by virtue of their ancestry, established themselves as Sikh gurus in their own right (Grewal 1980: 109–20). While other sources are not at all clear as to what exactly happened, traditional Sikh historiography has painted a graphic picture of the precise events of that Baisakhi day in 1699. Guru Gobind Singh invited five devotees to express their love and devotion by laying down their lives for him. Five followers responded, but instead of sacrificing them, Guru Gobind Rai designated these men as the *panj piare* ('five beloved') and initiated them into the Khalsa brotherhood by a rite that was entirely novel in the history of the Sikhs. Admittance into the Sikh panth had heretofore been by the rite of *charan di pahul*, whereby the initiate would drink water touched by either the guru's foot or the foot of a designated representative of the guru. The new rite, known as *khande di pahul*, instead referred to the administration of sweetened water (*amrit*), stirred with a two-edged sword (*khanda*), to the face and hair of a devoted follower of Guru Gobind Singh. Those to whom amrit was administered would then be part of the Khalsa brotherhood.

While accounts vary as to the central participants of this event, tradition maintains that Guru Gobind Singh's wives played an important role in the proceedings; a feminine element thus came to be added to this decisively male-dominated rite of initiation. According to most popular accounts, Mata Jito, the guru's second wife, came to the gathering out of curiosity, carrying sweets. The Guru instructed her to add the sweets to the water while he stirred the mixture with a two-edged sword. Macauliffe (1990, Vol. V: 95) relying on popular accounts notes: 'He had begun, he said, to beget the Khalsa as his sons, and without a woman no son could be produced. Now that the sweets were poured into the nectar the Sikhs would be at peace with one another, otherwise they would be at continual variance.' In a different rahit-nama, it was the third wife of Guru Gobind Singh, Mata Sahib Devi, who was responsible for the sweetened water (Padam 1974, cited in McLeod 1987: 230–1). An account from the early twentieth century, however, insists that it was Mata Sundri, the first wife of the guru, who added sweets to the water (Singh, B.C. 1903: 280). The *Chaupa Singh Rahit-nama*, emerging about fifty years after Guru Gobind Singh's death, added an entirely new perspective. It maintained that a man named Dharam Chand suggested to the guru that the water be sweetened, but that it was Chaupa Singh himself who prepared the mixture (McLeod 1987: 169–70). As these variances indicate, historical sources are not at all clear as to who actually took part in this pivotal event. Perhaps the repeated references to female contributes have more to do with sweets normally being associated with traditional feminine roles than with actual historical fact. Perhaps, as noted by Cunningham (1990: 65), it was 'as it were by chance', that his wife passed by, 'bearing confections of five kinds: he [the Guru] hailed the omen as propitious, for the coming of woman denoted an offspring to the Khalsa numerous as the leaves of the forest.' It is also possible that given that the rite was a resolutely 'male' act, later traditions, attempting to construct a more egalitarian perspective of the event, came to stress the feminine element of the occurrences of Baisakhi day, 1699. Nonetheless, traditional Sikh historiography is adamant that one of the guru's wives did indeed take part in the initiation ceremony introduced by Guru Gobind Singh, and that the impetus to her presence was the guru's insight into the necessity of a feminine element in the proceedings (Singh, N.K. 1993: 119).

Further, tradition notes that on this Baisakhi day, the guru called for all who were initiated into the Khalsa to take on the appellation 'Singh', to wear the five articles known as the *panj kakke*, or five Ks: *kes*, long hair; *kangha*, comb; *kirpan*, sword; *kachh*, a type of underwear; *kara*, a steel bracelet. They were also to ignore all caste affiliations, which to this point had caused divisions among them. A number of followers were initiated into the new order by the rite of the double-edged sword; many, however, rejected the guru's invitation, Brahmins and Khatris in particular. The appellation Singh was adopted by Khalsa initiates, as well as by Guru Gobind Rai, who was from then on known as Guru Gobind Singh. Further, a number of customs, some associated with non-Sikh communities, others prevalent among them, were firmly prohibited. These included the killing of female infants, hookah smoking, intercourse with Muslim women, and eating the meat of animals slaughtered in the Muslim fashion known as *halal*. The anti-Muslim proscriptions would understandably have stemmed from the increasingly troublesome relations between the Sikhs and the Mughals; moreover, the now religiously mandated Sikh warriors would certainly have been viewed as irritations by the Mughal rulers.

Guru Gobind Singh's harsh prohibition of the killing of female babies pointed to a practice which had most likely gone on largely unchecked since the guruship of Amar Das, the first Sikh guru known to have proscribed female infanticide (Grewal 1990: 51). The practice had evidently not ended with Guru Amar Das' injunction. In fact, according to Anshu Malhotra (2002: 56) it became a central feature of both the Bedi and Sondhi guru lineages. Female infanticide became the means by which these lineages rose above traditional caste biases among the Khatris. Her observations warrant extensive reference.

It is possible that by Dharam Chand's [Guru Nanak's grandson] time, the Bedis considered themselves to be higher within the Khatri hierarchy than they were hitherto held, as they were the descendants of the founder of the Sikh faith.... The Bedis belonged to the sub-section of the Bunjahi Khatris, below the Bari and the Dhaighar. Thus Nanak himself is said to have married within his Khatri sub-division as he married a Chona woman. The attempts by his followers to upgrade their status, one can speculate, may have led to tensions:.... Female infanticide can be said to have been adopted as a strategy for upward mobility, for doing away with a daughter meant never having to bow before anyone, even one nominally held superior.

The Sondhis, the descendents of the fourth guru onwards, who belonged to the sub-division of Sarin Khatris, a ranking low in the internal Khatri hierarchy, were also closely aligned with the practice of female infanticide. Sikh Jats, who had overtaken the Khatris in terms of actual numbers within the Sikh community, would have adopted the same means of upward mobility. The ensuing association between Jats and female infanticide can be clearly seen in the famous Punjabi saga of Hir and Ranjha. In its most illustrious version associated with the bard Waris Shah (1978: 44), the various methods utilized in the killing of infant daughters were spelled out. They included strangulation, poisoning, drowning, and suffocation. Shah (quoted by Garrett in Cunningham 1990: viii) goes on to lament the usurpation of prestige and power by this socially insignificant caste group:

> Thieves have become leaders of men.
> Harlots have become mistresses of the household.
> The company of devils has multiplied exceedingly.
> The state of the noble is pitiable.
> Men of menial birth flourish and the peasants are in great prosperity.
> The Jats have become masters of our country.
> Everywhere there is a new Government.

According to tradition, the *rahit*, or regulations, that were to govern this newly founded order, was given in its entirety by Guru Gobind Singh following the inauguration of the Khalsa. In all likelihood, it was given a rudimentary inception at this point and developed in time to reflect the needs of a later community. There were nine works dealing with the rules and regulations that were to govern the Sikhs, all of which were at some variance with one another; contemporary scholars date most versions to the nineteenth century (McLeod 1989: 23–42, Grewal 1966: 83–4).

While the evolving rahit will later be discussed in greater detail, suffice it to say that there is a good deal of uncertainty surrounding the events of 1699. What is clear is that the identity of the followers of Guru Gobind Singh underwent a profound transformation. Through their distinct names reflecting their new Kshatriya warrior status, the ritualized call to arms, and the correspondingly suspicious and increasingly malevolent rulers, a new version of the Sikh devotee came into being; the warrior-saint had fully developed as the new ideal of the Khalsa identity. According to Sainapati, a near contemporary to Guru Gobind Singh, a new understanding of liberation accompanied the new identity. Liberation now came to be associated with those who heeded the guru's call and styled themselves according to the identity constructed by him. As Surjit Hans (1988: 249) in his analysis of Sainapati's *Gur Sobha* has pointed out, those

who fail to come into the Khalsa fold are *manmukhs*. The word *manmukh* has been widening itself in Sikh theology. At the beginning it meant 'man oriented towards his empirical ego'; it began to cover the 'rivals' and 'those failing to become Sikhs of the Guru's'. The author [Sainapati] theologically invokes 'death' and 'hukm' in the tradition of the Gurus to condemn those who do not join the Khalsa.

As part of the new religious identity, the Khalsa was to be pre-pared to follow the guru into the throes of war. This translated into skirmishes with the surrounding hill chiefs as well as altercations with the Mughal rulers.

According to Carrol Smith-Rosenberg (1986: 49), body image and 'rules regulating its treatment and behaviour... correlate closely to social categories and the distribution of power.' What is of great importance in terms of Khalsa identity construction and gender analysis is that it is solely the male devotee, reborn in the order of the Khalsa as the new warrior-saint, that became the focus of all ritual and symbolic construction. Exterior symbols, weaponry, steel, and uncut hair became the signifiers constituting what it meant to be a 'real' Sikh. The double-edged khanda for instance, with which the guru stirred the sweetened water, is in symbolic terms a direct contrast to the *karad*, a single-edged utensil used for domestic purposes. The significance of the khanda, a military implement associated with masculine characteristics, contrasted to the karad, a domestic 'feminine' implement, is indicative of the process of masculinization that was central to the new order of the Khalsa. The interiority of the early gurus, which invited *all* to a profound relationship with the divine, simply did not fit into the masculine, soldier-saint following of the tenth guru. Caste, on the other hand, proved to be of little consequence for the new order. The Jat component of the Khalsa as well as participation by other lower-caste groups increased radically; many Khatris, however, refused to follow the new injunctions put in place by the guru. They preferred to maintain their identity as followers of Nanak, whose message appeared inconsistent with the aims and regulatory symbols of the Khalsa order.

Given the fervour of the newly founded order, it was this group which became the normative signifier of what it meant to be a Sikh; followers of the older ordinances became relegated to a secondary status within Sikhism. Women, excluded from the Khalsa brotherhood, were inadvertently depreciated as full-fledged followers of the Sikh tradition. An ethos developed which consis-tently widened the gulf between the 'true' Khalsa Sikh and those who were either not invited to join, namely women, or those who did not heed the guru's call. Females, by virtue of their gender and their consequent association with the old order, lost the right to be considered authentic and full-fledged members of the new world order of the Khalsa. Whereas the initiation rite known as charan ki pahul had invited all to full participation in the earlier Sikh panth, with the creation of the Khalsa and the newly-mandated rite of khande di pahul as normative, women were symbolically and ritually excluded from the 'brotherhood' and were relegated to marginal standing. *Chaupa Singh Rahit-nama*, the earliest rahit, strongly prohibited the administration of khande di pahul to a woman. It noted, however, that women could still be initiated into the Sikh panth, but were to be admitted by the older rite. Given the end of the guru lineage, the lectern supporting the *Adi Granth* was to touch the water, as opposed to the foot of the living Guru. Needless to say, the gulf between males, as possible adherents of the Khalsa military order, and females, as inadvertent adherents of the older Sikh panth, widened significantly.

Pierre Bourdieu's analysis of 'symbolic capital' and 'symbolic power' is useful in coming to an understanding of the increased symbolic and ritual distances between male and female Sikhs. He notes that symbolic capital is the site of fundamental power relations; for symbolic capital to be legitimate, however, it must first be recognized as such:

Symbolic power is a power of consecration of revelation .... [It]begins to exist only when it is selected and designated as such, a group, a class, a gender, a region, or a nation begins to exist as such, for those who belong to it as well as for the others, only when it is distinguished according to one principle or another, from other groups, that is, through knowledge and recognition (*connaissance et reconnaissance*) (Bourdieu 1989: 23).

Without doubt, the patriarchal value system was firmly established during the development of the Sikh community. Men, furbished with the cultural and social capital traditionally associated with their gender, were already placed in a powerful hierarchical position. Particularly in later developments, the key players of the movement, the gurus and the masands, were all men. Further, traditional male roles became increasingly valued and female roles devalued with the institutionalization and politicization of the Sikh panth. While there were exceptions to the rule, the ethos dominating the developing Sikh community was clearly patriarchal, hierarchical, and masculine. However, *symbolic* and *ritual* capital had not accompanied this development. Devotion to the guru, initiation into the Sikh panth, visiting the established places of worship (*dharamsalas*), ritual bathing and pilgrimage—these had been open to all members regardless of gender; the importance of gender as definitive signifier for the rewards of emancipation came about with the institution of the Khalsa. The stage was now definitively set for a 'theology of difference' based on gender, both ritual and symbolic, along with an already established cultural and social gender hierarchy. Thus was enacted a novel construct of gender difference in the development of Sikhism. The transformation from masculine to hypermasculine ethos was now complete.

THE 'WILES OF WOMEN'

If we look to the writings of Guru Gobind Singh which have been incorporated into the *Dasam Granth*, the *Pakhyan Charitra*, also known as the *Triya Charitra*, forms the bulk of the volume. Essentially, it is a collection of 404 tales about the wiles of women. John Campbell Oman (1973: 196–8) recounts a popular story in which a beautiful widow attempted to seduce the guru by disguising herself as a young sadhu who would reveal the goddess Devi to him at a specific spot at midnight. The guru, caught in an embarrassing situation, was shocked at her intrigue and managed to flee from the area. This was the famous occasion that prompted Guru Gobind Singh to collect and write down these tales on the guile of women. As Dharam Pal Ashta (1959: 156) notes, '[t]he chief merit of these tales is moral suggestiveness. While indirectly they instruct men in good moral behaviour, they warn the unwary against womanly enticements.' However, the collection also contains stories in which women play no part at all, as well as tales of heroic and honourable women. Woman is portrayed as victim, but also as inherently powerful over man. Yet, most of the themes are of love, sexual intrigue, and violence. In the depiction of sexual debauchery, women are often the seducers. One verse sums up their intrigues: 'There is no end to the fancies of these women, Even the Creator after having created them repented. Even he who has created the whole Universe accepted defeat, after he had probed into the secrets of women.' Further, the *Dasam Granth* enjoins the following: 'Whatsoever calamities befall a shrewd man, he will endure facing countless tribulations. But in spite of all this he will not disclose his secrets to women' (cited in Ashta 1959: 154, 156).

Many historians and theologians have downplayed the importance of this work; its actual authorship has also been a point of heated controversy. By and large it has been posited as unlikely to have stemmed from the tenth guru. This perspective must be traced to the early twentieth century. According to Macauliffe (1990, Vol. V: 260),

Several intelligent Sikhs were of the opinion that the tales and translations in the volume, as at present found, ought not to have been included in it, for many of them are of Hindu origin, others not fit for perusal and none comparable with hymns contained in *Adi Granth*. The Sikhs, therefore, maintained that the *Hikayats* or Persian Tales, and the whole of the *Triya Charitra* or stories illustrating the deceits of women, should be omitted and included in a separate volume which might be read not for religious purposes but for the entertainment and delectation of the public.

More importantly, however, Sikhs of the eighteenth and nineteenth centuries held the *Dasam Granth* at par with the *Adi Granth*. One of the first European accounts (Malcolm 1812: 173) of the Sikhs indicated clearly that the *Dasam Granth* was 'considered in every respect, as holy as the Adi Granth'. Given the 'Pakhyan Charitra's' stark condemnation of what was understood to be implicit in womanhood, the wiles-of-women narratives must be viewed as essential in configuring the construction of gender during the time of the tenth guru, particularly in the light of the specific male construct initiated by the guru through the Khalsa order. Women in the 'Pakhyan Charitra' symbolized the ultimate antithesis of the warrior-saint norm the guru was attempting to construct. Women had the power to turn the warrior-saint away from his true calling. According to Ashta (1959: 153), while these 'stories may not be a pleasant reading, but they do imply lessons of warning to the reader against feminine wiles.' Thus, regardless of whether its authorship can be attributed to Guru Gobind Singh or not, the work is of considerable importance in understanding gender construction in the immediate post-guru period; remnants of these attitudes toward women can also be traced directly to the *Chaupa Singh Rahit-nama*.

THE CHAUPA SINGH RAHIT-NAMA

If we turn to the Sikh rahit-namas, the codes of conduct that have evolved from the time of Guru Gobind Singh to the present time, we find an extensive amount of information pointing to an increased differentiation between women and men in the Sikh community. The *Chaupa Singh Rahit-nama* is the earliest of all the extant rahits. Though suspect today, given its overt deference towards the Brahmin caste and other 'anti-Sikh' interests and involvements, it is of considerable importance because of the time of its origin: fifty years after the death of Guru Gobind Singh. Further, it originated, at least in theory, with an esteemed member of the Guru's retinue, (ibid.: 180) Chaupa Singh Chhibbar. According to McLeod, the text was written around the middle of the eighteenth century. He notes that this 'does not necessarily identify the actual origin of the rahit sections, but it does demonstrate that for one section of the panth they were regarded as authoritative during the middle years of the eighteenth century' (McLeod 1987: 19).

The rules outlined for the Guru's Sikhs make it increasingly clear that women simply were not included in the 'regular' discipline outlined for the Khalsa. Many of the injunctions dealing with women relate to their associations with male Sikhs, especially male family members. 'A Gursikhni should sustain a placid and dutiful disposition. She should regard her husband as her lord. Other [male relatives] should be treated in accordance with their actual status—whether father, brother or son.' Further, a 'Gursikhni should never abuse or berate a man, nor should she fight with a man' (ibid.: 188, 189). While a Gursikhni should visit the dharamsala twice a day, she is never to read the Granth Sahib in a *Sikh* [italics mine] assembly. However, women can read the scriptures in a gathering of Gursikhnis (ibid: 187–9). Most specifically, anyone who administered initiation by sword (khande di pahul) to a Sikh woman must offer penance (ibid.: 186). As McLeod (1987: 240) has pointed out, a later work, known as the Piara Singh Padam text, reversed this prohibition, thus reflecting the concerns of a later period of Khalsa identity.

Notions of impurity, which the earliest Guru had strictly censured, were here also associated with women, as was a scepticism with regard to the credibility of women. Penance was also required of a man who ate food left over by a woman. Further, similar to Guru Ram Das' words, '[s]inful men, licentious and stupid, act as their women command. Lust abounds; thus do impure men take orders from their women and act accordingly' (*Adi Granth*: 304), the *Chaupa Singh Rahit-nama* warns that a 'Gursikh should never trust a woman, neither his own nor another's. Never entrust them with a secret. Regard them as the embodiment of deceit' (McLeod, 1987: 158). The nuanced ambivalence toward women during the early Guru period became radically accentuated through the polarization of the sexes brought about by the construction of the warrior-saint ideal—an ideal that applied only to the male Sikh.

The widening gulf between male and female Sikhs was apparent in other subtle ways. A true Sikh, Chaupa Singh noted, did not wear red (ibid.: 180). Kahn Singh expanded on this injunction in his famous work, *Gurumat Maratand*. He explained that because red was associated with women's clothing, it was thus 'inappropriate for the manly' (McLeod 1987: 236). Further, Sikhs did not dye their hands with henna, or apply collyrium to their eyes (ibid.: 180, 185). Again, as these practices were associated with the feminine, the injunctions were obviously meant for male members of the Khalsa. Joan Acker (1991: 167) has noted that in the 'gendering' process of organizational development, certain interactive courses must be taken to ensure that men retain the highest positions of organizational power. The aim is the construction of divisions along lines of gender. Second, and most intricately linked to the demarcation of men and women in the Sikh tradition, 'is the construction of symbols and images that explain, express, reinforce... those divisions. These have many sources or forms in language, ideology, popular and high culture, [and] dress.'

CONCLUSION

Accompanying the emergence of the militarized Khalsa was a polarization of gender; increasingly, attention came to be given to 'true' manliness, true warrior-saintliness. In Joan Wallach Scott's analysis of gender polarity, that which is dominant needs the secondary for its very identity (1988: 8). The dominant, normative pole can stand only in relation to the subordinate, against which it can be compared favourably. The primary concentration on true Sikh identity open only to males demanded that women subsidize that equation by being the negative or the opposite of that identity.

In other words, when one gender was predominantly fostered it could only be to the detriment of the 'opposite' gender. Thus to be a true Sikh in the eighteenth century required one's initiation into the Khalsa brotherhood, the wearing of external signifiers, military implements in particular, and taking on the appellation Singh. Moreover, the Chaupa Singh Rahit-nama maintained that a Sikh should never be called by only the first half of his name. Women, by virtue of their exclusion from the naming ritual, were not included in this injunction. To be a 'secondary' Sikh thus meant that one did *not* undergo initiation by khande di pahul, did *not* wear arms, and was *not* called Singh. More precisely, secondary Sikhs were not true men; they were either womanly (those men who refused to heed the Guru's call) or women.

Popular sources offer interesting and practical perspectives on this phenomenon. According to tradition, during the desperate situation following the battle of Anandpur, forty men resolved to abandon their Guru and return to their homes. Mai Bhago, the former wet nurse of Guru Gobind Singh's son Zorawer Singh, taunted the deserters and led them back into the battlefield in search of Guru Gobind Singh (Fenech 1996: 184). The men once again joined in the battle *alongside* Mai Bhago and fought to their death in the Battle of Muktsar. The only survivor was Mai Bhago, who was honoured for her bravery by being made a bodyguard of the Guru. According to Macauliffe (1990, Vol. V: 220),

The woman Bhago who remained with the Guru after the battle of Muktsar, in a fit of devotional abstraction tore off her clothes and wandered half naked in the forest. The Guru restrained her, gave her the *kachh* or Sikh drawers, and allowed her again to wear man's costume. She attained a good old age, and died in Abchalanagar (Nandar) revered by the Sikhs as a saint.

Central to this account is the issue of Mai Bhago being dressed in male attire, having donned the kachh, or breeches. Mai Bhago has been commonly used as an example of the inherent equality of women and men in the Sikh tradition; the Guru, it is said, welcomed all into his military brotherhood. And yet, the circumstances are fraught with ambiguity; the notion of equality is not as clear as many proponents would have us believe. One must question whether Mai Bhago's inclusion points to the equality between the sexes or to distorted notions of masculinity, femininity, and sexuality.

For only upon appropriation of male attire, only in the suppression of her femaleness, is she recognized as one worthy of honour. By the very fact that she is a notable historical figure *because* she is understood at the most basic level as a man embodied in female form, women are implicitly defined as marginal to society. This perspective speaks loudly about the Guru's appraisal of women in general who did *not* appropriate male identity markers. As a woman, it could only be upon the suppression of her sexuality, in her exchange of female for male attire, that Mai Bhago could continue as an acceptable member of the Guru's retinue.

Another fascinating aspect of this incident is the understanding that Mai Bhago taunted the deserting males. As Louis Fenech has pointed out in his study of the taunt in Sikh tales of heroism and martyrdom, women's taunt was often accompanied or replaced by the giving of a glass bangle to a male, *churian paunian*. The purpose of the bangle or the taunt was to present that particular male as effeminate. According to Fenech (1996: 183),

In essence such displays demonstrate that the male has been deprived of the force and vigour with which he is characteristically associated in Punjabi culture. He is in other words emasculated.... Within Punjabi culture referring to men as women, particularly by women, is a grave insult and is meant to persuade the males to demonstrate the contrary.

The incident of Mai Bhago donning male garb and her taunting of the forty deserters becomes all the more intelligible given the pronounced emphasis on male gender construction through the creation of the Khalsa during the late seventeenth century. Femaleness had become the direct antithesis of manliness; no greater insult could be offered to a male of the Khalsa than to compare him or his actions to those associated with women.

The equations of dominance and subordination, 'true' and 'secondary' membership within the developing Sikh community are of central importance when discussing subsequent constructions of gender. The era ushered in by Punjab's annexation into British territory was another important moment in history for the process of identity construction for the Sikhs. Assumptions of gender proved to be central to this process, for both the Imperial rulers and for the newly conquered Sikhs.

THREE

OF COLONY AND GENDER
The Politics of Difference and Similarity

We can write the history of the process only if we recognize that 'man'
and 'woman' are at once empty and overflowing categories. Empty because they have no ultimate, transcendent meaning. Overflowing because
even when they appear to be fixed, they still contain within them alternative, denied, or suppressed definitions.

(Scott 1988: 49).

To contextualize nineteenth-century British attitudes and
interactions with the Sikhs, it is necessary to understand the
interrelation between developments in India and those within
the social, cultural, and religious milieu in Britain before and after
the conquest of India. Significantly, constructions of gender in
Britain played a central role in policies developed by the British in
India. Deeply ingrained assumptions of gender in India, especially
the hypermasculine ethos that undergirded the institution of the
Khalsa, corresponded well with the prevailing Victorian sexual
ethos. As we shall see, these constructions furthered both British
and Sikh causes admirably.

According to Thomas Metcalf (1995), notions of the British as
an imperial people needing to govern others originated in the dis-
coveries and military victories of the Tudor state in the sixteenth
century. Viewing the Irish as little more than pagans and barbarians,
the British set out in the 1560s and 1570s to impose their rule
upon Ireland. For the first time, though not the last, the British
perceived themselves as the 'new Romans' with a mandate to civilize
unenlightened peoples. British patriotism gained momentum during
the eighteenth century with the uniting of the English, the Scot,
and the Welsh into 'one community set apart', especially in a united
participation in British expansion across the seas. Moreover, this ethos
of Enlightenment conferred an attitude of European superiority

over all other peoples. Antithetical to the assumptions of progres-
siveness and modernity underlying European self-perception, was
their understanding of those who were primitive, savage, *not* 'enlightened'—essentially, non-Europeans. As Metcalf (ibid.: 3–6) puts
it, such 'alterity, what one might call the creation of doubleness,
was an integral part of the Enlightenment project.'

Religious developments in Britain also added an important element to British imperialism. Reacting largely to Roman and Anglican
Catholicism, the Evangelical revivalist movement of the late
eighteenth and nineteenth centuries sought to foster a notion of
Christian manliness, or 'muscular Christianity'.[1] This understanding
was in direct opposition to Catholic tendencies, believed by the
revivalists to encourage effeminacy in men. The Catholic advocacy
of clerical celibacy, as well as conventions such as the use of
incense, flowers, and cassocks were perceived as striking at the
very heart of manliness (Knight 1997: 34, Wolffe 1991: 107–44).
Further, in the eighteenth century, women more than men were
likely to be involved in church or chapel activities. To combat the
notion that Christianity was only for the feminine (women) and
the effeminate (Catholics), new ways of presenting the gospel to
men were fostered in the nineteenth century. Underlying this trend
was the notion that a re-interpreted gospel would in turn make
men more 'manly'. This translated into a tradition of Christian
militarism that combined elements of the armed fighter with
Evangelical Christian fervour. Martial imagery in hymns such as
'Onward Christian Soldiers' and the foundation of Christian military groups such as the Salvation Army, complete with uniforms,
titles, and military ranks, were a part of the Evangelical ardency of
the time (Richards 1992: 87). However, it was not only Christianity
that was militarized, attitudes toward the military itself underwent
a profound transformation. Contrary to earlier notions of the
'rapacious and licentious soldiery', the new soldier was transfigured
into the hero, the dauntless champion of the imperialist cause
(MacKenzie 1992: 1). Positive attitudes towards war went beyond
their religious underpinnings; they were also deeply-seated aspects
of the intellectual, philosophical, and cultural trends of the age.
According to a popular dictum, 'Man is created to fight; he is
perhaps best of all definable as a born soldier; his life "a battle and
a march" under the right General' (Carlyle 1905, cited in MacKenzie
1992: 2).

Accompanying the 'Christianization' of the army and the divine right of imperial rule was a 'cult of manliness', a development grounded on the Evangelical focus on manliness which by the late nineteenth century had become a powerful middle-class moral code (Hyam 1990: 72–3). Notions of masculinity were intricately tied to patriotism and imperial destiny. Sir Robert Baden-Powell (1908: 309–15) was instrumental in the development of this sentiment; to make the upcoming generation 'into good citizens or useful colonists' was the rousing call of the Boy Scout movement. It translated into a preoccupation with competitive sports; football, cricket, and boxing came to be viewed as moral agents, capable of moulding the young boy into an upright combatant in preparation for the higher calling of imperial expansion. It was as Hyam (1990: 72) noted:

a shift from the ideals of moral strenuousness, a Christian manliness, to a cult of the emphatically physical (what later generations would call 'machismo'); a shift from serious earnestness to robust virility, from integrity to hardness, from the ideals of godliness and good learning to those of clean manliness and good form. Manliness, it has been said, moved first from chapel to changing-room.

That which did not fit into this Victorian construct of masculinity was labelled 'effeminate, un-English and excessively intellectual' (Newsome 1961, in Hyam 1990: 72). Britain, more than any other nation in the world, saw itself at the apex of true masculinity and imperial destiny.

This late-Victorian emphasis on manliness also had its feminine counterpart. Evangelical notions of womanhood had far-reaching effects on the expectations and ideals of women. Based on 'scientifically' resolved biological determinants, women were perceived as inherently fragile, passive, and emotional. As Metcalf (1995:93) explains, men 'were to be active in the public world, competing against each other for power and wealth; while women, from the sanctuary of the home were to nurture their husbands and children and so uphold society's values.' It became the 'manly' Christian's duty to render the framework within which to protect and provide for both his wife and children. This led to what Knight (1997: 26, 27) has labelled the 'excessive adulation of domesticity' that was based not only on religious sentiments, but also on Britain's rapid transformation from rural to predominantly urban and industrial

society. Industrialization and urbanization combined to 'produce a
rootless proletariat, disorientated by the breakdown of traditional community in an unfamiliar urban environment' (Smith 1994: 32); for
the first time in British and European society at large, people were
quite likely to find themselves living among virtual strangers.
The enlarging of the middle-class environment led to a novel signification of home and family. Women were elevated as guardians of
the faith who were more naturally spiritual than men; they were
the anchors that maintained the stability of the home as the world
changed rapidly around them. Life was increasingly divided into
public and private spheres. The public domain was where men
conducted their duties; the home was the place where women
carried out their responsibilities. Along with this division and the
elevation of domesticity and the family came notions of the purity,
gentleness, and frailty of women. Pre-industrial religion had
allowed women to take an active role in preaching activities. With
the sanctification of the home came a more conservative domesticity. Female assertiveness became inadmissible; instead of women's
grievances reaching the pulpit, they were redefined in private and
personal terms (Valenze 1985: 11). This mentality ultimately became the legacy of Victorian Britain. It had not been present in the
seventeenth and eighteenth centuries when women, men, and
children had worked together in family groups, living on a joint
income procured from the contributions of all. The nineteenth-
century construction of femininity, as well as transformed understandings of masculinity, had profound ramifications on the imperial
project as it progressed in India.

COLONIZATION AND THE POLITICS OF DIFFERENCE

The religious, economic, and social developments in Britain played
themselves out in complex and manifest ways. With the
inauguration of the British empire in India in the middle of the
eighteenth century, British colonizers were prompted to ask and
answer certain questions about their own identity as Britons, about
the essence of the newly conquered Indians, and about their
relationship to their Indian subjects. 'Conquest provoked the
questions, and it also provided the means for a more intimate
knowledge of India by which they could be answered' (Trautman

1997: 3). The questions asked and answered took dramatic turns during the course of the eighteenth and nineteenth centuries. What Thomas Trautman describes as 'Indomania' began in the eighteenth century with educated European gentlemen unreservedly enthused by the study of Sanskrit; in the similarities of Sanskrit, Greek, and Latin, they saw an intimate kinship between British and Indian civilizations. The earliest Orientalists, most notably Friedrich Max Müller, looked to the ancient Vedas to understand the origin of this kinship. Through their analysis of Vedic sources, Orientalists concluded that India's civilization was older and more original than that of Greece; the authority of scripture stemmed from its independence and antiquity in comparison to the Bible. It followed then that enthusiasm for India was ultimately an enthusiasm for Hinduism. But it was to a long-forgotten Hinduism of yore that the Sanskritists mainly looked for inspiration. Scrutinizing the Vedas, these inquirers deduced that at its archaic core, Hinduism, was basically monotheistic; the pantheon of images which was so distasteful in their Christian evaluation was understood as a later, more vulgar interpretation for the masses and the result of a corrupted Brahminical value system. Still, Hinduism in its contemporary context was the enigmatic link to the wisdom of Vedic antiquity and was thus a domain worthy of dutiful attention.

With the nineteenth century came the radically diverging Evangelical and Utilitarian movements. In India, they came to be represented chiefly by Charles Grant and James Mill. In conjunction, the two movements constituted the prevailing Anglicist policy of the nineteenth century. Trautman characterizes the profound change in British attitudes in the early nineteenth century as a move from 'Indomania' to 'Indophobia', constructed by Evangelicalism and Utilitarianism (ibid.: 99). Challenging the untrammelled enthusiasm of the early Sanskritists for Indian language, religion, laws, and culture, Charles Grant insisted with equal Evangelical fervour that it was only through aggressive Anglicization and Christianizing policies that India could be lifted up from its moral corruption. The cure, according to Grant, especially with regard to Hinduism as the crux of this degeneracy, was through Indians being educated in British arts, philosophy, and religion, in the English language. Comparing Indian and European morality, Grant ascertained that 'there is a difference analogous to the difference of the natural colour of the two races.' Despite representations of the Indian people as 'amiable and respectable', in reality, 'they are a people exceedingly depraved' (1796, cited in Trautman 1997: 102–3). This dual focus, on moral depravity and race, became the calling card of the reformist zeal of Charles Grant and subsequent Anglicists. James Mill advocated a secularized version of Grant's thesis—a call to progress that was based on an aggressive policy of modernization. The reformation of India based on Anglicist policy was to be a strictly one-way assimilation process, as opposed to the early Sanskritist position that had advocated a thorough immersion into the cultures, languages, and religions of India. Thomas Babington Macaulay (1835, in de Bary 1964: 601) summed up the Anglicist policy when he promoted the formation of an elite native class that was 'Indian in blood and colour, but English in taste, in opinions, in morals, and in intellect.'

One of the cornerstones of these new developments was the rise of social Darwinism in Europe in the 1860s and the subsequent collapse of the six-thousand-year-old Biblical chronology of human history. Contrary to what had previously been known, racial differences among human beings had progressed over a time scale of vast proportions. In India, this translated into a new perspective with regard to the formation of Indo-European languages; these were fairly recent developments and were therefore less consequential. The focus thus shifted from philological exploration of human history to 'indubitable' scientific rigour in the form of biological inquiry, now understood to be the new master key to unlocking the mysteries of ancient history.

The Aryan race theory or Aryan invasion theory, was an ingenious tool of the nineteenth century utilized to understand the contemporary conditions in India. Max Müller, the chief spokesperson for the early Sanskritists, had earlier used it to show that the civilizing process of the Aryans had culminated in the south of India with peaceful colonization by the Brahmins. Müller (1847, cited in Trautman 1997: 176) had suggested that they 'followed the wiser policy of adopting [for] themselves the language of the aboriginal people and of conveying through its medium their knowledge and instruction to the minds of uncivilized tribes' as opposed to the vanquishing, destroying, and subjection which took place in the north of India from whence the invaders came. This interpretation of historical events came to be contradicted with novel versions of the invasion theory in the nineteenth century. Having taken on a distinctly biological flavour, the theory asserted that the 'higher civilization and the superior physique' of the Aryan invaders became soiled as they advanced further south and eastward though their intermingling with the uncivilized; their higher creeds came eventually to be corrupted by 'foul Dravidian worships of Siva and Kali, and the adoration of the lingam and the snake' (Taylor, cited in Trautman 1997: 185).

The divine right to rule the loathsome Dravidians, increasingly characterized as a weakened, morally corrupt, and effete race of people, was not difficult for the nineteenth-century imperialist mindset to justify. Yet, with the final annexation of Punjab and the subsequent encounter with the frontier peoples, the colonial project needed to restructure its attitudes regarding the vast differences between its Indian subjects and their colonial masters. Through a complex interplay of the Victorian ideals of masculinity, biological understandings of race and colour, British perceptions of Indians as weak and beleaguered in general, and antithetically, the hardy, masculine, and 'martial' Indian races of the north, the colonizers sought theories which would better explain the Indian condition. Claiming simply to be maintaining an ancient Indian tradition, the British made rigid distinctions between the so-called martial and non-martial Indian races. The former were correspondingly represented as 'masculine' and the non-martial races as 'soft' and 'effeminate'. But, as Mrinalini Sinha (1995: 8) has pointed out, this distinction had less to do with an indigenous Indian tradition than with a 'colonial understanding of the ways in which certain attributes of masculinity were supposedly distributed in traditional Indian society.' In essence, this notion drew sustenance from the colonizers, as the martial races were those who most closely matched British perceptions of themselves. The benefits and rewards inherent in being classified by the British as belonging to the martial races were widely known by those who were *not* included in this rubric. The Khatris of Punjab, originally classified as Vaisyas in the Census of 1901, held great protest meetings, and claimed instead to be direct descendents of the Kshatriyas of ancient Hindu mythology, the great warrior-caste lineage. Census superintendents were accordingly instructed to include the Khatris under the Kshatriya warrior caste in their classification project. The anthropologist Sir Herbert Risley notes (1915: 113) with not a small degree of imperialistic self-satisfaction that the decision 'served to illustrate the practical working of the principle that the sole test of social precedence prescribed was Indian public opinion, and that this test was to be applied with due consideration for the susceptibilities of the persons concerned.'

Risley developed an elaborate scheme to scientifically prove that definite differences between the conquered peoples of India existed. Based on indices such as head size, stature, and colour, he analysed the inhabitants of north-west India: (ibid.: 49)

We are concerned merely with the fact that there exists in the Punjab and Rajputana at the present day, a definite type, represented by the Jats and Rajputs, which is marked by a relatively long (dolicho-cephalic) head; a straight, finely cut (leptorrhine) nose; a long, symmetrically narrow face; a well-developed forehead, regular features, and a high facial angle. The stature is high and the general build of the figure is well proportioned, being relatively massive in the Jats and relatively slender in the Rajputs. Throughout the group the predominant colour of the skin is a very light transparent brown, with a tendency towards darker shades in the lower social strata.... In respect of their social characters the Indo-Aryans, as I have ventured to call them, are equally wholly distinct from the bulk of the Indian people. They have not wholly escaped the contagion of caste, but its bonds are less rigid among them than with any other Indian races, and the social system retains features which recall the more fluid organization of the tribe.

While in the earlier Indophobic milieu any intimations of possible kinship between Indians and the British were loudly refuted, in the newly conquered people of Punjab, the colonizers found remnants of ancient ties which inextricably bound them. They found more elements of kinship with the Jat Sikhs than with any other group. The British saw in them a reflection of themselves in an earlier, less civilized age (Cunningham 1990: 114). Beyond perceived ties of colour, race, or notions of gender, the prevalent village community and its peasant population caught the British imagination. George Campbell (1893: 46–7) compared the eighteenth-century Sikh rulers in Punjab to the princes of medieval Germany. He was amazed that the Sikh Jats could create a 'complete and fully organized feudal system'. The only explanation he could offer was that the 'feudal system which prevailed in Europe is a sort of natural instinctive habit of the Aryan race when they go forth to conquer' (see also Dewey 1972: 291–328).

MANLINESS, MORALITY, AND THE POLITICS OF SIMILARITY

Early accounts of the people of Punjab focus largely on what the British considered a 'new' breed of men—'handsome... resembling Hindoos in general, but with a finer muscular development, and a more robust appearance' who were skilled in martial arts and unsurpassed as agriculturalists (Steinbach 1846: 212). The British had begrudgingly admired the Sikh ruler Ranjit Singh, who had for years withstood the advances of the British. Upon his demise, his successors, lacking Maharajah Ranjit Singh's administrative and political skills, could not hold off the advancing British army. After two Anglo–Sikh wars in the 1830s and 1840s, the development of the area described as 'the Land of the Five Rivers' became the locus of British activities. Concerted efforts were made to understand the inhabitants of Punjab, even before the establishment of British rule. Given the legacy of the ten Sikh gurus, purity laws and Brahminic influences were downplayed by the Sikhs; Hinduism, described by Risley (1915: 252) as having 'an unedifying mythology, a grotesque Pantheon, a burdensome ritual, a corrupt priesthood', and above all, tainted by a 'palpable idolatry' had a weakened hold on Punjab's inhabitants. Martial aptitude, especially honoured by the British, had been fostered by Guru Gobind Singh with the creation of the Khalsa. In this regard the Sikhs, at least in terms of Khalsa ideology, were perceived as vastly different and superior to their Hindu co-religionists (Malcolm 1812: 189). They were also superior to Muslims. The effects of Islam on a man, while leading to 'manly' characteristics, also filled him, according to Ibbetson, with 'false pride and conceit, disinclined him for honest toil, and renders him more extravagant, less thrifty, less contented, and less well-to-do than his Hindu neighbour' (cited in Thorburn 1983: 16). The Jat Sikh also reigned supreme as an example of a caste group that had overturned rigid Brahminical codes of hierarchy and had risen in stature through its embrace of the tenets of Sikhism (Barstow 1984: 168). Further, the Jat as peasant par excellance was acclaimed for his agricultural competence. Most importantly, in the area of cultivation, Punjab represented for the British a rich minefield of revenue acquisition for the insatiable imperial coffers.

Similar to the early Orientalist enterprise, British administrators turned to Sikh sacred scriptures in an attempt to understand the *true* nature of Sikhism. Given their own Christian framework, they responded warmly to the Sikh scriptural vision of 'the One'—true, ineffable, and everlasting—and contrasted this with the baffling array of the Hindu pantheon. As an early army account notes, 'There is no branch of this sketch which is more curious and important, or that offers more difficulties to the enquirer, than the religion of the Sikhs. We meet with a creed of pure deism, grounded on the most sublime general truths' (Steinbach 1846: 119). Early missionaries furthered this identification, once again favourably contrasting Sikhism with Hinduism. The Reverend E. Guilford (1915: 28–9) purported that a study of·Sikhism yielded not a few points of contact with the great truths revealed in Jesus Christ.

The *Shabd* of the Granth is in truth no other than the Eternal Logos—'The true Light that lighteth every man coming into the world', who has not left Himself without witness in any age or nation... [However] [t]he mass of Nanak's followers have not risen to his ideals, for they are still bound by the grave-clothes of Hindu superstition... yet the influence of his teaching has been such as to mark the Sikhs, as a nation, as being far in advance of any other people of India in spiritual conceptions, and in moral ideals and aspirations.

Christian missionaries believed that the reforming spirit inaugurated by Guru Nanak was now to be fulfilled by the truths of Christianity: the theological contributions of the Sikh Gurus were not in themselves enough to guide Sikhs to their fullest potential. Nonetheless, the very recognition of analogies between Christianity and Sikhism paved the way for further points of relationality. Fitzpatrick and Clark (1886, cited in Singh, N.K. 1992: 246) appointed to Punjab in 1851, expressed this point clearly:

Though the Brahman religion still sways the minds of a large proportion of the population of the Punjab, and the Mohammedan of another, the dominant religion and power for the last century has been the Sikh religion, a species of pure theism, formed in the first instance by a dissenting sect from Hinduism. A few hopeful instances lead us to believe that the Sikhs may prove more accessible to scriptural truths than the Hindus and Mohammedans.

For the British mindset, the martial overtones of the Sikh religion were particularly engaging; the militarized/masculinized enterprise of Protestant Christianity corresponded readily to Sikh delineation of the Ultimate as *Sarab Loh*, or 'All Steel', depictions of God that had assumed significance since the militarization of Sikhism. During the early guru period, the Ultimate was most commonly referred to as *Akal Purakh*, the 'Timeless Being', reflective of the mystical and elusive understanding of the Supreme Being stemming from the North Indian Sant parampara. The change 'significantly affected the subsequent understanding and promulgation of Sikh doctrine.' In the transformation to *Sarab Loh*, divinity was 'made manifest in the burnished steel of the unsheathed sword' (McLeod 1989: 52). Martial imagery had thus become central to Sikh doctrine and most specifically to the initiation rite, whereby sweetened water was to be stirred by a double-edged sword, *khande*. In its highly masculine and martial imagery, orthodox Sikhism compared favourably with Hindu devotional practices, specifically the effeminate veneration of female deities and a corrupt and abusive priesthood. The lack of a formalized priesthood in Sikhism also corresponded well with Protestant notions of a priesthood of believers, especially given the highly disparaged clerical order of Catholicism that was deemed as most responsible for the feminization of Christianity. In essence, Sikh religious symbols, martial implements of a highly masculine nature, their religious administration, and their uniform, militarized dress code complemented the nineteenth century's Evangelical ethos in Britain. Certainly, there was little that could be construed as effeminate in the religious imagery, practices, and rites of the Khalsa Sikhs.

However, the earliest accounts of the British denote intrigue and even dismay with regard to the variance present in the classification 'Sikh'. This translated into censure when variations of Sikh identity did not fit into British attempts to create a powerful Sikh military machine. For British administrators, the tenets of Guru Gobind Singh were responsible for the creation of martially astute men (see Falcon 1896: 14–15). Thus the British turned to the Sikhs of the Khalsa, the 'true' Sikhs, describing them as 'generally speaking, brave, active and cheerful, without polish, but neither destitute of sincerity nor attachment'. Those Sikhs who were not of the Khalsa brotherhood Steinbach (1846: 113–15) described as, 'Full of intrigue, pliant, versatile, and insinuating, they have all the art of the lower classes of Hindus, who are usually employed in transacting business: from whom, indeed, as they have no distinction of dress, it is very difficult to distinguish them'. The Sikhs who were signified as Nanak Pautra, or descendents of Guru Nanak, he depicts as having the 'character of being a mild, inoffensive race... They do not carry arms; and profess, agreeably to the doctrine of Nanac, to be at peace with all mankind'.

These descriptions of the types of Sikhs are remarkable for the way in which much of the burden is carried by the adjectives. The Khalsa Sikh was early on identified primarily with the Jat Sikh (Falcon 1896: 65, Franklin 1803: 74). He was admiringly described as, 'generally tall and muscular, with... erect carriage... They make admirable soldiers... inferior to no native race in India' (Barstow 1984: 166). The images of those other than the Khalsa Sikh were derogatory, namely, they were 'insinuating', 'full of intrigue', 'pliant' and 'mild', and 'of somewhat soft material' (Steinbach 1846: 114–15).

It is significant that the same Khatri trader class is also described by Falcon as 'an intelligent, fine race', while the Jat Sikh was not in any way devalued though characterized as 'too slow to understand when he is beaten', 'impatient of education, as slow witted, as simple in his habits and ideas as when Ranjit Singh formed him into a semblance of a nation'. British ideals of masculinity, sportsmanship, and militarism formed the parameters of the discourse on gender in the nineteenth century; these descriptions reflected those values. Very intellectual men had little place in the British imperial ethos of the nineteenth century. As G.A. Henty, the nineteenth-century boys' fiction writer, stated in *Through the Sikh Wars*:

Give me a lad with pluck and spirit, and I don't care a snap of the fingers whether he can construe Euripides or solve a problem in higher mathematics. What we want for India are men who can ride and shoot, who are ready at any moment to start on a hundred mile journey on horseback, who will scale a hill fort with a handful of men, or with a half a dozen sowars tackle a dacoit and his band (cited in Richards 1992: 93).

Given British contentions of true masculinity, Khalsa Sikhs, characterized as *not* mild and *not* soft, represented points of similarity between Khala Sikhism and the British ideals of masculinity. In the light of colonial interpretations of the religious militancy of the Sikhs, the British foresaw Khalsa Sikhs as fitting into their own interests in the fortification and peace-keeping efforts in Punjab and the whole of India. It was believed that under the firm guidance of the British, the rather lawless and turbulent Punjabis could be moulded into an efficient fighting machine. The Khalsa Sikh was

identified as a natural soldier, one who under genteel British
influence and authority could stand among the finest of native
soldiery. It was thus to the Khalsa Sikhs that the British turned
their attention and efforts. However, the British noted with some
alarm that these true Sikhs were on the decline. As early as 1853,
Sir Richard Temple prophesied that 'the Sikh faith and ecclesias-
tical polity is rapidly going where the Sikh political ascendancy
has already gone.... They rejoin the ranks of Hinduism whence they
originally came' (cited in Fox 1990: 8). Given their penchant for
Census classifications, the British administration noted that the
Singhs, the true Sikhs, would soon be crushed by the long arm of
Hinduism. The Census of 1881 confirmed their suspicions when a
significantly smaller Sikh population was enumerated than in 1868
(ibid.: 9).

Harjot Oberoi has questioned the oft-touted decline in the number of Sikhs in the nineteenth century. The 1868 Census suffered
severe limitations as not all districts in the province of Punjab were
included in British numeration efforts. Further, there was no indication as to what was meant by the classification 'Sikh'. Punjabis in
the first Census, of 1855, were delineated as either Hindus or
Muslims. By 1868, Sikhs were included in the enumeration but
the definition of 'Sikh' remained unclear. By 1881, only the true
Sikhs, who maintained the external indicators of the Khalsa identity, were classified under the rubric 'Sikh'. All others, including
Sikhs who cut their hair as well as numerous Sikh sects, the
Nanakpanthis, Ramdasis, Nirmalas, Udasis, and other groups, were
classified as Hindus (Oberoi 1994: 208–13). According to Oberoi,
the cosmology of the Sikhs in the eighteenth and the early nineteenth
century embraced a wide variety of religious experience and
expression. Sikhs could choose their rites, rituals, and beliefs. This
latitude was 'reflected, for instance, in the fact that if a Sikh so
desired, he or she could in the same year go to a khanaqah of a
Muslim pir like Sakhi Sarvar in western Punjab, undertake a
pilgrimage to the Golden Temple in central Punjab, and visit
Hardwar to take a dip in the holy Ganges. This sort of ritual exercise
caused no ripples within the Sikh sacred hierarchy.'

The British mindset, however, could understand religion only
within the boundaries of Western religious authority, that is, scriptural authority, that could be easily classified as binding for all.
The religions of India were anomalies to British sensibilities, with

their indulgent intermingling of popular traditions, scriptural authorities, and varied rites. Thus the constrained and tightly boundaried Christian sensibilities of the colonizers set out on a powerful, dual-pronged project of privileging scripture and equating tradition with it, over the everyday realities of Indian society. According to Lata Mani (1990: 90–1), this project must be understood as a significant aspect of colonial discourse in India.

It meant that officials could insist, for instance, that brahmanic and Islamic scriptures were prescriptive texts containing rules of social behaviour, even when the evidence for this assertion was problematic. Further, they could insitutionalize their assumptions... by making these texts the basis of personal law. Official discourse thus had palpable consequences.

Mani delineates colonial or official discourse as a mode of understanding the Indian society that emerged within colonial rule. Over time, it came to be shared by officials, missionaries, and the indigenous elite. This official discourse was, however, utilized by various groups for different, often ideologically opposite ends. The British administration, which admired the martial resonance of the Khalsa ideology, turned to the tenets of Guru Gobind Singh for guidance and took it upon themselves to stem the tide of the Hinduization of Sikhism through their recruitment tactics. Sikhs who were not of the Khalsa faith were characterized as *already* desecrated by the menacing arm of Hinduism. The true and martial variety of Sikhism was overtly nurtured. Recruits into the army were required to undergo Sikh initiation rites before becoming members of the Indian Army (Griffin *et al.* 1940). Macauliffe portrayed the initiated Sikh thus: 'A true Sikh will let his body be cut to pieces when fighting for his master. The Sikh considers dying in battle a means of salvation. No superiority of the enemies in number, no shot, no shell can make his heart quail, since his Amrit (baptism) binds him to fight single-handed against millions' (1990: xix–xx). In insisting that recruits undergo initiation rites before entering the British military system, the British considered themselves to be the protectors of the faith, alone responsible for the continuance of the true martial Sikh spirit in Punjab. It was the hypermasculine, militarized Khalsa Sikh that the British related to, and who, more than any other Indian, fit into British designs of maintaining imperial stability in India.

The timing of Punjab's annexation into the British empire is central in the discussion of gender construction in the nineteenth century. Gender and racial ideology had become a powerful binary yardstick in the nineteenth century in helping to mark the contrast between the ruler and the ruled. The new breed of Indian, the Jat Sikh in particular, was conspicuously contrasted with the Bengali. According to British estimation, the Bengali had responded to imperial educational schemes better than any other group in British India, but had fallen short of the accompanying objective of cultural and religious assimilation and unceasing loyalty to the British. English-educated Indians, who in the mid-nineteenth century were predominately from Bengal, were particularly detested by the colonizers. They were known collectively as *babus*, formerly a term of respect among Indians, but used by the British as an epithet of degradation. With scant memory of Macaulay's design of Anglicizing the Indian, Bengalis were ridiculed for aping British ways. Highly primed in the thought of English liberalism, the babu increasingly challenged the claimed superiority and authority of the Raj. Turning their attention instead to the unpolished though manly frontiersman of the north, the British formed an alliance based largely on perceived differences between the northerner and the Bengali. In fact, the British army took great pains to maintain the image of the manly unpolished Sikh. Whether because of the Sikhs' diet, which included meat as opposed to the stringent vegetarianism of Bengali Vaishnava Hindus, the climatic differences between Bengal in the east and Punjab in the north (a more rigorous climate producing a more rigorous breed of men), or Sikh and British affinity in terms of their love of games, horsemanship, and sports, the British were inextricably drawn to the Punjabi Sikhs. Moreover, dandyism of any sort was to be discouraged among the Sikh soldiery (Falcon 1896: 106, Steinbach 1846: 212). On the other hand, Bengalis had little use for the more masculine tendencies of the British soldier. They 'do not hunt, shoot, [and] play games', these were instead pursuits which the Sikhs shared with the British (Sinha 1995: 42). Bengali failure in sportsmanship was conclusive proof of the crucial difference between the effeminate Bengali and the sport-loving Anglo ruler. In comparison, Parry (1921: 36) offered glowing descriptions of the athletic prowess and sportsmanship of the Sikhs. Further, the Sikhs had little use for stringent purity laws, which allowed for untrammelled British and Sikh fraternizing.

Perhaps most importantly, it was in Bengal that the seeds of discontent towards British rule had been sown in the nineteenth century. The sepoys of the Bengal Army in the Mutiny of 1857 had acted on the build-up of Indian resentment. Bengali activity at this crucial event was viewed as indicative of their subversive nature and exceeding ungratefulness. The inhabitants of Bengal, close kin to the 'foul Dravidian' race which produced effeminate males, were increasingly contrasted with the representatives of the Aryans, the martial races of the frontier. A British newspaper summed up the contrast thus: 'I fancy most of us would not object to being taken before a fine Sikh *Hakim* for instance. Is it the Sikhs who are clamouring for our loss of liberty? or is it any of the warlike races of India?' (*The Englishman*, 2 March 1883, cited in Sinha 1995: 40). Given their belief in the unmitigated difference between themselves and the Bengalis, the British turned to their similarity with the Punjabi Sikhs; the Bengalis came increasingly to represent everything that was anti-British and excessively effeminate in India.

The perception of Bengalis as effeminate was not only a construct of the nineteenth century. Richard Orme writing in 1770 characterized all natives as somewhat effeminate, but insisted that the Bengalis were 'still of weaker frame and more enervated character' (cited in Sinha 1995: 15). Macaulay, perhaps best known for his pronounced attacks on the Bengali character, wrote in the early nineteenth century:

The physical organization of the Bengalee is feeble even to effeminacy. He lives in a constant vapour bath. His pursuits are sedentary, his limbs delicate, his movements languid. During many ages he has been trampled upon by men of bolder and more hardy breeds.... His mind bears a singular analogy to his body. It is weak even to helplessness for purposes of manly resistance; but its suppleness and tact move children of sterner climates to admiration not unmingled with contempt (quoted in Strachey 1911: 450).

Sir John Strachey, writing almost a century after Macaulay, concurred:

It has often been said, and it is probably true, that Bengal is the only country in the world where you can find a great population among whom personal cowardice is looked upon as in no way disgraceful. This is no invention of their enemies; the Bengalis have themselves no shame or scruple in declaring it to be a fact.... But for the presence of our power, Bengal would inevitably and immediately become the prey of the hardier races of other Indian countries (ibid.: 452).

Colonial discourse increasingly attempted to distinguish the sexually enervated Bengali male from the virile frontiersman in the newly annexed British colony of Punjab. Citing determinants such as diet, the hot and humid climate of Bengal, and the social organisation of Hindu society (the Brahminic hierarchy of the caste system in particular), property relations, marital arrangements—especially with regard to 'marrying immature children, the great blot on the social system of the upper class of Bengal'—British writers made much of their perceptions of the differences between the Bengali and the martial races. Contemptuous of Bengali demands for self-rule in the late nineteenth century, British rule in India was justified precisely because of the vast differences *between* Indians, particularly between the Bengalis, the Sikhs and other 'races'.

I used no terms of exaggeration when I said that a native of Calcutta is more of a foreigner to the hardy races on the frontiers of northern India than an Englishman. To suppose that the manlier races of India could ever be governed through the feebler foreigners of another Indian country, however intellectually acute those foreigners may be—that Sikhs and Pathans, for instance, should submit to be ruled by Bengalis—is to suppose an absurdity (ibid.: 548).

Along with British compulsions to distinguish between the various group of Indians came an overarching urgency to produce knowledge that would clarify the differences between the natives and the British. Perhaps even more importantly for our purposes, one outcome of this exercise led to what Metcalf (1995: 113) has called the 'ordering of difference', which inadvertently proposed that some groups of Indians indeed were not *as* different from the British as others were. Jeffrey Richards in his analysis of popular boys' fiction in the late nineteenth century has focused on G.A. Henty's novels to demonstrate British attitudes towards the native populations of India. Henty's novel of 1906, *A Soldier's Daughter*, acknowledged that the Sikhs and Gurkhas counted among the finest fighters in the world, yet Henty was compelled to prove that the British were superior to all others. Given prevailing social Darwinist theories, Henty weighed the martial instinct of the British against other races. Ultimately, the British race was superior for the British possessed this instinct more naturally than did others (Richards 1992: 98–100). British observers noted that the martial prowess of the Sikhs stemmed from a *religious* impulse; for this reason the British fostered the Khalsa identity over all others, though, ultimately, the natural *racial* military instincts of the British were still superior to those fostered by the Khalsa ideal. Further, as already pointed out, the Aryan race theory played an important role in this ordering of difference and similarity. The Punjabi Sikhs, particularly the Sikh Jat, were representative Aryans with ties to the West and concerted efforts were made to substantiate this ancient kinship. MacMunn writing in the early twentieth century made an explicit connection between Britons and the Sikh Jat. He recounted the words of advice from a British officer to Dalip Singh, the son of Maharajah Ranjit Singh, who was sent to England after Punjab's annexation: 'You will be among your own people there, for you are a Jat and the men of Kent are Jats from Jutland' (MacMunn 1932: 14). Others also made this identification, noting that the Sikhs 'maintain with honour the integrity of the British race' (Parry 1921: 122).

The Mutiny of 1857 clinched the British association with the Punjabis. Inflamed by rumours of East India Company's stipulations to use pork and beef fat to grease cartridges, the sepoys of the Bengal Army throughout northern India revolted. Mutinous soldiers seizing Delhi and raising anew the standard of the Mughal empire were joined by other discontented groups throughout the country. Sikh royalty, on the other hand, sent in troops to contain the uprisings. To the Sikhs the British now owed allegiance, for they had stemmed the tide of insurrection and had thus allowed the imperial army to tighten its hold over the mutinous natives. The revolt of 1857 was ruthlessly suppressed; sepoys, even if implicated only by suspicion, were blown from cannons; villagers were haphazardly shot; Delhi, the former Mughal capital, was devastated. Indians were thoroughly demonized by British observers and presented as disloyal, depraved, and most significantly, as violators of Western women. The brutal suppression of the revolt reflected the degree of vulnerability felt by the British in India. Magnification of events, particularly regarding the molestation of white women, as well as utter demonization of Indians allowed the British to avoid taking any responsibility for the uprising (Metcalf 1995: 43–5).

Needless to say, the events of 1857 severely intensified the perceived chasm of difference between the Indian and the Briton. As the revolt was assessed, it developed a more nuanced characterization of those who were loyal to the British and those who were disloyal. The Sikhs, through their propitious display of loyalty, moved into a position of privilege and honour. Strachey (1911: 509–10) noted that the 'mutinies of 1857 showed conclusively that the native states are a source to us, not of weakness, but of strength. In the words of Lord Canning, "these patches of native government served as a breakwater to the storm which would otherwise have swept over us in one great wave".'

Notions of chivalry along with nineteenth-century British understanding of true manliness and femininity played an important part in the politics of similarity between the British and the Sikhs. The latter, as loyal British subjects, managed to fit into this scheme as true men, chivalrous and loyal, maintaining the honour of British women by supporting the British in quelling the rebellion. For the British, the real test of masculinity lay in the chivalric protection of white women from Indian men, for the threat to the white woman's honour was understood as the ultimate affront to Britain itself. The mutiny became the 'essential knightly moment', the critical event in which the British 'went forth to slay the dragon and save the pure damsel immured in the tower' (MacKenzie 1992: 118). Most importantly for the purposes at hand, through what has been characterized as the 'great heroic myth' of the Indian empire, the Sikhs, by way of implication, became enmeshed in British notions of chivalry and loyalty. For, while the widely held notion of the native threat to the white woman's honour came to be refuted by Britons themselves after the quelling of the rebellion (MacMillan 1988: 102), the mutiny inevitably led to an intensification of British political strategies of difference and similarity that were already in place (Richards 1992: 97). The Bengali regiments, as the instigators of the mutiny, were disbanded after the suppression of the revolt; the East India Company was abolished, and Queen Victoria proclaimed the sovereign of India. The relatively few British troops in India since the middle of the nineteenth century were increased, while Indian troops decreased in number (Ballhatchet 1980: 3). In the wake of these changes, the British administration initiated a cautious recruitment process of potential Indian soldiery. Those who fit under the classification of the martial races were systematically

chosen to join the ranks of the Indian army. The Sikhs, characterized as the pinnacle of the martial races, reaped the benefits of
their propitious display of loyalty to the British for years to come.
Punjab chiefs who had stood by the British during the uprising
were given monetary and territorial rewards, and Indian honorary
titles were meted out to loyal princes and officials (Latif 1994:
582–3). Sikhs came to hold a coveted place in the Indian army
and their numbers in it came to be highly disproportionate to their
actual minority status in India.[2]

CONSTRUCTIONS OF WOMANHOOD—THE BRITISH IN INDIA:

Once what can be summed up as the 'politics of similarity' between
the Sikhs and the British was established, the colonizers spared
little effort to expand and strengthen these convictions. Points of
similarity were extended to include feminine constructs as well as
the masculine constructions outlined earlier. In comparing the
earliest British accounts with later representations, one senses a
marked difference in the tone of the descriptions. Malcolm (1812:
139–40), writing half a century before Punjab's annexation
expressed the earlier view:

The conduct of the Sikhs to their women differs in no material respect
from that of the tribes of Hindus or Muhammedans.... Their moral character with regard to women, and indeed in most other points, may, from
the freedom of their habits, generally be considered as much more lax
than that of their ancestors, who lived under the restraint of severe
restrictions, and whose fear of excommunication from their caste, at
least obliged them to cover their sins with the veil of decency. This the
emancipated Sikhs despise: and there is hardly an infamy which this de-
bauched and dissolute race are not accused (and I believe with justice) of
committing in the most open and shameful manner.

The contrast of this description with that of the superintendent
of the Census of 1901 is remarkable: 'No one who has seen the
peasantry, especially the Jat peasantry, in their villages, at fairs and
the like, could for a moment suggest that women and girls in this
province are treated, generally, with cruelty or intentional neglect.
Sikhs, especially, treat women well' (cited in Risley 1915: 177).
The change in this latter description is conspicuous, raising questions

as to how and why this transformation came about. The positive evaluation of Sikhs and their treatment of women was particularly striking, given consistent Census reports depicting conspicuously fewer females than males in Punjabi Sikh society. Female infanticide had long been associated with Jat and Khatri Sikhs. The Census Report of 1881 tabulated the number of females per 1,000 males for each religious community. For girl children under the age of five, the Sikhs enumerated 839, Hindus, 941, Muslims, 962. The numbers decreased significantly for all three when females of all ages were compared to males: Sikhs, 765, Hindus, 834, and Muslims, 864 (ibid.). In the Census Report of 1901, the proportion of girls to boys among children under the age of five ranged from 96 per cent among Muslims and 92 per cent among Hindus, to 76 per cent among Sikhs, with some Sikh-populated tracts falling as low as 62 percent (Strachey 1911: 346). In 1870, the government passed a law enabling the registration of births and deaths among the classes most suspected of infanticide. While the numbers of females did increase over the next fifty years, the Census reports continued to show lower numbers of females among the Sikhs than among other groups. By the end of the nineteenth century, despite evidence to the contrary, the British were satisfied that their intervention had been successful and withdrew the Act.

Risley, in particular, was baffled by the connection between the so-called martial races and the high incidence of female infanticide, and went to great lengths to justify the practice among the Sikh Jats and Rajputs. Distinguishing the practice of infanticide among the martial races as different from the 'savage type' practiced by the Nagas and Khonds, Risley noted that the more 'refined' type of infanticide was associated with a sense of honour; a daughter was made away with 'in the belief that no one will be anxious to marry her, and that the family will be disgraced if she grows up an old maid' (Risley 1915: 174). With the inclusion of honour, highly esteemed by Victorian values, infanticide as practiced by the martial races could be partially understood and apparently excused. Ibbetson (quoted in Risley), while concluding that the life of a girl was undoubtedly less valued than that of a boy among the Sikhs, pointed to 'the contagion of Hindu ideas, among all other classes of the Punjab people without distinction of race, religion, or locality as responsible for this state of affairs'. Ultimately, given the politics of similarity fostered by the British with regard to the Sikhs, when blame for the incidence of female infanticide was conferred in any way, it came to be transferred to the pre-eminent scapegoat of all India's social problems, Hinduism. Others turned to social Darwinism to explain the possible long-term benefits of female infanticide. 'The idea has been thrown out that the practice of killing female infants, if persevered in for many generations, might induce among the surviving women a hereditary tendency to bear more boys than girls' (Risley 1915: 177). Once British kinship with the Sikhs had been established, the colonizers maintained a most positive portrayal of their Aryan kinfolk, establishing convoluted explanations for even their most contradictory conduct.

Further, the Sikhs and the Bengalis were conspicuously contrasted with regard to marriage and consummation practices. The degeneracy of Bengali society was readily traced to their early marriage practices. Unlike the more 'purely Aryan' population of the north, Bengalis lacked manly self-control; early, unnatural sexual activity was responsible for the effeminacy of Bengali manhood and the enervation of Bengali society in general (Sinha 1995: 156). On the other hand, Sikhs, though espousing child marriage, extended the time of consummation until it was no longer harmful to the girl's health (Steele 1929: 16). Ibbetson (cited in Risley 1915: 193) insisted that although there were exceptions, child marriage in Punjab was free from the harmful effects found in Bengal. 'Wherever infant marriage is the custom, the bride and bridegroom do not come together till a second ceremony called *muklawa* has been performed, till when the bride lives as a virgin in her father's house. This second ceremony is separated from the actual wedding by an interval of three, five, seven, nine, or eleven years, and the girl's parents fix the time for it.' Martin noted in 1838 that the 'Pamar Rajputs, among whom the custom of early consummation is adopted, form a striking proof of the evils of this custom.' Among them, he observed not one good-looking man; most had the 'appearance of wanting vigour both of body and mind' (quoted in ibid.: 194–5).

Undoubtedly, the high incidence of female infanticide among the Sikhs had resulted in a great demand for wives. High bride price was perhaps the *most* important factor in the higher age of marriage for Sikh girls (Falcon 1896: 50). Still, the British largely chose to ignore the actual reasons for the higher ages of marriage and underscored only their benefits to the Jats. Ultimately, the 'healthy sense' of the warrior races was contrasted with the Bengali 'demon of corrupt ceremonialism, ever ready to sacrifice helpless women and children to the tradition of a fancied orthodoxy' (Risley 1915: 194). Another observer agreed emphatically, noting that delayed marriages offered positive results on the lives of Indian women. 'The women who have made the most mark in Indian history have been Sikhs, Mahrattas[sic], or Mahommedans; and the reason is probably found in the fact that among these races the marriage of girls is generally deferred to a reasonable age (Griffin, in Poole 1892: viii).

The Sikh custom of somewhat later consummation of marriage corresponded more closely to British sexual practices. Until the late nineteenth century in Britain, the age of consent for sexual activity by females had been twelve; it was raised to thirteen in 1875. Hyam has argued persuasively that prostitution was an acceptable 'intermediate technology' devised to offset the unusually high age at marriage for men in the eighteenth century. Child prostitution too was prevalent in eighteenth-century Britain. As late as 1857, in fact, two hundred child prostitutes under the age of twelve were recorded as working in Liverpool alone. The intense British focus on marriage practices in India stemmed partially from the psychological need to justify their own affairs in Britain and to compensate for British moral standards, both in Britain and in India. The keeping of an Indian *bibi*, or mistress, was commonplace with most Britons until the late 1700s. The age of their Indian sexual partners was not of great concern to British soldiers. The increased numbers of Evangelical missionaries were largely responsible for changes in British sexual practices in India. Further, the Mutiny of 1857, as well as the appearance of British women in India with the opening of the Suez Canal in 1869, widened the distance between the ruling British and their subjects. As a result, the keeping of Indian mistresses was severely censured by army officials (Hyam 1990: 115–20). As British self-perceptions placed them at the pinnacle of social, moral, and physical development, their own achievements had to be understood as stemming from 'correct' social patterns. Again, with the Sikh Jats in particular, Britons found the justification for their own societal norms and values.

Another aspect distinguishing Jat women from their Bengali counterparts, was what the British viewed as their ability to contribute to larger society. Edward Pollard said this about the

'Hindoo' woman: 'unwelcomed at her arrival and often harassed and kept in subjection till her death, *she can contribute little to the welfare of her people* [italics mine].' Pollard (1908: 155) contrasted her with the highly effectual 'mother of the primitive Aryan or Indo-European stock'. According to the Aryan race theory, the Sikh Jats and the Rajputs were the closest remnants of the great Aryans that invaded India. Trumpp (cited in Beames 1869: 137) had unequivocally noted that there 'is no doubt that these Jats, who appear to be the original race in the country, belong to the real Aryan Stock.' In the female Sikh Jat the British had the mother of the Aryan stock in their midst and she in particular grasped their attention, particularly her physique, her stamina, and her participation in agricultural labour. Barstow (1984: 166) noted that Sikh Jat women helping in the fieldwork 'form a marked contrast to Rajput and Mohamedan females, who, being secluded, are *lost* to agricultural labour [italics mine]'. Another administrative report noted that '[t]he women work as hard as the men do if not harder. The heavy tasks of bringing in wood and fuel and water fall on them; they have to cook the food, and carry it daily to the fields; they have to watch the crops; to them the peeling of the sugarcane and picking of the cotton belongs; and when there is nothing else to do, they must always fill up the time by tasks with the spinning wheel' (Purser and Fanshawe 1880, cited in Chowdhry 1990: 307). In terms of monetary gains inherent in the revenue-rich province of Punjab, the contributions of the female Jat to the agrarian milieu procured her proclamation as an economic treasure, resulting in great benefits to British coffers. Popular Punjabi proverbs attested to the benefits of marrying a Jat: 'A Jat wife for me, as all other women are a waste of money' (Darling 1928: 35). Other observers noted that the actual status of Sikh Jat women was little more than that of a servant, nonetheless insisting that 'she is far better treated than her Mussalman or Hindu sister' (Parry 1921: 25). The fact that Sikh women were not 'lost' to the attainment of agricultural stability and development, making their situation similar to that of lower-class rural women in Britain, contributed largely to this positive evaluation of Sikh women and traditional Sikh attitudes toward women.

Another measure comparing Sikh Jat females favourably with their Bengali upper-caste sisters was the fact that for the most part, Sikh women did not observe complete purdah restrictions. For the

British, purdah represented a fundamental and derogatory element separating English domestic ideology from that of India. The self-proclaimed position of the British at the apex of the scale of civilization was intricately tied to the status of their women (Christian Literature Society 1892: 9). As a genteel race, they were at the forefront of the ennobling of women. In stark contrast to the position of British womenfolk, Indian females were viewed as de-nobled, humiliated, and degraded. Purdah and the *zenana* (seclusion) restrictions were important indicators of this abasement; they were also indicative of the wider moral degeneration of India (Metcalf 1995: 94). Victorian religious and social sensibilities spawned an understanding of woman as the helpmate of the man; the ennobled wife, at least for the educated upper class, was to be the intelligent companion of her husband's daily life, she was to confer upon him sympathy and encouragement within an atmosphere of relaxation. She was also to give gentle guidance to 'stimulate him to a course of noble conduct' (Christian Literature Society 1892: 3).

The Bengali woman, wholly separated from her husband's everyday life, was the direct antithesis of this ideal. One British observer spoke contemptuously of the 'natives who practice polygamy, treat their wives as caged birds, kept in the dark chiefly for the creation of sons' (Sinha 1995: 45). The seclusion of the Bengali woman was perceived as inducing in Indian women an unhealthy preoccupation with sex and enfeebling passivity (Borthwick 1984: 228). On the other hand, only a small percentage of the highest caste in Punjab observed purdah. Roughly 80 per cent of the Sikh population lived in rural villages as agricultural peasants. Sikh Jat females, though veiled in public (something which British Victorian sensibilities would have approved of), did not generally practice purdah, and with some restrictions, could freely move about in their field duties. Thus, from a British utilitarian perspective, they were in many ways functional helpmates for their husbands. Moreover, Jat women were not only highly effective as contributors, their independence also allowed for exemplary management of resources (Berstow, 1899: 166–7). While British observers repeatedly critiqued Hindu and Muslim practices, they were appreciative of the fact that female Jats did not languish unproductively behind closed doors.

Once again the colonizers turned to the sacred writings of the Sikhs to understand the true position of women in Sikh society.

Macauliffe in particular, spurred on by singular, positive scriptural references towards women, sought to present Sikhism in contrast to Hinduism. With regard to the 'tyranny of purdah', he went to great lengths to show conclusively that Sikhs stood outside the pale of Hinduism through 'the high moral and enlightened teachings of the Gurus', and had much to offer women in Punjab (Macauliffe 1990, vol. I: xiii).

The plight of widows, and primarily the practice of sati in India, was for the British the most crucial indicator of the moral, racial, cultural, and religious difference between them and Indians, and ultimately, of their own superiority. The image of the abject victim, thrown upon the raging flames of her husband's pyre or entering the flames on her own accord, loyal, stoic, and reserved, was one that filled the British imagination with fascinated abhorrence. More than any other aspect of Indian society, the discourse on sati allowed for British notions of superiority to reign with certainty and purpose. They took on the role of heroic knights sent to India to save innocent Indian damsels in distress. British notions of masculinity exerted themselves with renewed vigour as the rescue of these unfortunate women served as an apt indicator of their own moral and physical superiority over the Indian male, who was ultimately responsible for this blight on Indian society. The abolition of sati in 1829 by the colonizers thus made manifest a prime objective of British ideology, namely, the reformation of overt Indian depravity. Women as weak, passive, and helpless victims became the focus of British efforts to uplift Indian society from its excessive degeneration. But the debate on sati had more to do with British compulsions of showing their moral superiority over the mores and values of Indians, and over an indigenous Indian elite pursuing a cohesive nationalist identity as 'keepers of tradition', than with the actual status of Indian women. Lata Mani has noted that women were the *site* on which tradition was debated and re-formulated. As the nineteenth century progressed, on a symbolic level, the 'fate of women and the fate of the emerging nation' became 'inextricably intertwined. Debates on women, whether in [the] context of *sati*, widow remarriage or *zenanas*... were not merely about women, but also instances in which the moral challenge of colonial rule was confronted and negotiated' (Mani 1990: 90, 118). As with other issues, the British turned approvingly to the Sikhs of Punjab to contrast their practices with those of the Bengalis, most closely allied to the utter debasement of widows. While sati had been common practice among the earlier Sikh rulers of Punjab, its incidence among the general populace was rare. Through Sikh scriptural prohibitions against sati, officials equipped themselves with yet another point of similarity between themselves and the Sikhs. Guru Amar Das had commented, 'They are not *Satis* who are burnt alive on the pyres; Rather *Satis* are they who die of the blow of separation [from their husbands]' (*Adi Granth*: 787).

Comparing the plight of widows in Bengal to what was construed as the favourable position of widows in Punjab, the British directed their attention to the tradition of *karewa*, or levirate widow remarriage, common among the Jats of Punjab. Karewa referred to the acceptance of a widow as wife by one of the younger brothers of her deceased husband; failing him, the husband's elder brother, and, failing him, his agnatic first cousin. Henry Prinsep (1834: 199) described the ceremony: 'The eldest surviving brother of the deceased places a white robe over, and the *neeth*, or ring in the nose of the widow, which ceremony constitutes her his wife.' This custom was characteristic of an extensive assemblage of practices widely upheld in Punjab, which by and large stood outside the realm of conventional Hindu law. As Sir Robert Egerton observed in 1878:

The most fundamental basis for the division of the population in this part of India is tribal rather than religious, and should rest, not upon community of belief or ceremonial practice, but upon ancestral community of race, in which, whether it be genuine or only superstitious the claimants of a common origin equally believe (cited in Gilmartin 1981: 152).

British administrators recognized early in their mandate that the preservation of tribal laws in Punjab would not only justify their presence in Punjab, but would also appease the wider populace. They also realized that many of these customs could be utilized to further British designs in Punjab. Thus the Punjab Laws Act of 1872 was passed, which gave tribal, or customary law, precedence over the laws of Hinduism and Islam, which formed the basis of legal authority in most other parts of British India.

Once again, the English discovered remnants of their own distant and not-so-distant cultural and religious past in the practice of karewa. Turning to similar Mosaic injunctions in Deuteronomy 25 and to the early customs of their European kin, they enthusiastically maintained that karewa was a legitimate alternative to the otherwise beleaguered life of the widow. Early British accounts praised the practice, particularly with regard to young Sikh female widows of 'masculine disposition, want of modesty, and of delicate feeling', especially 'in a society amongst tribes notorious for the laxity of their morals, and for the degeneracy of their conceptions' (Steinbach 1846: 215–22).

The British purported to support the practice of karewa because of their beneficent concerns for the status of widows in Punjab. Yet as early as the mid-nineteenth century Steinbach noted with the most telling of insights that the custom

acts as a counteractive to the many evils attendant on female rule. If the free will of the widow were consulted, it is scarcely to be doubted she would prefer the possession of power and the charms of liberty, to the alternative of sacrificing her claims to her brother-in-law, and taking her station amongst his rival wives [italics mine] (ibid.).

Ultimately, the issue revolved around the partition of land holdings upon a landowner's death, the possibility of which was held reprehensible to the rural Jat, whose land accorded him honour and prestige. The break-up of land and resources was perceived as inevitable if the widow were allowed to have her way. Thus, from the perspective of the British administrators, karewa had to be safeguarded because stability in rural society was pivotal to their continuing positive relations with the rural Punjabis. British apprehensions towards the widows of Punjab were clearly indicated in legal records. '[T]he widow will only waste the property when she obtains absolute control', thus necessitating courts to take the stand that 'women are not qualified to manage their lands themselves' (Kensington 1893, cited in Chowdhry 1996: 68).

Yet the legal system put in place by the new rulers also brought with it novel ways and means for the rural women of Punjab to contest the new laws. Even though their challenges usually failed, the system did give women a platform from which to assert their legal rights (Chowdhry 1997: 316–17). To the chagrin of the British, the number of malcontent widows challenging the legality of their new (lack of) rights assumed such proportions that government intervention was felt to be necessary. Though the courts did make some exceptions in cases involving cultivating castes where women were active in agricultural work, the general trend was to uphold the custom of karewa, thus preserving an effective method of regulating a widow's right of inheritance and maintaining landholdings. Given the high demand for Punjabi males in the British Indian army, it was imperative that the agricultural assets of the recruits' families not be jeopardized by the claims of widows (Chowdhry 1990: 317). As George Campbell, a British official, attests in the 1870s, British officials were forced at times to go to great lengths to assert their authority over the provocative widows.

A special source of dispute was the obligation of widows (under the law, as understood by the men at least), to marry their deceased husband's brothers. They had a contrary way of asserting their independence by refusing to do so. I am afraid the law that I administered was rather judge made law; my doctrine was that if they refuse they must show reasonable cause. The parties used to come before me with much vociferation on the female side, and I decided whether the excuse was reasonable. But if the man seemed a decent man, and the woman could give no better reason than to say 'I don't like him', I said 'stuff and nonsense, I can't listen to that—the law must be respected', and I sometimes married them there and then by throwing a sheet over them after the native fashion for second marriages. So far as I could hear those marriages generally lived out very happily (1893: 89).

Yet the administration was eventually forced to recognize the inherent discrepancies between the newly codified 'customary' practices, particularly those associated with the custom of karewa and inheritance rights, and the negative consequences of the rigidity of their laws. Increasingly, though reluctantly, the new code came to be acknowledged as counterproductive to British claims of raising the status of women in India. According to the High Court Justice Sir Frederick Robertson in 1907, the rights of women had 'in the opinion of many... suffered unduly of late years under too universal application of the "agnatic theory"' (cited in Uberoi 1996: 159–60).

The clearly male-defined posture taken by the Raj with regard to the suppression of women in positions of authority, even those at the helm of land holdings, can be traced to the history of Punjab prior to its annexation. The British were well aware of the record of successful female rule in Punjab. Upon the death of a husband or son during the *misl* (confederacy) period of earlier Sikh rule, women had often taken over the leadership. George Thomas had written appreciatively of Bibi Sahib Kaur, a 'woman of masculine and intrepid spirit', who bravely defended the capital city of Patiala during his expedition of 1798. He was sufficiently impressed by Sahib Kaur to assert that she was 'a better man than her brother', Raja Sahib Singh, who had fled the city during the siege (cited in Gupta 1980). Rani Askour and Rani Rajinder were other noteworthy Sikh women rulers and, according to Lepel Griffin, 'it would appear that the Phulkian chiefs excluded by direct enactment all women from any share of power, from the suspicion that they were able to use it far more wisely than themselves' (Griffin, Introduction, in Poole 1892: viii). Perhaps most importantly, the colonial regime had come full force against Maharani Jindan, a powerful female leader characterized by Dalhousie as the only person of '*manly* understanding of the Punjab' who for a time successfully withstood the advances of the British army [italics mine] (Dalhousie 1849, cited in Yadav 1966: 167). Nonetheless, despite a begrudging admiration, it was to Jindan, 'whose evil passions... brought about [her] ruin and that of the State', that British officials credited the first Sikh war and the 'downfall of the monarchy which Ranjit Singh had so laboriously built up.' The blame was squarely placed on Jindan's 'unbridled passions and the intrigues of her lovers' (Griffin, Introduction, in Poole 1892: x). Jindan represented to the Victorian imperial mindset the ultimate antithesis of feminine purity and frailty. For obvious political reasons, as well as tightly boundaried Victorian gender constructions, Jindan was intensely maligned by British officials. Hardinge reprovingly observed in a dispatch that she reviewed her Sikh troops unveiled and dressed as a dancing woman. Further, she sent gifts to courtesans and, although attending to religious observances during the day, her nights were spent in the grossest of debaucheries (1845, cited in Hasrat 1977). Despite Hardinge's overt criticism of Jindan, he conceded that she possessed considerable energy and spirit, and a singular devotion to the affairs of the state. Rajanikanta Gupta, an insightful nineteenth-century Bengali writer, bears repeating, given his insistence that the inimical estimation of Jindan by the British had everything to do with the fact that she was a woman. Had Maharani Jindan

been satisfied with her normal feminine role away from the action, she would have been well received by English historians.... The English, accustomed to universal admiration and respect for their bravery and political wisdom, found that she refused to be overawed by them... Her regular interference in the administration of the realm wounded the political ego of the English; they therefore reacted sharply to whatever the queen had intended to achieve in Punjab and made her into the villain of the piece (cited in Banerjee 1988: 33–4).

British attitudes towards female jurisdiction were closely aligned with the already prevalent ethos of hypermasculinity reigning supreme among the Sikhs, as well as with Sikh apprehensions towards female rule. During the complex settlement proceedings with Sikh chiefs after the Mutiny of 1857, the issue of possible female incumbency played a considerable role in the negotiation process. A petition to the British sent by the Phulkian chiefs entitled 'Paper of Requests' insisted that 'women should not be allowed to interfere in the affairs of the State either on the pretext of the Chief being young or upon any other plea, and that no complaint of any sort preferred by the women of the families of the Chief be received by the British Government.' The commissioner responded warmly to this request, adding that

the exclusion of women from the Council or Regency or from any participation in public affairs was 'a wise and sensible provision', and that nothing but evil could accrue from the nominal supremacy of women, uneducated and secluded as they were in the country... He observed that as a rule the Government did not interfere in the matters of complaints from women but in extraordinary cases the Government might be compelled to interfere on humane grounds (1859, cited in Arora 1982: 41).

Not surprisingly, given previous altercations with the ever-insubordinate Maharani Jindan, the government of India accepted this request of the Phulkian chiefs in principle.

The Politics of Similarity and its Discontents

Somewhat hesitantly, given the tenuous politics of similarity between the British and the Sikhs, the latter were often portrayed by the British as intrinsically immoral, most particularly with regard to their sexual mores. British administrators, steeped in a Victorian ethos with its exaggerated oppositions of masculinity and femininity and corresponding puritanical sexual codes, were troubled by what they perceived as sexual depravity among the Sikhs. Cunningham in the mid-nineteenth century explained this sexual depravity thus:

[T]he sense of personal honour and of female purity is less high among
the rude and ignorant of every age, than among the informed and the
civilized; and when the whole peasantry of a country suddenly attain to
power and wealth, and are freed from the many of the restraints of society,
an unusual proportion will necessarily resign themselves to the seduc-
tions of pleasure, and freely give way to their most depraved appetites
(1990: 159).

Besides commenting on the absence of honour among Sikhs in
relation to their womenfolk, Cunningham was presumably referring
to homosexual practices observed among the Sikhs, especially in the
court of Maharajah Ranjit Singh. Prinsep (1834: 85) had earlier commented on the prevalence of homosexual activities in the court, and
among Sikhs in general. The British propensity for masculine virility
as opposed to their obvious opprobrium for weakness in men had
everything to do with their belief that effeminacy led naturally to
homosexual behaviour in men (Sinha 1995: 19). To the chagrin of
the British, however, homosexual practices were associated more with
the manly and the 'resolute', than with the effeminate races (Wurgaft
1983: 50). Further, the incongruity of British self-perceptions as a
truly masculine race and their observations of the sexual depravity
among those most closely aligned to them did not bode well for the
colonizers. Thus, while Cunningham's rigid ethical sensibilities
recoiled from the sexual customs of the Sikhs, he was quick to exon-
erate them, noting that 'those who vilify the Sikhs at one time, and
describe their long and rapid marches at another, should remember
the contradiction and reflect that what common-sense and the better
feelings of our nature have always condemned, can never be the
ordinary practice of a nation' (Cunningham 1990: 159). Fortuitously
for British self-understanding, the formulaic boldness and robust-
ness characterizing the Sikh male could outweigh any disturbing
contradictions with regard to his sexuality.

Sikh women, though admired when contrasted to Bengali
women, given their sturdiness and procreative abilities in the
development of the manly races, could hardly be aligned with
widely held Victorian notions of the frailty of women. In the words
of Lepel Griffin, '[t]he characteristics of women which disqualify
them for public life and its responsibilities are inherent in their sex
and are worthy of honour, for to be womanly is the highest praise

for a woman, as to be masculine is her worst reproach' (Griffin 1892, cited in Sinha 1995: 35). Thus the sturdy Punjabi Jat female by her very nature was an affront to the deeply held Victorian assumptions of the British. Perhaps most importantly, Sikh women, in direct opposition to Victorian notions of women as naturally devout and virtuous 'angels of the household', were perceived as ultimately responsible for the degeneration of the Sikh faith. Uneducated, they were unable to give the abstract faith of Sikhism the estimation it deserved. According to British observations, Sikh women were more likely than Sikh men to turn to the dreaded Hindu tradition, which was 'easy to understand' and were able to give 'a colour and life to their religious exercises' not imparted by the dry recital of obscure passages of the Granth. As women were highly superstitious, the influence of the Brahmin also weighed more heavily on the women than on the men (Falcon 1896: 21). For the British as the self-defined 'keepers of the Sikh faith', Sikh womanhood, steeped in Hinduized practices, constituted an unwelcome impediment to the purification project of Sikhism.

Counteracting the folly of Sikh women through education came to be understood as the most expedient means to the reform of a degenerate society. Accordingly, the Panjab Educational Department was instituted in 1856 with specific guidelines for the education of females. Yet progress was painfully slow, especially among the rural population, which forced the government to appeal initially to the higher classes of Sikhs to support the cause of female education. Baba Khem Singh Bedi, the influential head of Guru Nanak's lineage became a staunch supporter of British efforts to educate females in the province (see Sidhu 1985). By the end of the nineteenth century the educational torch had been passed on to the Singh Sabha reform movement. The Sikh intelligensia, carefully moulded and educated to conform to British political designs, benefited greatly from the politics of similarity that had progressed under the tutelage of the Raj. The response of the Singh Sabha with regard to the condition and practices of Sikh females went far beyond that of education. Enthused by the Victorian customs and ethos of the British, these reformers also adopted, and in some cases modified, the prevailing gender constructions of the Raj. The ramifications of the melding of Victorian gender constructs with the hypermasculine Sikh ethos of the nineteenth and early twentieth centuries through the newly forged Sikh elite were profound and far-reaching. Gender construction proved to be pivotal to the very enterprise of Singh Sabha reform.

Notes

1. The phrase 'muscular Christianity' was first used in 1857 in a *Saturday Review* column by T.C. Sandars. See Fasick 1994: 96.
2. The process of recruitment culminated with the event of World War I, where the proportion of Sikhs in the army was more than three times the ratio of Sikhs in Punjab; Sikh proportion in the army was nearly twenty times their representation in the general Indian population. See Fox 1990: 143.

FOUR

CONTEXTUALIZING REFORM IN NINETEENTH-CENTURY PUNJAB
Continuity and Change

The last of the vast Indian frontier to be conquered by the British in 1849, Punjab, was without doubt teeming with economic, political, social, and religious uncertainty. The British attempted to surmount the obvious difficulties of controlling the turbulent, widely dispersed population of the newly annexed province by establishing a benevolent, semi-military, authoritarian form of government. The framework of Punjab's administration has been described as a paternalistic, benevolent authoritarian system which closely regulated the conduct of society in order to achieve its new rulers' objectives (Lee 1995: 65, van den Dungen 1972). The experienced and carefully chosen officials who gathered to oversee the Punjab project were invested with both administrative and judicial powers. The task of the architects of the Punjab school of administration, John and Henry Lawrence, was to ensure peaceable transition from Sikh to British domination with the singular intent of designing an administration that would ensure an attitude of loyal submission from the majority of Punjab's population. According to Henry Lawrence, 'promptness, accessibility, brevity and kindness are the best engines of government.... Be considerate and kind, not expecting too much from ignorant people' (Innes 1898: 115).

British procedure in the administration of Punjab initially had two foci: the placation of the bulk of the population largely comprised of rural peasants' and the conciliation of the aristocracy which had lost its rulership. To secure the loyalty of both groups, the British administration endeavoured to address their concerns and needs with remarkable foresight and benevolence. Given that the political stature of the Sikhs had diminished with the annexation of Punjab and the British admiration for the military prowess of the 'manly' Sikhs, Punjab administration conferred special privileges on the peasantry and Sikh aristocracy. The loyalty of the Sikhs during the uprising of 1857 only enhanced their relationship with the administration. It was thus in the continued search for allies amongst the rural bulk of the population that the world's largest irrigation system was built, transforming the region from one of the poorest agricultural areas to the granary of India. Agricultural colonies were also developed and then populated by ex-servicemen of the Indian army, as rewards for their loyalty to the British. The Sikh Jats in particular, well established for their manliness and loyalty in British perception, benefited greatly from the benevolent patronage of the Raj. Their well-known abilities as agricultural cultivators as well as their categorization by the British as the pinnacle of the 'martial races', paved the way for their preferential treatment by the Punjab administration in the form of land grants in fertile regions and low land revenue demands, particularly in the agricultural colonies. Further, the aristocratic leaders of Punjab, especially after lending support to the British during the Mutiny, benefited from their auspicious show of loyalty by receiving *jagirs* (assignment of land revenue in lieu of salaries), honorary ranks, titles, and positions in local government. Leading religious families were also patronized, as were *mahants*, the custodians of gurdwaras and shrines. British patronage of the Sikh religious elite remained advantageous to the political designs of both for many years to come. For example, Baba Khem Singh Bedi supported the British during the Mutiny by raising troops to stem the tide of insurrection. His continued support of the British administration in Punjab took many and varied forms. He pioneered vaccination projects amongst his followers, supported and sponsored female education, served as an honorary magistrate from 1877 onwards, and was knighted shortly before his death in 1904. Further, in return for British patronage, the mahants of principal religious shrines issued *hukamnamas* in support of the Raj in times of political crisis. Through a complex web of patronage, the British established a successful framework for ensuring the intense loyalty of the Sikhs. According to Henry Lawrence (Innes 1898: 92):

The Sikhs *have* come to terms, and *have* settled down, because they have been treated well *by us*.... The Sikhs perhaps care as little for their

Government as do other natives of India; but like others they care for themselves, their jagirs, their patrimonial wells, gardens, and fields, their immunities and their honour. And in all these respects the Sikh and Jat population had much to lose. The Sikh position must not be mistaken. They are a privileged race, a large proportion have jagirs and rent-free lands; all hold their fields on more favourable terms than the Mussalmans around them.

From the 1860s onwards, with the attainment of political stability and improved communications and irrigation systems, agricultural prices and land values increased significantly. Newly introduced crops and the ability to export goods on railway lines led to vast riches for Punjab's cultivators; they soon ranked amongst the wealthiest of the continent. Punjab's administration went to great lengths to revise earlier policies that were responsible for increasing indebtedness in the greater part of India, through low revenue demands and extensive land grants to the Punjab peasantry.[1] The Punjab government 'unlike any traditional oriental despot... allowed most of the increased agricultural profits to remain in the cultivators' hands. It pitched its revenue demand as low as possible' (Talbot 1988: 54).

DISSENSION AND CONTROL: THE PUNJAB ADMINISTRATION AND KUKA REFORM

Alongside the well-manoeuvred schemes of the British to ensure loyalty from their Sikh subjects emerged a movement that scorned the British and their efforts to appease Sikh loss of liberty, though on a relatively small scale. The Namdharis were a Sikh sect led by Ram Singh from village Bhaini, in Ludhiana district. His followers were called Kukas, or shriekers, given the impetuous shrieking, dancing, and removal of turbans that occurred when they entered a state of mystical ecstasy. Estimates vary as to the actual numbers in the Namdhari sect, but they claimed a membership of nearly one million adherents by 1871. Other estimates place the figure much lower (Jones 1994: 92). One reason for this discrepancy can be traced to the lack of clear distinctions between the sect and the wider Sikh community; this may have led to the overlapping of categories. However as Namdhari ideology became increasingly militant, the Sikh establishment tried to conclusively distance itself from the movement.

Various attempts have been made to interpret the Namdhari movement. Punjab administrators in the 1870s, confronting what they understood as fanatical anti-British behaviour, characterized the Namdharis as a wild Sikh sect. Indian nationalists eulogized the Kukas as the first anti-imperialist group in Punjab. More recently, Kukas have been presented as a millenarian community arising in response to specific socio-economic circumstances, with close ties to Sikh cosmological assumptions (McLeod 1979: 164–87, Oberoi 1992: 157–97). As a millenarian reform movement, its primary focus was the restoration of ritual purity and holiness. The latter approach is helpful in that it moves beyond mere maligning or elementary glorification of the group; it also necessitates an examination of what the movement meant for its adherents, the significance and utilization of symbols, imagery, behavioural codes, and the socio-political circumstances.

Little is known about the sect's founder, Ram Singh, who was born in 1816. As a youth he assisted his father, who was a carpenter. At the age of twenty he left Bhaini to join Ranjit Singh's army but, disillusioned by the deterioration of the Sikh empire after the death of the Maharajah, Ram Singh left the army just before the Anglo-Sikh war of 1845 and returned to his native village. He became known for his intense spirituality and miraculous powers, and quickly acquired a following. In 1855, Ram Singh opened a shop to earn a living, while at the same time collecting around him a nucleus of disciples, mostly former soldiers of the Lahore regiments. Upon Ram Singh's declaration that he was the reincarnation of Guru Gobind Singh, he was rejected by many orthodox Sikhs who maintained that the line of living gurus had ended with Guru Gobind Singh in 1708.

By the 1860s, the government was taking a keen interest in Kuka activities. Initially, British attitudes towards the Namdharis were favourable, commending them for their strict morality and high ideals. In 1867, the Inspector General of Police reported that the reform movement had purely religious motives (Singh and Singh 1989: 68–9)[2]. The positive Kuka reforms outlined by administration officials were precisely those aspects of a degenerated Sikh society decried by the British in the early nineteenth century. British observers had particularly critiqued the position of widows, caste observances, alms-taking, the centrality of popular though unorthodox religious rituals, and the effects of drinking among

Sikhs. In time, added British interest and concern stemmed from repeated reports of Kukas desecrating and demolishing village shrines. Namdharis rejected outright the veneration of dead saints, a central aspect of popular religion in rural Punjab. They were also vehement in their beliefs in the need for cow protection. By 1871, Kukas were being hanged on charges of murder of butchers. More importantly, Kukas refused to endorse the new administrative and political system introduced by the British. They spurned transportation on the extensive railway built by the new rulers, rejected government employment and educational opportunities, and ignored British postal services and judicial system (Ahluwalia 1965: 67, Singh, J. 1985: 55).[3]

While for centuries India had exported fine cloth to the world, in 1813, under pressure from Britain's Lancashire textile industry, the British government imposed a high tariff on the import of Indian textiles. British goods, however, had virtually unlimited entry into India. The consequences for the Indian textile industry were shattering. Weavers who had supplied fine muslins and brocades to the aristocracy in India and the world were no longer in demand; thriving textile towns were laid to waste (Tharu and Lalita 1991: 146–8). The Namdharis displayed their aversion to English textiles and the English textile industry by wearing distinct indigenous clothing made out of white Indian fabric. Their stance was a crucial indicator of their unqualified condemnation of the commercial system put in place by the new rulers.

Their overt anti-British, anti-Western sentiments and the increasing incidents of violence by Namdharis against kine butchers intensified the apprehension of the Punjab administration. This concern led to British awareness of a need to come to a deeper understanding of the Sikh religion, which had ostensibly given birth to the rebel movement. The government turned its attention to Sikh scripture, calling upon the services of Ernest Trumpp, a renowned German Indologist. In essence, the administration wished to ascertain whether Ram Singh's anti-establishment ideology had its basis in Sikh scripture. Ernest Trumpp was hired by the Secretary of State in 1869 to translate the *Adi Granth*, though the project had been planned as early as in 1859 after the annexation of Punjab. However, the perceived threat of the Namdhari movement lent an urgency to the need to translate Sikh scriptures. Accordingly, in 1869, no effort was spared to carry out this project. The translation was published in 1877 after Trumpp's return to Munich in 1872 (Trumpp 1970). While the Sikhs reacted negatively to his translation, the administrators, in consultation with Trumpp, concluded that the political bias of the Kuka creed was far removed from the harmonious message of the Sikh scriptural tradition (Singh, N. 1992). Satisfied that the untainted core of Sikhism's ideology was not incompatible with their designs, officials went to great lengths to support a purified rendering of Sikhism.

The Genesis of the Punjab Intelligentsia

As part of this process, an educational and literary society was initiated in 1865 by G.W. Leitner, the newly-appointed principal of Government College, Lahore. The Anjuman-i-Punjab was a multi-faceted movement with numerous aims. These included the revival of ancient and classical studies by traditional scholars trained in Western methods of critical thinking and the creation of modern literature in the vernaculars through the translation of European and Western works. One of the initial ventures of the society was the establishment of a free public library in Lahore. Within a year the library had acquired 1,431 volumes through donations from British officials and monetary contributions from the landed gentry. Given that print material was still fairly uncommon in Punjab during the late 1800s, the library became a focal point for the growing numbers of the Lahore literati (Oberoi 1994: 231–2). The 'Orient movement', another offshoot of the Anjuman, endeavoured to establish an Oriental university to give a more popular, indigenous character to the existing system of education by making the vernaculars of India the medium of instruction for the European sciences. The Anjuman also promoted close association with the natural leaders of Punjab through the representation of chiefs, leading zamindars, priests, and mahants in the management of educational institutions. These objectives were put in place to bridge the cultural-political gap between the rulers and Indians, as well as to address the immense discontinuity between the small number of educated Indians and the vast bulk of illiterate peasants. Further, the Anjuman was influential in the formation of Punjab University College in Lahore in 1869. Leitner played a key role in this endeavour, subsequently moving to the position of Registrar of the Senate, an appointed body that was responsible for the higher-education needs and strategies for the region. However, Leitner's bid for an Oriental university was not successful; Lahore Oriental College with 'provincial' status was created in its stead. It began as a school in 1865 and acquired college status in 1872–3. It too was run by the senate of Punjab University College. Leitner's Anjuman-i-Punjab became the informal manager of the educational complex consisting of Oriental College, Punjab University College, and Government College, Lahore. It became immensely popular with the Punjabi aristocracy as well as with Europeans. The participation and support of the latter in particular gave the Anjuman a position of prominence, which in turn led to lavish donations in support of the university stratagem by wealthy Punjab chiefs (Singh, N. 1992: 35–8).

The year 1872 saw the culmination of the Namdhari agitation; it ended with the massacre of Kukas by the British and the subsequent exile of Guru Ram Singh to Rangoon, Burma.[4] On 15 January 1872, 120 Namdharis attempted to invade the town of Malerkotla to avenge the killing of cows by Muslim butchers. They were met by well-armed state troops who had been warned of the plan in advance. On the same day, troops from the Sikh principality of Patiala captured sixty-eight Kukas and transported them to Malerkotla. There, L. Cowan, the officiating Deputy Commissioner of Ludhiana district, ordered forty-nine of the offenders to be blown from cannons without trial. The following day, T.D. Forsyth, Commissioner of the Ambala division, had sixteen more Namdharis blown from guns, this time after a brief trial. The administration deemed the immediate and brutal suppression of this group, which it characterized as conflicting with the interests of civil society, legitimate and suitable (Singh and Singh 1989: 213–17).

The year following the altercations between the Raj and Namdhari Sikhs was an eventful one for the Sikh community. Needless to say, Sikh leaders were well aware of the possible plunge of their community from the lofty heights of British estimation. Fearful of losing their favoured status, they went to great lengths to demonstrate their unwavering loyalty to the Raj. A group of well-respected Sikhs addressing the Lieutenant Governor in Amritsar in 1872 denounced the Kukas as a 'wicked and misguided sect' who had injured the hard-won honour and loyalty of the Sikh community in the estimation of the government through 'their misconduct and evil designs', and 'well-nigh leveled with the dust the services we [the Sikhs] had rendered to the government, such as those for instance performed in 1857' (*The Englishman*, 23 March 1872, cited in Singh, K. 1991: 133). Also, troops of the Sikh maharajahs of Patiala, Nabha, and Jind had amply assisted the British during their altercations with the Kukas in January of 1872. The Maharajah of Patiala subsequently ordered the arrest of all known Kukas in his state.

Around the same time, in 1873, when four Sikh students at a Christian mission school in Amritsar pledged their intent to convert to Christianity, a wave of alarm reverberated through the Sikh community. Sikh leaders feared a headlong race of their brightest and most educated minds to the religion of their new rulers. They were faced with a double predicament: fear of losing the patronage arising out of their favoured standing with the British, and a growing need to cement the bonds of their community to check the movement towards conversion to Christianity. Having taken part in various cultural, educational, religious, and social associations, Sikh leaders were well aware of the methods and benefits of group formation. Foremost among these groups were the Anjuman and the Brahmo Samaj. To 'belong to the Brahmo Samaj or to rank amongst its sympathizers was to belong to the intellectual aristocracy of Lahore. The Brahmo Samaj Mandir, was, thus, the only place where one could hope to meet Indians of advanced views on religion and social reform' (Singh, G. 1965: 40–1).

Armed with newly acquired organizational skills, the Sikhs subsequently initiated the process by which a common platform was established to protect and bolster Sikh interests. The Sri Guru Singh Sabha, Amritsar, was inaugurated in 1873 as the first purely Sikh association aimed at expressing the indisputable loyalty of Sikhs towards the British as well as the reformation of the degenerated state of Sikhism. It represented the needs, values, and loyalties of a select, highly placed group of men; notable aristocrats and religious leaders including *pujaris, gianis, granthis, Udasis,* and *Nirmalas* attended the first session of the Amritsar Singh Sabha.[5] Certainly, this segment of society was most anxious to maintain ties of loyalty towards the British administration given the privileges it received. While there had been other groups dedicated to the reformation of Sikhism, such as the Namdharis and Nirankaris, their efforts had been limited to sects and groups considered heterodox or on the periphery of the Sikh faith (Webster 1979,

Singh, H. 1979, Singh, G. 1978). In contrast, the newly established Singh Sabha was composed of well-respected political and religious leaders, well within the fold of Sikhism.

British administrators looked upon this reformatory process within the Sikh community with favour. They had long expressed their dissatisfaction with what they considered to be inconsistency between the pristine ideals of Sikhism and its actual state in the nineteenth century. More importantly for their purposes, the leaders of the Amritsar Singh Sabha had professed and exhibited their allegiance with the British cause; thus English officials viewed the formation of the Sabha as a propitious vehicle for furthering their own educational, social, and political agenda. The lack of education among Sikhs was an obstacle that the administration had sought early on in its mandate to remedy. According to the Census of 1881, the Sikhs were 'the most uneducated class in the Punjab' (Census Report of India, Part I: 38–9). The Punjab administration made concerted efforts to convince the education-wary Punjabis, particularly the Sikh Jat population, of the need for a solid educational foundation for both males and females. While Sikh Jats hesitantly endorsed education for boys, girls' education remained a more contentious issue. However, the effects of a purely English-based education on the Bengalis were already making themselves known in the form of nationalist rhetoric and opposition to the Raj. Education authorities attempted to evade similar developments in Punjab by supporting and developing a system which had as its foundation the vernaculars of Punjab, as opposed to a wholly Anglicized scheme in Bengal (Leitner 1971).

In line with the religious reform initiatives of the Singh Sabha, admission to Leitner's Oriental College was initially restricted to students whose parents were hereditary religious leaders. It was hoped that this would yield new religious leaders and teachers who would be influential in the moral and religious renewal of Punjabi society. Correspondingly, the students' traditional standing in the Punjabi community was expected to raise the prestige of the college. Further, Leitner started a Punjabi class at Oriental College in 1877–8, where Gurmukhi and the *Adi Granth* were taught. The class was officially labelled the 'Bhai class'. During 1878–9, there were a total of seventeen boys in this class, and nine of them were sons of granthis, mahants, and pandits (Singh, N. 1992: 39) Although there was some opposition to the apparent bias of the so-called religiously neutral college,

Leitner's unquestionable authority allowed for the continuance of the class. Orientalist objectives to develop and further indigenous languages *and* the attainment of the two-fold Singh Sabha demand for the upliftment of Punjabi and Western-educated interpreters of Sikh scriptures was thereby fulfilled. To further secure the loyalty of Punjab's landowning class, Aitchinson College was founded in Lahore in 1886 to educate the sons of the principal landowners. Admission was by and large restricted to Punjab's rural elite. As was the case with Oriental College's Bhai class, students here were given preferential treatment by the administration. The restricted access to Aitchinson College inculcated in its students a sense of emotional attachment and loyalty to the Raj. (Talbot 1988:57).

Following closely on the heels of the overt sanctioning of Sikh reformative efforts at Oriental College, the government decided in 1879 to raise the status of Punjab University College to university. This controversial decision was for some indicative of attempts to conclusively distinguish Punjab's educational policy from that of Calcutta University; Delhi College, an affiliate of the Calcutta (Kolkata) institution had earlier been closed by the government. The fears of Punjab's Brahmo Samaj and others of the intelligentsia who were products or supporters of the Calcutta system, revolved around questions regarding the nature of Punjab education. Would Punjab University simply be an extension of Oriental College, which sought to downplay the English language and Western sciences through its concentration on Indian classical studies? At the announcement of the college's status change in 1879, Viceroy Lord Lytton referred to the distinctions between the principles of the Punjab scheme of education and those upon which the University of Calcutta was operating. First, he noted, vernacular languages would be the medium of instruction. Second,

the object of instruction shall be to develop the sentiment of enlightened loyalty by association with it all those sentiments of natural reverence, duty and self-respect which every race inherited from the highest types of its own special character, whatever that character may be; and of whatever the religion may be; natural sources instinctively revered (cited in Singh, N. 1992: 40).

For some, these distinctions only accentuated their concerns that the administration was attempting to isolate Punjab from Bengal, and from the nationalist movement led by educated Bengalis, by denying the people of Punjab the facilities for higher, English-based education that were already in place through the Calcutta system, and which had previously led to successful bidding for government employment by Bengalis. The controversy led to an open division in the Anjuman-i-Punjab. One faction supported Leitner's and the government's decision. The second faction, believing Western, English-based education to be the panacea for India's problems with regard to social reforms and Indian advancement in government ranks, resolutely opposed the underlying designs of the decision. The ardent Anglicist, Sayyid Ahmed Khan, and his Aligarh Movement, independent of the Anjuman's internal opposition, became the chief spokesperson against the Orientalist agenda in Punjab and a leading critic of Leitner. He insisted that 'the regeneration of India depends entirely upon the spread of English education among the natives' (Aligarh Institute Gazette, 27 November, cited in Singh, N. 1992: 44). Indeed, the Punjab administration dreaded the spread of anti-British sentiment believed to have been engendered by the a religious, liberal, utilitarian thought which had taken root among the educated elite of Bengal. Believing that the threat of the free-thinking, effeminate Bengalis was minimal in comparison to a possible anti-government backlash of the manly Punjabis, the authorities insisted that government-sponsored education be accompanied by a thorough religious curriculum. The Anjuman's news organ, *Akhbar-i-Anjuman-i-Punjab*, an Urdu weekly, insisted (on 10 December 1880) that 'the Government should patronage only those men who distinguish themselves both in Eastern and Western Science and adhere to their religion, and not the so called votaries of Western Science who are free thinkers and whose conduct is calculated to promote disaffection towards the Government' (ibid.: 45).

Simultaneous to the linguistic and religious revival of the Sikhs in the higher centres of learning was the inauguration of the Arya Samaj reform movement in Punjab. In the years between 1863 and 1872, Dayanand had been transformed from *sanyasi* to social and religious reformer due in large part to his increasing interaction with Anglicized Indians. In 1872, he had been invited to Calcutta by Debendranath Tagore, which had resulted in close contact with Brahmo Samaj leaders. Though he had established sabhas in both Gujarat and Maharashtra, they had had little impact on their respective societies and had soon folded up. Accepting the invitation of a number of Brahmos, Hindus, and Sikhs, Swami Dayanand arrived in Punjab in 1877. It was only then that the Arya Samaj movement took hold, becoming the most influential of the various groups attempting to reform Punjabi society. Swami Dayanand's iconoclastic monotheism and egalitarian message flourished in a region where Brahminic authority had a weakened hold on both religious and cultural establishments. A number of influential Sikhs took part in Arya Samaj activities during the initial stages of expansion. The alliance quickly soured, however, when Swami Dayanand and his followers made a series of fiery attacks on Sikh gurus and the Sikh religion in the name of Vedic revival. Furthermore, Dayanand insisted that Sikhism was one of the numerous sects of Hinduism. 'They do not worship idols, but they worship the *Grantha Saheb* which is as good as idolatry.... Just as the priests of temples ask their devotees to see the goddess and offer presents to her, similarly the Sikhs worship the book and present gifts to it' (Upadhyaya 1960: 522–3, 525). Singh Sabha leaders responded quickly and identified the Arya Samaj movement as the most immediate threat to their reform initiatives; they also recognized the need for their expansion beyond Amritsar. The Lahore Singh Sabha was established in 1879, followed by successors in the surrounding districts. By 1899, there were 120 Sabhas in operation. While a large number of Sikhs left the Arya Samaj to join the Singh Sabha movement, a number of highly influential Sikhs remained within the Arya ranks. Bawa Chhajju Singh retained his position as editor of the *Arya Messenger*; his brother Bawa Arjan Singh was in charge of another publication, the *Arya Patrika*.

Leitner's successful bid to endorse the teaching of the Gurmukhi script and the Punjabi language at Oriental College was heartily supported by Singh Sabha leaders because they believed that the close linguistic association of Punjabi and Sikhism would only bolster their attempts to reform their tradition. Only through Punjabi could the masses be educated in true Sikh practices and beliefs. The establishment of a Sikh education committee soon followed the Lahore Sabha's inauguration and included Leitner, other British officials, and Sikhs. To take action against the Sikhs' educational underdevelopment, the leaders moved to initiate their own institutions. Thus, in 1880, the Lahore Singh Sabha started the first denominational school.

The concrete mobilization of the Singh Sabha movement also led to the adoption of certain principles (Barrier 1970: xxiv–xxv):

The purpose of the Singh Sabha is to arouse love of religion among Sikhs.

1. The Sabha will propagate the true Sikh religion everywhere.
2. The Sabha will print books on the greatness and truth of the Sikh religion.
3. The Sabha will propagate the words of the Gurus.
4. The Sabha will publish periodicals to further the Panjabi language and Sikh education.
5. Individuals who opposed Sikhism, who have been excluded from Sikh holy spots, or who have associated with other religions and broken Sikh laws cannot join the Sabha. If they repent and pay a fine, they can become members.
6. English officers interested in Sikh education and the well being of Sikhism can associate with the Sabha, also those who support the Panjabi language.
7. The Sabha will not speak against other religions.
8. The Sabha will not discuss matters relating to the Government.
9. The Sabha will respect well wishers of the community, those who love Sikhism, and those who support truth and education in Panjabi.

Though the numerous Sabhas were held together by the common threads of linguistic concerns, education projects, restoration of Sikhism to its original state of pristine purity, and loyalty to the Raj, they varied considerably in character and specific interests. In due time these interests began to clash and two distinct models began to emerge. The first was led by the Amritsar Singh Sabha, which derived much of its strength from the wealth and status of its constituency—the aristocratic and religious orthodoxy, the latter represented by families of guru lineages, mahants, pujaris, and other heterodox groups. Members of the Amritsar Sabha tended to be conservative, holding fast to the assumptions and privileges of the upper and respected religious classes. This group was representative of what Harjot Oberoi has labelled Sanatan Sikhism. Sanatan Sikhs had little use for a monolithic and closed understanding of what it meant to be Sikh; the Khalsa ideal initiated by Guru Gobind Singh was for them simply one of many Sikh identities. '[H]eterogeneity in religious beliefs, plurality of rituals, and diversity in lifestyles were freely acknowledged... [and] several competing definitions of who constituted a Sikh were possible' (Oberoi 1994: 24). This fluid understanding of Sikh identity was challenged by the Lahore Singh Sabha, which was composed of what Bruce Lawrence calls the 'elite consumers of the new knowledge'. The new knowledge was based on Western enlightenment ideals and incorporated into the teachings of their British educators (Lawrence 1989: 98). The consumers of these ideals were professionals, many from lower castes, who had risen in status due to the opportunities offered by the British educational system. But their new-found status did not necessarily bring with it acceptance from the wider Sikh populace. On one occasion, upper-caste Sikhs had refused to accept *karah prasad* (sacramental food) from the hands of Ditt Singh, who though of Mazhabi (low) caste, had become a potent force in Sikh reformative circles due to his education. As a result, he became a veritable force in the castigation of the Amritsar Singh Sabha and of Sanatan Sikhs in general. Another powerful Lahore leader was Gurmukh Singh, who had risen to prominence as the first professor of Punjabi at Oriental College. His father had served as a cook in the palace of the Rajah of Kapurthala, and due to a scholarship provided by the king, had received an education normally reserved for those of the upper echelons of society. These individuals from the lower classes, had risen to positions of eminence due to their educational qualifications, but they were still denied acceptance by the upper classes because of the prevailing caste prejudices, particularly by the traditional elites—the aristocrats and the religious orthodoxy. The incongruence between the age-old dogmatism of caste and their new middle-class world view was a potent factor in determining their reform initiatives (Bhatia 1987: 207).

The men who benefited most from the system of education put in place by the British became the powerful elite in a society where 93 per cent of the society was illiterate. The Census of 1891 indicates that 19, 274 out of the approximately twenty-three million inhabitants of Punjab could speak and write English. Oberoi (1994: 262) maintains that '[b]ilingual skills and western education became a form of capital in a colonial society that could be effectively used to acquire power, privilege and the ability to strike political bargains.' It was this group that found the traditional attitudes and elitist premises of the Amritsar group to be demeaning and demoralizing. Thus the Lahore faction's comprehensive reform initiatives were based on an insistence on the equality of all Sikhs, focusing particularly on the elimination of caste distinctions within Sikhism.

Though attempts were made as early as 1880 to bring the Lahore and Amritsar Singh Sabhas under one executive body, given the antithetical composition of the two groups, the final and well publicized breach between them happened in 1883. There were, however, instances of cooperation between the feuding groups, particularly during times of perceived threat, as in the vitriolic attacks on the Sabhas by extremist Arya Samajists, and through the establishment of important institutions, such as Khalsa College in 1897. By and large, however, the vested interests determining the objectives of the two groups increasingly widened the chasm between them. It was only in 1902 that the Chief Khalsa Diwan was formed as the umbrella organization of all existing Singh Sabhas. By the turn of the century, the need to address the issue of the duplication of programmes and projects of the two factions had become increasingly apparent. According to Barrier (1970: xxix), collaboration was possible because by then, many of the founding fathers had died and much of the bitterness and personal feuding had diminished.

The Lahore Singh Sabha's approach to comprehensive reform in the nineteenth century, increasingly demoted the more conservative, orthodox religious establishment's reform objectives as less meritorious, and publicly denounced them as such. These attacks were met with bitter rebuttals by the Amritsar Sabha. Whereas the pujaris of the Golden Temple had issued a *hukamnama* (letter of command) in 1879 urging all Sikhs to join the Singh Sabha, by 1883 an official hukamnama from the Akal Thakhat decried the activities of the Lahore leaders as being injurious to Sikh interests (Bhatia 1987: 153). Nonetheless, given the wider appeal of the Lahore Sabha's initiatives, most other Singh Sabhas too severed their connection with the Amritsar group. The members of the Lahore group were certainly well-versed in the tactics employed by the potent missionary machine in Punjab, especially its proclivity to spread Christian tenets through the written word, which initiated widespread Sikh participation in the increasingly prevalent print culture of the day. According to Marshall McLuhan, those involved in the forging of the print culture became the principal powerbrokers of society (McLuhan, in Oberoi 1994: 262–4). Without doubt, power dynamics inscribe themselves in language and these new elites utilized the widely available printing press to further their cause (Minh-ha 1989: 51–2). The doors of communication were thrown open by the new proprietors of literary power, allowing for a virtually unlimited capacity to disseminate opinions, designs, and 'enlightened' world views. Leaders channelled vigorous energy into publishing, printing, and writing. Despite the great surge to set up presses and papers, many of these attempts failed quickly due to lack of experience and proper financing, particularly prior to 1900. Notwithstanding these and other difficulties, there were over twenty Sikh newspapers and journals by 1910. The Khalsa Tract Society, founded in 1894, produced small, cheap volumes on Sikh theology and social conditions. By 1902, 192 works had been published and distribution had risen to over half a million copies. Further, notable writers such as Bhai Ditt Singh, Bhai Mohan Singh Vaid, Bhai Teja Singh, and Bhai Vir Singh wrote voluminously and diversely. Their output included theological and scriptural commentaries, novels, tracts, and treatises, most of which attacked prevalent social conditions among Sikhs. Taking a stand on the contentious issues of the day, they were resolute in the belief that their efforts were beneficial in serving to reform and uplift the Sikh community.[6]

Indian Reform, the Missionary Undertaking and the 'Women's Question'

Pivotal to the efforts of the newly established Singh Sabha movement, as well as those of other reform groups, was a call to return to the fundamental principles of their respective traditions. The degenerate condition of women—Sikh, Hindu, and Muslim—became a central tenet for the process of reorganization and interpretation by each reform movement. The imperial masters had long pointed to Indians' depraved attitudes towards women as moral justification of their presence and rule in India. Missionary activities had also been spurred on considerably due to this conviction. According to an early missionary report, the degree of attention devoted in this country to work amongst women and girls, was one of the most striking features of missionary work. Zenana missionary activity, women's education, and women's medical missions were a focal aspect of the varied and multifarious Christian missionary efforts in Punjab. Regarding India's 'problem', one account aptly sums up missionary attitudes toward Indian women's status and societal roles (A.D. n.d.: 29–30):

On the threshold of this subject we meet with a paradox, but that is to be expected. In no country is woman more despised than in India, and in no country are there so many goddesses.... In no country has woman more power, and yet she has no recognized place in society. Religion gives her no position, yet she is the upholder of religion.... Surely the poignant grief of Sita, Savitri and others should have vindicated wifely devotion for all time—if times had not changed, and fetters had not been forged, and wrongs had not been inflicted, as the years went by, until now it is quite true that woman is no longer the helpmeet of man. She has sunk too low to help him. She drags him down, and herein is India's undoing. A proverb has it that a cart cannot run on a big wheel and a little one. No more can it, and if man is the big wheel and woman the little, nay, more often the broken wheel, he cannot pursue his course in safety.

The Indian woman was thus in desperate need of reform; Western women's example and work with Indian women was viewed as one way to bring light to the darkness of the latter's lives. The anonymous writer continued:

There is a mighty tide of good influence pouring into India with the Christian women of the West, representatives of many missionary societies. And there is a return wave, for, last but not least, there is a noble band of Indian lady pioneers, who are surely the means in God's hand to raise their wronged sisters.... Of the signs of the times there is not much more to say. It is enough that the decisive hour has struck, and that India's women are on the point of gaining their lost freedom.

Not all Indians concurred with this belief. Many were shocked by European manners, particularly the offensive behaviour of women baring their shoulders and freely dancing at gatherings. Without doubt, these behaviours did not encourage Indians to abandon their traditional customs of the seclusion of 'respectable' women. Ballhatchet (1980: 5–6) notes further that the British found it insulting that Indian gentlemen did not bring their wives to social gatherings where Indians and Britishers mixed. Also, by the end of the nineteenth century, prostitution by European women was becoming a problem. In Calcutta, Bishop Thoburn of the Methodist Episcopal Church noted in a speech in 1893 that it 'is a striking fact that the most shameless characters in the city are not Indian but persons imported from Europe...' (ibid.: 131).

In Punjab, the missionary establishment was closely aligned with the larger government machine spreading its influence through rigorous control mechanisms set up throughout the state. Gone were the early British ideals of the necessary detachment of the church and the state that were clearly in evidence in Bengal during early missionary expansion efforts.[7] Due in large part to the increase in Christian missionary activity and to the Evangelical revival in Britain, there was a major change in sexual attitudes in the Raj in the late eighteenth century. In the wake of the religious revival in Britain came the rise of the powerful purity campaign which resulted in a repressive new sex code among the British. Punjab, as the newest and last frontier to be conquered, witnessed the purified attitudes of the British more pointedly than areas vanquished earlier. In Punjab for the most part, British administrators supported the missionary enterprise. Subsequently, they also applauded the efforts of religious reformers, presenting them as compelling evidence and a direct manifestation of their exemplary influence upon Indian society. Farquhar (1924: 433–4) wrote about the purifying force of Christianity:

While the shaping forces at work in the movements have been many, it is quite clear that *Christianity has ruled the development throughout.* Christianity has been, as it were, a great searchlight flung across the expanse of the religions, and in its blaze all the coarse, unclean and superstitious elements of the old faiths stood out, quite early, in painful vividness. India shuddered, and the earlier movements were the response to the revelation.... In every case the attempt is made to come up to Christian requirements. Frequently the outcome is extremely slender, yet the purpose can be seen. Christianity has been the norm, and no part of the most orthodox movement is fully comprehensible except when seen from the Christian point of view.

Further, the partial restructuring and redefinition of the overall condition and roles of women in the name of reform, were perceived, at least by a small minority of the educated indigenous elite, as a clear indication of their adherence to the ideals of 'modernity'. James Mill, in his influential *History of British India* noted that among 'rude people, the women are generally degraded; among civilized people they are exalted.' As societies advanced, 'the condition of the weaker sex is gradually improved, till they associated on equal terms with the men, and occupy a place of voluntary and useful coadjutors' (1968: 309–10). Commenting on Indian society in the early nineteenth century, Mill had insisted that 'nothing can exceed the habitual contempt which the Hindus entertain for their women.... They are held, accordingly, in extreme degradation' (also Forbes 1996: 12–19). This widely-known evaluation of Indian society became a pivotal initiative for the transformation of their 'degraded' nation by Indian reformers in the nineteenth century. The very notion of 'reform' pointed to the inherent uncontaminated origins of their respective religious traditions. The concern with women's status was a major aspect of the Bengal renaissance, when the educated elite engaged in a rediscovery and refurbishing of their own past. Rammohun Roy is lauded as the first of the Indian reformers to question the position of women and engage in the re-interpretation and rewriting process that marked the nineteenth century's reform procedure with regard to the status of women (Roy 1964: 581–4).[8] He was a tireless critic of social norms, particularly with regard to the practice of sati. His influential tract entitled 'Abstract of the Arguments Regarding the Burning of Widows Considered as a Religious Rite' summarized his writings on the subject (Ghose 1982: 367–84). Seeking ways to explicate the superstitious and highly ritualized aspects of Hinduism increasingly denoted as degenerate, Roy was at the forefront of the reform impetus calling for a return to Hinduism's core, the Vedas and the Upanishads. The combination of his early Hindu classical training and his ease with Western ideas led Roy and others of the educated indigenous elite to apply the principles of reason and individual rights (common to both Hindu and Western thought in their view) to the problems facing Indian society. Evoking both principles, and, purified versions of history as the basis for social renewal, reformers decried the evil customs that had crept in, such as child marriage, polygamy, and sati, as disharmonious with nature. Accordingly, India needed to recover from a degenerate age, one fallen from a past Vedic 'golden age' when women had led fulfilled lives and held positions of high status. The prominence given to India's past glory was in large part adopted from early Orientalists and was utilized by these intellectuals to refute James Mill's interpretation of India's status as low on the hierarchy of civilizations. It was precisely the discovery of their golden past that made it possible for the indigenous elite to prescribe change, particularly with regard to the women's question.

For Muslims as well, reform was not confined to Western influences in the nineteenth century. As Gail Minault has pointed out, particularly in North India, Muslims had their own tradition of cultural re-examination and reform dating as far back as the seventeenth and eighteenth centuries. The nineteenth and twentieth centuries, however, witnessed a renewed vigour among Muslim literati to 'rid Indian Islam of medieval accretions and to re-examine the sources of the faith to find new wellsprings of strength and inspiration, whether political, religious, or cultural' (1986: 4).[9]

Most significantly, the reconstruction of the past by reformers of the various religious traditions was not confined within the select realm of British Orientalism. Instead, it was being widely disseminated by leading spokespersons of all Indian religions through vernacular newspapers and pamphlets made possible by the introduction of the printing press in India. As Uma Chakravarti (1990: 32) notes:

the indigenous literati were *active agents* in constructing the past and were consciously engaged in choosing particular elements from the embryonic body of knowledge flowing from their own current social and political concerns.... [A]ll this meant that apart from a general increase in historical consciousness, the past was beginning to be classified and analyzed more rigorously to argue the debates of the present.

Undoubtedly, the newly emerging intelligentsia, composed as it was of both traditional and modern elements, perceived itself to be the legitimate interpreter of tradition, both of the past and the present.

The status and position of women were crucial aspects of this interpretive process. As already noted, the 'higher' morality of the imperialists and the superiority of Western ideology was sought to be effectively established by accentuating the low status of Indian women. In seeking to improve women's position, reformers were reacting to the implication of their moral inferiority and depravity put in place by imperial rule. R.C. Dutt reported that passages drawn from the Vedas indicated that women were educated and highly 'honoured in ancient India, more *perhaps than among any other ancient nation on the face of the globe*... [italics mine]' (1972: 170–1). Dutt focused on Rajput and Maratha heroes, who were linked to ancient Kshatriya warriors such as the Pandavas. The Kshatriyas were then linked to the Aryans who were the original conquerors in history. Whatever was good among the later Aryans was thus associated with the Kshatriyas. Genuine Indianness for a reformed

Hindu, thus lay in martial, Hindu, and Aryan elements of the past. These identities were central to the resurrection of the Vedic *dasi*—virtue, vigour, militancy, and the manliness of her male counterparts (Chakravarti 1990: 44–9). Rajput women were presented as the embodiment of virtue and valour, especially during the period of Muslim rule. British writers too were instrumental in this process of idealization, identifying the Rajput women of ancient times as the Rajput Amazons. Colonial constructions of race, particularly the Rajput–Aryan connection (and thus the close identification of the British with these Aryan remnants), were central to British fascination with the ancient Rajputs (MacMillan n.d. see 'The Ruby of Hazrat' and 'The Rajput Amazon').

Correspondingly, these female Kshatriyas, given the educational opportunities open to them, could be viewed as the intellectual companions of their husbands. They were also the source and inspiration of martial valour, making no demands on their menfolk and enabling them to sacrifice their lives with honour. Thus was developed the ideal of the Indian helpmate, wholly agreeable in the forfeiture of her own needs, and ever ready to sacrifice her life in the name of honour, courage, and resistance to the forces which contested Aryan rule and the honourable position of womenfolk (Chakravarti 1990: 51–2, based on Dutt 1943). In essence then, indigenous reformers developed a feasible counterpart to the helpmate of Victorian ideals. The Indian reformers of the late nineteenth century viewed women and the status of women as transformable through persuasive arguments, social action, education, and ultimately, through legislation. By and large, women themselves were not collaborators in these designs. Indeed, they were often portrayed as being opposed to their own liberation. As Forbes has pointed out, without 'first-hand accounts by these women, their reluctance to change in the ways prescribed by their husbands and fathers could be read as nascent feminist resistance, an intelligent reading of their true interests, or plain and simple opposition to any change' (Forbes 1996: 20–1). Male reformers were unwilling to relinquish their position in the patriarchal system that they endeavoured to change; nor were they open to a redistribution of economic power. 'They dreamed of a world where women would be educated and free from some of the worst customs of the society—child marriage, sati, polygamy. But at the same time, these new women would be devoted to home and family' (ibid.).

POSITIONING PUNJAB'S WOMANHOOD—INDIGENOUS POLITICS AND
PRINCIPLES IN THE COLONIAL MILIEU

The Singh Sabha movement has been lauded as the first among the
Sikhs to confront the women's question in the nineteenth century
(Dhillon 1995: 32–7). However, as early as 1853, at the initiative
of British officials, local chieftains, landlords, merchants, and
aristocrats gathered to deliberate on issues pertaining to the position
of women in Punjabi society. Central to this and subsequent
gatherings was the eradication of female infanticide and sati and
limiting dowries and other marriage expenses. Tracts and pamphlets
followed, publicizing government policy and its condemnation of
these customs. Hindu, Sikh, and Muslim leaders were acutely
humiliated by British denunciation of societal conditions;
willingness to support British initiatives regarding the eradication
of misogynist practices offered them an opportunity to gain the
approval of their new masters (Jones 1988: 48). Some years later,
in 1872, Sikhs and Hindus came together to form the Amritsar
Dharm Sabha which took as its aim the eradication of all 'evil
practices... which are opposed to the Shastras and to intelligence,
which are in vogue among the Hindus' (ibid.). Significantly, the Sabha
also focused on customs and behaviours traditionally associated
with women as substantial problem areas. These included practices
such as dowry, mourning and marriage rituals, prostitution,
women's songs, and garb. With regard to prostitution, the Sabha's
annual report of 1873 notes that while even women from
respectable families had sometimes become public women, the
efforts of the Sabha to stop the practice had been successful (cited
in ibid. 1988). Assuredly, the high incidence of prostitution in
Punjab, as well as its honorable position in the nineteenth century,
is supported by Jacquemont's report on the city of Amritsar a
number of decades earlier. He had noted that '[t]he prostitutes have
theirs [quarter], which is not the most magnificent, but is certainly
the best kept, in the city.... Public opinion does not regard them as
degraded, as with us. They are never exposed to insult, and it would
be a grave lack of good manners not to return the salutation which
they never omit to give to respectable passers-by' (Garret 1971:
27). The departure from these earlier attitudes towards prostitution
can best be understood as fundamentally motivated by a need to
better align Punjabi and Victorian British ideals; only thus could

the vested interests of these early Sikh reformers, as well as those of the British administration, be fulfilled. Certainly, British sexual attitudes had changed, due in large part to a rigorous Victorian ethos transforming sensibilities towards prostitution in England.

The Amritsar group also tackled issues such as women bathing in public places. Lakshman Singh recounts in his autobiography that women had earlier frequented the surrounding rivers to bathe. His mother and her friend went out for their daily baths in the river Leh over a mile away from their homes, returning before dawn. These were the daily practices of the women of the elite echelons of Punjabi society who, given their relatively high status, would have had *higher* standards with regard to seclusion and modesty in comparison to women of the lower classes. The Amritsar Dharm Sabha passed a resolution that women were no longer to bathe naked at ponds, wells, rivers, or canals, but should instead bathe in the privacy of the home, behind a curtained area. If no such bathroom was available, women were to bathe wearing a *chadar* or *dhoti*. Further, Punjabi women were not to sing love songs or utter obscene words at the time of marriages, in public places, or behind a curtain (Jones, 1988: 49). John Campbell Oman (1908: 161) reports that the *panchayats* of the Khatri caste in Lahore imposed a fine upon any Khatri whose wife partook of the customary singing of 'obscene songs in streets of Lahore'. Significantly, the Dharm Sabha also insisted on a dress code for women: 'First, a ghagra with a wide girth; second, a pyjama under it; third, a kurta; fourth, a dopatta; fifth, a chadar made of long cloth' (Jones 1988: 50).

The Dharm Sabha also condemned the traditional customs of women during festivals and other occasions of celebration or mourning. Mourning rituals included the uncovering of heads or breasts; these were no longer to be carried out in the market places. The period of *kanagat,* or *sraddha,* was a ritual timeframe within which deceased persons were remembered and honoured by family members. The deceased honoured in this way included the father, mother, grandfather, grandmother, and sons over eighteen (Lewis 1965: 213). During kanagat, the women of a locality, according to their position and status, would don their best clothes and jewellery and collect as a group. They would then stand in a public place and hurl insults and abuses on women from another locality. The subjects of their affronts would inevitably be the husbands, parents, and relatives of the other group. Kanagats often included physical fighting between women and were a source of entertainment for the men who gathered to watch the proceedings. Jones (1988: 50–1) notes that this was a 'ritual occasion on which women could vent their accumulated frustrations' (see also Marriott 1955: 192). Needless to say, kanagats were heartily censured by the Dharm Sabha. Another rite assailed by the Sabha was that of *sada talla*, a fertility ritual where women gathered at the Tek Chand Garden and the Guru Bagh in Amritsar

... while there are in front of them thousands of men of all classes, collected together to see this entertainment or drama, and these women bare their bodies up to their breasts and then start rolling on the ground with great zest and enthusiasm, shouting with their mouths in loud voices: 'I have laid down on a wheat field, may my womb become fertile'. During this action of theirs almost the whole of their bodies become naked. The women believe that by this action of theirs, they become pregnant immediately thereafter (Jones, 1988: 51).

This rite the Sabha declared to be shameless and evil. Its members were exhorted to wield control over their female family members and relatives to ensure its abolishment. Harjot Oberoi (1994: 139–203) has analysed the varied and manifold rituals that were a conspicuous aspect of the 'enchanted universe' of the nineteenth century, particularly in rural Punjab. Popular religious rituals were legitimate instruments of agency for women in a society that was largely controlled and defined by men. In the rural milieu, where people were so dependent on seasonal fluctuations, these rituals were mechanisms of control and a means to comprehend the disparities of life. The peasants' dependence on the forces of nature for their livelihood was particularly manifested in the riverine tracts of the province. The Ravi, the Beas, or 'the harlot' Sind could in one moment flood their banks and wipe out entire crops, homes, and even settlements. The river god was known as Khwaja Khizar, and offerings of grain and *gur* (unrefined sugar) were made to appease his wrath (Darling 1928: 66). The populace also turned to miracle saints and conducted pilgrimages to their shrines. One account notes that the 'greatest shrine in the Western Punjab is that of Sakhi Sarvar.... Men, women and children, Sikhs, Hindus and Mohammedans alike, come from all districts in the Punjab' (Falcon 1896: 17). Further, cultic practices were abundant; spirit possession and magic endowed the vast illiterate masses with agency and at least partial influence on the forces surrounding them. Sohinder Singh Bedi's documentation of rural religious practices based on Punjabi folklore maintains that there were many types of magic performed in Punjab for the welfare of the community, but there was also an invocation of black magic that called upon evil spirits for anti-social purposes. 'It is performed with the evil intention of taking revenge, causing harm to someone.... For this purpose the witch or wizard invokes dark, supernatural powers and achieves full mastery over evil spirits' (Bedi 1971: 41). Women in Punjab who achieved mastery over evil spirits were known as *dains*; men as *ojhas*.[10] As Oberoi (1994: 142) notes, 'the focus of religiosity was not on analysis but on pragmatic results. Whereas scriptural religion is concerned with explaining reality, popular religion seeks to manipulate reality to the advantage of its constituents, be it through the intercession of spirits, magic or other rituals.' Popular religious forms conjoined the various religious communities in Punjab resulting in the cultural, social, and religious fluidity which characterized nineteenth-century Punjabi society. According to the Census of 1891, the religion of the Indian masses had little resemblance to the more orthodox forms of religions. It was labelled animism by authorities and its main object was to get power over the spirits by magic, gifts, or homage (Strachey 1911: 315–16).

While the restrictions put in place by the Amritsar Dharm Sabha in 1872 reflect an absorption with the popular religious ethos in all levels of society, not only rural but urban, it was in the urban centres that the practices were initially confronted. The desire to do away with what the reformers considered to be irrational or useless behaviour on the part of their womenfolk was in no small part connected with the image of the Punjabi that the Dharm Sabha wished to present to the new rulers. According to its annual report:

[Y]ou can get honour only when you have modesty first. Our rulers, who are Englishmen, also feel happy on seeing good characters and respectable persons. What I mean to say is that this great shamelessness and immodesty has spread among the women folk of this city, on seeing which other people ridicule us. Let us adopt measures, by means of which this blot giving us a bad name might disappear (Jones 1988: 2).

The arena of women's rituals, previously outside the jurisdiction of male authority and experience, became increasingly viewed as contributing to immoral behaviour; these rituals were thus perceived as largely responsible for all that was wrong with Punjabi society. Women's decadent conduct was understood as lacking proper rites and behavioural patterns. New ideals of morality, affected largely by the mores, needs, and practices of the British, were thus intrinsic to the re-ordering process put in place by the male reformers. The pointed concern and embarrassment of the Amritsar Dharm Sabha with regard to the immoral behaviour of their womenfolk can best be understood in the light of their acute fears of women's actions jeopardizing British approval and support. Their honour was at stake, threatened by the annual feminine rites that traditionally made room for women to emerge from the underside of the patriarchal hierarchy customarily ordering their lives. These rituals had traditionally allowed for acceptable outlets for the accumulated anger and frustration experienced under the system. However, respectability, along with a renewed sense of honour, had become the watchwords by which the reformers reorganized their own lives and the lives of their womenfolk.[11] As one feminist historian proposes:

[o]ne comes to change one's view on a particular group not so much because former beliefs have been rationally demolished, but rather because one believes (for a number of reasons) that it is no longer proper to hold a particular view, at least not publicly.... Other than through the use of disreputable images, attitudes are changed through a general alteration in a society's thought patterns so that a previously accepted view now becomes 'old fashioned' or 'superstitious' (Smith 1976: 378).

The irrational feminine rites used by women to explain, control, and order their circumstances came increasingly to be perceived by the reformers as needing to be transformed to be more in line with their own, and their rulers', rational and enlightened world view.

Carroll Smith-Rosenberg (1986: 49) has argued that a concern with body image and with rules regulating its treatment and behaviour closely correlates to social categorization and distribution of power.

Differences in the rules governing the body (dress and sexual codes, freedom of movement, and so forth) will demarcate social differences and positions of relative power. A concern with social control will dictate a system of rigid bodily and sexual restrictions governing the group to be socially controlled. And so, social and sexual politics interact.

Dharm Sabha regulations about women's bodies, actions, and dress were indicative of a novel apportioning of social power relations among male and female Sikhs and Hindus in Punjab. The education of females increasingly came to be viewed as the panacea for the degenerate condition of their society, the way to ensure that women complied with the new demands and expectations of these reformers; these efforts also aligned with the designs of the British, ostensibly to uplift India's woman-kind. Early reformers and religious leaders in Punjab were thus offered the opportunity to gain positive recognition from the administration.

DISSENTING VISIONS OF GENDER REFORM—GURU RAM SINGH AND THE NAMDHARI SIKHS

Not all reformers in the mid-to-late nineteenth century benefitted from alignment with the British. The Namdharis' efforts at redefining and creating a new moral order included a radical restructuring of attitudes, roles, and rituals pertaining to women. Most studies of the Namdharis have simply extolled rather than adequately analysed how and why Guru Ram Singh's innovations came about with regard to women. The framework provided by both McLeod and Oberoi in their analyses of the Namdharis as a millenarian movement can be extended to include an examination of gender construction. But Harjot Oberoi's examination of the Kuka order as a millenarian 'brotherhood of the pure' excludes any analysis of gender construction. In the light of the radical transfor-mation of gender roles in the development of the new moral order envisioned by the Namdharis, any analysis of the movement as millenarian must also posit an explanation for the changes it introduced with regard to the role, status, and ritual organization of women (Oberoi 1992: 160–1, McLeod 1979: 164–87).[12]

The head of the Namdhari sect, Guru Ram Singh, resolutely censured the widely prevalent practices of female infanticide. A large number of his followers were of the lower castes, especially Jat Sikhs, widely known to practise infanticide, despite injunctions against the killing of daughters—injunctions which were closely associated with the creation of the Khalsa from early eighteenth century onwards. Ram Singh, well aware of the extent of the practice, issued circulars to his devotees harshly attacking the custom. In a letter to Daya Singh, he said, 'Teach your children and do not kill infant girls as infanticide is a great sin. Excommunicate those who are cruel enough to put their children to death' (Appendix B, in Singh, J. 1985: 4). The Bedis and the Sondhis, revered guru lineages, were particularly associated with the practice and were especially scorned by Guru Ram Singh, despite their esteemed position in Sikh society. Sikh religious leaders responded by a unanimous denunciation of the practices of the Namdharis. Nihangs, Akalis, Bedis, and Sondhis even attempted to refuse Guru Ram Singh and his followers admission into important religious shrines; they were, however, eventually persuaded by government authorities to allow the Namdharis to enter the shrines. While the orthodoxy censured Namdhari practices as being alien to true Sikhism, the pujaris were in turn chastised by the Namdharis for supporting common 'un-Sikh' practices of female infanticide, drinking, and meat eating. Ram Singh concluded that they could not possibly be Sikhs, as they did not live according to their own scriptural precepts (Singh and Singh 1989: 57–62).

The Namdharis also attacked the practice of selling and exchanging females, which was particularly widespread in Ludhiana, the area surrounding Guru Ram Singh's headquarters. The practice resulted in inordinately high rates of prostitution in the region. According to an early nineteenth-century document, 'Ludhiana has the reputation of furnishing women to all the British regiments stationed there. In a population of not more than 20,000 there are 3,000 prostitutes—that is nearly half the female population are engaged in this occupation' (Garret 1971: 21–2). Although many of these girls were stolen or bought from the surrounding hill country, girls from the district were bartered as well. Malcolm Lyall Darling (1928: 55) describes one such incident: '[A]n Amritsar Jat bought a widow and daughter (also Jats) for Rs. 600. He sold the daughter, who was in her teens, for Rs. 1,200 and six months later got Rs. 300 for the widow, clearing Rs. 900 in all.' According to Darling, this trafficking in women persisted well into the twentieth century and became a lucrative moneymaking scheme for Punjabis in the area. The official British position was opposed to the practice but appeared unable to eradicate the custom. Darling noted that the 'risk is small: if awkward questions are asked, there always witnesses enough to prove satisfactory antecedents; and even if a former husband appears, the worst to be feared is a suit, which is not necessarily lost' (ibid.: 54). Guru Ram Singh's vehement censure of the buying and selling of daughters is best understood within the context of the prevalence of these practices in the region.

Both the Niranakris and the Namdharis claimed credit for introducing novel forms of marriage practices and rituals which disposed of the services of Brahmins and rejected the customary practice of dowry among the Sikhs in the mid-eighteenth century. The marriage ceremony known as *Anand* was first initiated by the Nirankaris in 1855. They introduced the practice of going around Sikh scriptures as opposed to the sacred fire of both orthodox Sikh and Hindu marriage customs. The Namdharis included the reading of Sikh scriptures but also incorporated the sacred fire into their marriage ceremony. The Namdharis also initiated mass marriages for adherents in order to bring down wedding costs. Both groups, however, excluded the services of the Brahmin for marriage rituals. Guru Ram Singh launched his programme of marriage reform in June 1863 in the village of Khote, where a large number of Namdhari disciples had gathered for an inter-caste marriage. Along with other couples, Guru Ram Singh married the daughter of a carpenter to a boy of the Arora caste. The village Brahmins were quick to protest the alternative introduced by Ram Singh since their earnings and authority rested on their sole guardianship of religious and social rituals. A report was consequently made to the authorities about the Namdhari gathering in the village and the Deputy Commissioner of Ferozepore proceeded to Khote to investigate the activities. Fearing a headlong clash with the religious authorities, the Namdharis left Khote. The reformed rites continued with Guru Ram Singh himself presiding at marriage ceremonies.

It was, however, Namdhari critique of dowry practices that was particularly consequential to the prevalent attitudes toward women. Extravagant dowries had led to great indebtedness among the Sikhs in Punjab and contributed significantly to negative attitudes towards girls. According to one source, '[t]he girls are sacrificed in order that loans for their marriage expenses may not encumber the land descending to the sons. The birth of a daughter is regarded as the equivalent of a decree of Rs 2,000 against the father...' (*Jullundur Gazetteer* 1904, cited in Darling 1928: 56). Ram Singh exhorted his followers to arrange inexpensive marriages without incurring debt on dowries (letter to Daya Singh, in Singh, J. 1985: 44).

According to British officials (reported in the Census of 1891: 156), it was precisely these modifications which induced 'men to come forward and join [the Namdharis]'. The 'moderate expenditure at marriage ceremonies and the immunity enjoyed from brahmanical oppression and exaction,' made these ceremonies appealing. Remarriage of widows was another aspect of the reforms initiated by the Namdharis, one warmly endorsed by the British.

It was in the area of religious rituals that the Namdharis radically extended the role and status of women in the nineteenth century. As already noted, initiation rites into the Sikh panth had been in place since the time of the first guru, but had been transformed into a strictly male rite by the time of the tenth guru. Guru Ram Singh embraced the traditional Khalsa cosmology with a number of significant exceptions: all adherents were required to wear white, wear a *malla,* or wooden rosary, and, men *and* women were to be initiated in an identical manner. The traditional colour of the Khalsa on the other hand was blue and was strictly associated with Sikh males; females were explicitly forbidden to wear blue (Falcon 1896: 59). Blue garb worn by the males of the Khalsa effectively separated the 'true Sikhs' from all others; women in orthodox Sikh circles were thus essentially excluded from the ranks of true Sikhs. Conversely, all Kukas were required to wear white, regardless of gender, thereby making a radical break with the colour differentiation that traditionally segregated Sikh women and men. Moreover, Guru Ram Singh's innovation with regard to the malla as another quintessential Kuka Sikh symbol was a requirement for all adherents (Singh, J. 1985: 52). While there are varied accounts of how many women were initiated into the Namdhari order, sources concur that this radical break with tradition did indeed take place. Kuka tradition had twenty-five women receiving Khalsa initiation at village Siahar in Ludhiana district in 1863 (Kavi 1979: 37, Jolly 1988: 89). Further, by their rejection of the esteemed and monopolized position of the Sondhis, Bedis, and Udasis, the traditional guardians of the major Sikh centres where initiation ceremonies were carried out, Namdhari innovations not only opened initiation to women but also made these rites more accessible to all. Obviously, many rural Sikhs had simply been unable to travel to the traditionally revered shrines.

In his reformatory efforts, which continued after he was exiled in Burma, Guru Ram Singh in his letters repeatedly pointed to *Prem*

Sumarg as 'the foundation of the Sant Khalsa' (Singh, J. 1985: 45).
While the work claimed to have been written by a younger
contemporary of Guru Gobind Singh, exact details as to the
authorship and dating of *Prem Sumarg* are unavailable.[13] Given the
centrality of the work to Ram Singh's reforms, a brief analysis of
Prem Sumarg is in order. Traditional historiography insists that the
Sumarg dates to the early decades of the eighteenth century. This
would render the work one of the earliest compositions after the
death of Guru Gobind Singh (Grewal 1968: 82). While J.S. Grewal
(1996: 153) is doubtful that the extant text was actually written in
the eighteenth century, he believes that it could be based on an
earlier work from that era. Recent scholarship, however, has
questioned this dating of *Prem Sumarg*, positing instead that the
work must be understood as a mid-to-late nineteenth century
composition revealing unmistakable nineteenth-century reformist
and colonial influences.[14] The work reflects concerns such as ritual
identity attempting to distinguish Sikhs from Hindus, marriages
that were to be solemnized without the services of Brahmins and
accompanied by the reading of Sikh scriptures, inter-caste and
widow remarriages. Moreover, in the ideal Sikh state posited by
the *Sumarg*, Gurmukhi script was to be given official status. This
had simply not been an area of concern in the eighteenth century;
neither were hygienic conditions, wholesome food, and spacious
houses, all advocated in the *Sumarg* (Singh, R. 1965: 32–72, 103).
Most importantly, *Prem Sumarg*'s vision of the Sikh social order
included explicit instructions with regard to the initiation of women
by khande ki pahul. While there are no primary sources referring
to Guru Ram Singh's specific injunctions regarding women's
initiation, his repeated reference to *Prem Sumarg* would support
the claim that Guru Ram Singh initiated women in the same manner
as men. Significantly, his reliance on *Prem Sumarg* could suggest a
possible connection between the author of the *Sumarg* and
Namdhari ideals and/or following. Guru Ram Singh had admirers
that extended beyond the lower-caste, who formed the bulk of his
following. Giani Gian Singh, the author of the voluminous and
influential *Panth Parkash*, who wrote in the second half of the
nineteenth and into the early twentieth century, though an adherent
of the Nirmala sect, wrote respectfully of Baba Ram Singh and
designated him a prophet (Singh, B. 1976). In this regard it is
perhaps significant that *Prem Sumarg* appears to be written from a

distinctly urban perspective. In the social stratification outlined by the writer, the most superior of occupations was that of trader; agriculturists came next in the hierarchy (Grewal 1996: 160). Unfortunately, given the paucity of scholarship specifically on *Prem Sumarg*, the possible connection between its authorship and the Namdharis must for now remain in the realm of conjecture.

With a growing number of adherents, Ram Singh divided Punjab into districts and placed each area under an agent who bore the Muslim title of *suba* (Fuchs 1992: 313). The Namdhari leader extended the traditional roles of women, offering them full access to these leadership positions. The duties of the subas for both women and men included travelling, preaching, and other proselytizing activities. The decision to appoint women to this administrative position is particularly significant in the light of the Russian Prince Alexis Soltykoff's observations in 1842 that the custom of purdah had spread to such an extent that courtesans were the only women to be seen in Punjab towns (see Khera 1979: 53). One particularly successful female suba known as Hukmee was twenty years old when her preaching and proselytizing achievements were reported. Subadar Hukmee worked in Amritsar and Hoshiarpur, where she preached 'with great success converting a large number of Sikhs to Kookaism' (Ahluwalia 1965: 66). Guru Ram Singh's decision to appoint Hukmee as suba can only be interpreted as a challenge to the prevailing Sikh attitudes towards women, especially towards young women as needing the protection of the confines of the home. It also points to a decided attempt to transform and enlarge the scope of women's roles among Sikhs in Punjab. The initiation of females into the ranks of subadar was cause for great contention among the orthodoxy. Traditional Punjabi folklore maintained that 'three things are bad: grinding for a man, threshing for a buffalo, and travelling for a woman.' Another proverb continues, 'she who stays at home is worth a lakh and she who wanders out is worth a straw' (see Singh, G. 1981: 361). British officials, highly suspicious of Namdhari activities by this time looked upon these developments with great interest. Well aware of Sikh attitudes regarding women's roles, they interpreted the falling popularity of Guru Ram Singh as stemming directly from his resolution to appoint women to the position of subadar (Singh and Singh, 1989: 90). Moreover, the officials were alarmed at the increasing number of women joining the movement; women and children often accounted for one-third to one-half of the adherents at fairs and other gatherings. According to British sensibilities the movement allowed for 'much too free intercourse between the sexes' and officials played no small part in advancing rumours of sexual immorality among Kuka adherents and their leader. Official records charged that Namdhari women were 'loose', and that Guru Ram Singh, through his adulterous affairs had contracted venereal disease (ibid.: 4, 147, 338). The allegations regarding Guru Ram Singh's immoral lifestyle were subsequently withdrawn though the charges of loose conduct against Kuka women remained.

In the light of traditional early nineteenth-century attitudes toward women in social and religious spheres, the opening of ritual and leadership activity to women, can only be understood as an extension of women's roles and a transformed attitude towards women. Further, women's activity on many different religious and political levels, including what was called political insurrection by the British authorities, indicate a radical transformation of roles beyond abstract ideology and reform rhetoric. Correspondence from Guru Ram Singh from Burma was often addressed to the women and children in his following as well as to the men. Further, his exhortations with regard to the Kuka path to liberation, including the memorization of Sikh scripture and constant prayer, were addressed and applicable to both men and women. Notably, of the sixty-six prisoners rounded up by the authorities upon the murders of Muslim butchers, two were women. British sensibilities would not allow them to be blown from cannons along with the other sixty-four Kukas, and they were subsequently released.[15] In terms of ritual activity beyond the initiation rites for female Kukas, women as well as men were included in Guru Ram Singh's guidelines of ritual purification in preparation for prayer (Singh, J. 1984: 49).

CONTEXTUALIZING WOMEN'S REFORM IN THE NINETEENTH CENTURY: CONTRASTING PERSPECTIVES

The Namdhari movement had as its ideological core a need to distinguish itself from the wider civil society. This translated into a strict moral code defining and distinguishing for the community what was pure and impure, separating right from wrong, and what was sacred from the profane. The cosmology of orthodox Sikh society lent itself well to Guru Ram Singh's vision and must be understood as pivotal to the leader's re-interpretation and reformation thereof. However, the difference with regard to these regulations and rites lending themselves to the formation of purity must also be underscored. Significantly, the inclusion of women at virtually all levels of religious and political activity figures largely in the construction of difference between Kuka and orthodox Sikh society. The incorporation of women in leadership roles and religious rites, as well as their inclusion in regulations underlying the construction of difference circumscribing Kuka understanding of the pure in their vision of a moral order, is central to understanding the large influx of women into Kuka ranks. Whether the women streaming to Kuka meetings were simply attracted to Guru Ram Singh's message of emancipation without undergoing initiation or were official adherents of the order is unclear. However, the repeated references of the British to the large numbers of women at Kuka gatherings point to a radical departure from normative customs observed within Sikh orthodoxy. Their numbers would suggest a profound vacuum in terms of the traditional attitudes and circumscribed female roles in nineteenth-century Sikh society.

The Namdhari movement must be appropriately contextualized within the traditional patriarchal norms and values of Sikh society in the nineteenth century without exalting the movement as gratuitously women-centred. Yet it must also be pointed out that traditional research into Namdhari history has not adequately come to terms with the suppositions inherent in the restructuring of attitudes and roles pertaining to women within the Namdhari world view. Women were an integral component in the renewed and purified universe that the millenarian Namdharis saw themselves as forging. In contrast, the reformative efforts of the Amritsar Dharm Sabha simply attempted to do away with many of the same women's rites and beliefs condemned by Guru Ram Singh. The Dharm Sabha did not create alternative rituals, nor did it expand existing male-oriented rites to include women. In essence then, Punjabi females were left with few alternatives to fulfil their need to order their everyday lives. In spite of the avowedly male-centred framework within which the Namdharis operated, in creating an enlarged space for women in terms of purity issues and ritual activity, as well as augmenting women's traditional roles in Namdhari political affairs,

Guru Ram Singh opened doors for women's direct involvement in the transformed moral universe which Namdhari ideology attempted to create. Conversely, the efforts of the Amritsar Dharm Sabha must be understood as stemming from a profound need to *extend* male control over those areas traditionally under the dominion of women. Significantly, the Amritsar Dharm Sabha, initiated at the same time as when Namdhari agitation and its suppression was at its peak, castigated women who followed gurus, insisting that female devotion to a guru would undermine the authority of husbands. The resolution condemning women's adherence to a living guru may well stem from the large influx of women into Namdhari ranks (Jones 1988: 50).

Studies on the reform process within Sikhism in the nineteenth century have tended to focus on the movement championed by the Raj, the Singh Sabha movement. This reform endeavour was, as noted earlier, initiated by individuals who by virtue of their assimilation into the British educational framework had moved up the social hierarchy into positions of power and prestige, traditionally reserved for members of the aristocracy and religious orthodox leadership. The exploits of these new elites have tended to strike the imagination of a great number of scholars. Much of Sikh historiography has, on the other hand, underplayed the reorganization process undertaken by the Kuka leader Ram Singh and his predominantly lower-class adherents. Also significant from a colonial perspective, the reforms undertaken by the Namdharis, particularly those pertaining to women, were deemed reprehensible given the rigid Victorian ethos informing the gender constructs of the British authorities. In the light of the negative reports regarding the large influx of women and their conduct at Kuka gatherings, British intentions to uplift the status of Punjabi women must indeed be held suspect. The parameters of these intentions with regard to women had to do with British and British educated reformers' compulsions to subdue and control the population of Punjab.

Uma Chakravarti has criticized the tendency of historiography to concentrate on the activities of upper-caste male reformers, those individuals who worked broadly within their own traditions through a process of redefinition and 'recasting' of women into roles amiable to their 'reformed' sensibilities. The predominately lower-caste Namdhari movement has generally not been given the attention or the recognition it warrants. Yet there were profound implications involved in the Namdharis' conspicuous critique of dominant class ideologies and gender. Further, while the elite reformers of the upper echelons loudly touted their objectives pertaining to the women's question, there was virtually no challenging of the extant patriarchal framework. The control of women through the imposition of novel restrictions and carefully defined spaces for women became matters of central importance for the new elite. Conversely, Namdharis not only challenged the religious status quo with regard to women, but also supported their assertions by radically enlarging women's space and involvement on all levels.

Dayanand's Arya Samaj Movement and Singh Sabha Reforms— Contesting Claims and Rhetoric

The Arya Samaj, though founded after the initiation of the Amritsar Singh Sabha, was the most far-reaching and influential of the reform initiatives in Punjab with regard to the question of women. As noted earlier, Sikhs and Hindus played active roles in the formation of the Arya Samaj during the late nineteenth century. Consequently, Dayanand's vision of the role and status of women affected both communities. Swami Dayanand, like Roy and others of the Bengali literati, was centrally implicated in the re-interpretation of the past and the rewriting of Indian history. He differed from the universalism of the Brahmo Samaj in his insistence on the superiority of the Vedas and the Vedic religion over all others. Understandably, this led to irreconcilable differences between Arya and Brahmo leaders. Dayanand did, however, follow in the footsteps of his Brahmo predecessors in his belief that the key to a correct understanding of the position and role of women was to the found in the Vedas (Banga 1996: 245–7). Dayanand's vision was based on a return to the 'golden age' through the purification (*shuddhi*) of all peoples, as well as through the procreation of superior offspring. While Hinduism traditionally lacked a conversion ritual, Dayanand introduced the shuddhi ritual to purify and re-admit into the faith Hindus who had converted to Islam or Christianity, as well as those of the 'untouchable' castes. In the first decade of the twentieth century, the Aryas purified a number of Rahtias, a Sikh caste of 'Untouchables' (now called Dalits). Sikhs of the Singh Sabha movement also adopted the shuddhi reconversion rite, largely to contest the conversion activities of the Arya Samaj.

Given the centrality of his concern regarding the furtherance of the race, the role and sexuality of women was of immense concern to Dayanand. Thus, the *Satyarth Prakash,* or 'light of truth', is specific about the rules and regulations for ideal conception, ideal child-rearing practices, and ideal womanhood. For the conception of children, Dayanand gave concise descriptions and regulations for the timing and circumstances surrounding the sexual act between marriage partners. Central to his concern was the outcome of a superior rank of progeny. He cautioned: 'The sex rules should be strictly followed by the husband and the wife. Efforts should be made not to waste the seminal fluid preserved through *Brahmacharya* as best children can only be born of the best generative elements' (Upadhyaya 1960: 137). Another example was in his explicit instructions regarding the nursing of infants—important, given his understanding of racial purity and the necessary potency thereof:

As the body of the child is made out of the elements of the mother's body, the mother gets weak at the time of child-birth; therefore, it is best that she does not feed the child at her breast. The nipples of the mother should be anointed with such ointment as might check the flow of milk. This will rejuvenate the mother within a month. Till then the husband should exercise self-restraint. The husband and wife who live up to these principles are sure to be blessed with excellent progeny, long life, and gradual progress in strength and valour and all their children will be the possessors of the best kind of strength, and valiance, long life and righteousness.

Dayanand also vehemently criticized other issues affecting females such as child-marriage, prostitution, and the lack of female education. These were viewed as largely responsible for the inferior rank and state of Hindu progeny (fallen from the superior state of the original Aryan race), which had ultimately led to the degenerate state of Hindu society. The *Satyarth Prakash* was insistent that all children be educated. The duration for girls' education, however, was much shorter than for boys, the minimum being eight years as opposed to seventeen for boys. Further, the curriculum for girls included supplements for special training suitable for the household duties they were to be responsible for after marriage. Certainly, girls were not to be educated for any professions outside the home, with the exception, as the need became increasingly urgent for female teachers, for teaching in girls' schools.

With regard to marriage, Dayanand's understanding of societal rejuvenation was based on the notion of monogamous marriages, restraint, fidelity, and compatibility with regard to giving birth and raising superior offspring. The minimum age of marriage for girls, after completion of education, was sixteen years; a higher age at the time of giving birth was believed to lead to better progeny. Domestic harmony too was presented as conducive to the good socialization of children. Thus, the compatibility of marriage partners was essential to Dayanand's societal vision (Banga, 1996: 245–7).

Central to the regulations pertaining to women as well as men was a profound need to control sexuality. Thus while both girls and boys were entitled to education, their physical segregation was imperative. The schools themselves had to be separated by a minimum of three miles, and teachers and all other employees of these schools needed to be of the same gender as the students. Dayanand wrote,

No boy of five years of age should be allowed to enter a girls' school, nor a girl of that age in a boys' school. It means that as long as they are *Brahmcharis* (male students) and *Brahmcharinis* (female students), they should keep themselves aloof from eight kinds of sensualities—looking at the person of opposite sex, contactual relation, private meeting, conversation, love-story-telling, intercourse, contemplation of a tempting object and company... (Upadhyaya 1960: 56).

Needless to say, while the larger concern for the propagation of the Aryan race implied that both men and women were included in his observances, the function of women as primary procreators was of particular importance to Dayanand's vision of reform.

The Singh Sabha movement, inaugurated in the late nineteenth century, has been presented as being induced and undergirded largely by the immutable forces of Sikh scripture. The British administration, however, viewed the reforms pertaining to the women's question sweeping the province as directly tied to their own moral superiority and influence. British influence on the Singh Sabha movement is undeniable, particularly in the light of the preferential treatment given the Sikhs by the Raj. Correspondingly,

Singh Sabha leaders exhibited admiration and unequivocal support towards their rulers. However, many of the reforms pertaining to women put in place by the new elite had their foundation in the vision and reconstruction of society by those outside the pale of orthodox Sikhism. The Namdhari and Nirankari movements, as well as other local reformative groups such as the Amritsar Dharm Sabha, played significant roles in shaping the reform efforts of the Singh Sabha movement. While Namdhari and Dharm Sabha reforms have already been discussed, Nirankaris were also highly influential in their reform efforts. As already noted, the Anand marriage ceremony originated with the Nirankari reformers; they were also highly critical of dowries, child marriages, and elaborate marriage ceremonies. They also posed little threat to the British authorities, and given their largely urban base, had minimal influence on the wider Sikh population, particularly the mass rural populace (Webster 1979; Jolly 1988). Precisely because of their urban bearings, the Nirankaris figured significantly in the initiatives of the Singh Sabha, whose influence, as will be argued, was largely restricted to a small minority of Sikhs, most particularly those living in the urban centres of Punjab. Given the jeopardized position in which the Kukas had placed the Sikhs, reformers fearing a backlash that would erode their preferred status made certain that they distanced themselves considerably from the Namdhari movement's reform ventures in particular. Thereafter, and most predominantly, Singh Sabha reform initiatives regarding Sikh women were largely in response to the highly developed gender ideology of the Arya Samaj. Increasingly aware of the threat as well as the successful initiatives of the Arya Samaj, they incorporated many of the premises of Swami Dayanand's vision, all the while insisting that their initiatives were solely and securely founded in Sikh scripture and tradition. By the beginning of the twentieth century Singh Sabha leaders also began to claim credit for the successful ventures of the Arya Samaj, positing their gurus' injunctions against idol worship as laying the foundation upon which Swami Dayanand had been enabled to build his reformative vision (*Khalsa Advocate*, 20 May 1905)

For the Sikhs, by the end of the nineteenth century, calls for reform were securely embedded in a need to protect and separate Sikh identity from those of the other religious communities. Increasingly, members of the new middle class within all faith traditions in Punjab began to utilize these newly established religious societies and institutions for their own personal gains. These included jobs, status, prestige, and prosperity for themselves and for their respective communities. In essence, 'secular battles began to be fought with communal weapons'. While elsewhere the middle classes combatted communal discord in the name of Indian nationalism, communalism in Punjab acquired a more secure footing. Yadav gives the composition of the Punjabi middle class and the circumstances within which it was cultivated as accounting for this contrast with regard to communal differences. In Bombay, Madras, and Calcutta (now Mumbai, Chennai, and Kolkata, respectively) the middle class had grown largely out of the new phase of finance capital and its respective industries, trade in particular, which resulted in the middle class becoming less dependent upon and more competitive with the British bourgeoisie and government. In Punjab, the middle class was more of a 'go-between contractor class' which was inaugurated through the break-up of the feudal economy and the subsequent British exploitation of the Indian market. This took place through the construction of a requisite infrastructure, roads, bridges, public buildings, railways, irrigation works. 'Hence they [the middle class] were closely connected with the British by economic interests and therefore could not be expected to adopt an independent line of action in matters political.' Hindus, Muslims, and Sikhs vied with one another to protect their communal interests, not through agitation against their colonial masters, but through close collaboration with them. Through their respective organizations, members of the various groups began to demand special privileges for themselves. While the forces of communalism did increasingly dominate the political arena in Punjab, they were by and large restricted to the urban middle classes, particularly during the earliest years of the twentieth century. According to Yadav, only a small percentage of the population, about 2 per cent, were directly involved and affected by the communal antagonism in Punjab at the turn of the century. If his appraisal of the situation is correct, this left about 98 per cent of the population still living in peace and amity in the villages, towns, and cities of Punjab (Yadav 1986: 201–2).

What became increasingly vital for these groups then, particularly for the minority populace such as the Muslims and Sikhs, was the creation of religious distinction and distance between themselves and the larger Hindu population. For until the nineteenth century, religious identity had not been confined to one particular religious tradition, especially with regard to religious rites, pilgrimages, and festivals. However, by the end of the nineteenth and beginning of the twentieth century, communal interests fostered a heightened compulsion to establish uniformity of tradition and novel boundaries between religious rites, practices, and individuals of the various faith traditions. David Gilmartin points out that with colonial rule came a weakening of kinship structures in urban areas; forces of individualism transcended ties of kinship. With this realignment process followed new ideological commitments to communal affiliations as opposed to the intense tribal ties that characterized rural regions (Gilmartin 1981: 161). While the British widely supported rural communities, by the turn of the twentieth century the interests of the Raj lay less in maintaining rural kinship ties than in the active realignment of these tribes by their religious affiliation. The Alienation of Land Bill in 1900 attests to this shift. For instance, under the Bill, the government separated Hindu Jats from Muslim Jats; members of these groups were prohibited to transfer land between themselves. There were, however, critics of the British government who insisted that the distinctions made by the government were erroneous; that they would simply intensify communal unrest and turn brotherly relations into discord (Barrier 1966: 74–5).

For the Sikhs, the shifting winds of heightened communalism translated into a process of 'Sikhizing the Sikhs', a redefining of the parameters of true Sikhism. Well moulded by British assumptions of scriptural authority as the essence of true religion, Singh Sabha reformers increasingly turned to fastidious interpretations of Sikh scripture and novel interpretations of Sikh history as the basis of their reform endeavour. Alongside this scriptural focus came the urgent need for education. Literacy for all, males and females, the urban as well as the rural populace, became pivotal to support and perpetuate the system of belief and the behavioural expectations of this new elite. And to this end they intensified their attention and efforts.

Integral to the safeguarding of religious identity by the Singh Sabha in the late nineteenth and early twentieth centuries was the women's question. Sikh women as the traditional bearers of tradition and observers of popular religious forms became important sites upon which the margins of Sikh identity were constructed. Women, however, were seldom included in these transformational endeavours; the process surrounding the proper construction of Sikh women's identity was executed almost exclusively by middle class males *for* their womenfolk.

NOTES

1. For an analysis of the negative consequences of the British tax structure. See Tharu and K. Lalitha 1991: 146–7.
2. This volume is a collection of official police and government reports about the Kukas from 1863 to 1880.
3. Jaswinder Singh 1985 is a useful volume of translations of the correspondence between the exiled Guru Ram Singh, in Burma, and his adherents in Punjab, as well as of official documents pertaining to the guru and his followers.
4. Guru Ram Singh was transported to Allahabad on 18 January 1872, and from then, lived in exile in Burma until his death on 29 November 1885.
5. For an excellent analysis of the forces generating and sustaining the newly established Singh Sabha. See Oberoi 1994: 207–304. This volume remains the most comprehensive and well-balanced study of the Singh Sabha reform movement.
6. For an invaluable summary of the literary achievements of the Singh Sabha leaders, see the introduction to Barrier 1970.
7. The early British presence in India, the East India Company, spurned missionary attempts to advance quickly through the Indian subcontinent. It was only with the Charter Act of 1813 that controls over missionary activity were relaxed. See Viswanathan, 1989: 36.
8. Historians have questioned the practical manifestations of Roy's convictions in his own relationships with women. See Forbes 1996: 10.
9. Minault points to the work of Shaikh Ahmad Sirhindi and Abdul Haq Muhaddis Dehlavi in the seventeenth century and of Shah Waliullah of Delhi in the eighteenth century as the forerunners in the Muslim quest for renewed practices and ideologies.
10. Jacquelin Singh (1991: 164–5) gives a fascinating fictional account of the power of a sorceress in contemporary rural Punjab, in this case, a local sweeper named Veera Bai.
11. The strong sense of honour attached to Punjab's womenfolk is

reported in many early accounts. One such is by Mufti-Ali-Ud Din of Lahore, in 1854, about social conditions at the time of Ranjit Singh. See Gurbux Singh 1976: 135–6.

12. For accounts eulogizing Kuka contributions towards the emancipation of women, see Bali and Bali 1995: 44–7, 74–81, Bajwa 1965: 28–30, and Kavi 1979.

13. With regard to the discrepancies in the dating of the *Sumarg*, see Hans 1982. J.S. Grewal, apparently convinced by Hans' claims with regard to this 'modern forgery', initially included a chapter on *Prem Sumarg* entitled 'A Theory of Sikh Social Order' in his influential *From Guru Nanak to Maharaja Ranjit Singh*, excluding it from subsequent editions. See Grewal 1972: 72–83.

14. An extant manuscript of the *Prem Sumarg* is dated *summat* 1931 (AD 1874). This date has been posited as the actual time of its composition. See Gurpreet Kaur 1988: 319.

15. An earlier Kuka attack on Malodh Fort also included women. See 'The Kooka Outbreak', cited in Singh and Singh 1989: 394.

FIVE

EDUCATION, GENDER CODES, AND POLITICS

What gender is, what men and women are... do not simply reflect or elaborate upon biological 'givens' but are largely products of social and cultural processes.

(Ortner and Whitehead 1981: 1)

Feminist historiography is based primarily on the notion that each aspect of reality is gendered. As such, it seeks to determine how the categories of female and male are historically constructed over time. It moves beyond a timeless, biologically determined understanding of gender to a construct that is fluid and constantly changing. As one historian maintains, women 'do not have a fixed place in this frame; indeed, the frame is not even fixed. The frame is constantly shifting, as norms, cognition and even relationships are negotiated and renegotiated' (Friedl 1994: 92). Needless to say, feminist historiography may be *feminist* without being exclusively focused on women's history. To return again to the analysis of Joan Wallach Scott, gender refers to an on-going, fluid process whereby sexual difference acquires a socially or culturally constructed meaning. A historical focus on gender thus goes far beyond the mere addition of women to the pre-existing narrative; it fundamentally changes one's understanding of history. Traditional historiography has not examined the development of the various reform movements among the Sikhs from a gender perspective.[1] Yet, the process of gender definition was crucial to the very formation, ideology, and rhetoric of the emerging elite, the new middle class—including the reformers, who were greatly influential in defining gender for their times.

The rhetoric of the social reformist discourse with regard to the women's question often cloaks the active charting of a very different political agenda. In the case of the British, the image of the oppressed

Hindu woman served a political function as affirmation of European superiority and justification of the imperial enterprise. In reaction, nationalists elevated the Indian woman; her place in the home represented the uncontaminated purity of Indian tradition. Thus, 'woman' became the site upon which larger claims were made and contested, though these claims varied and were dependent on the specific reformist discourse. Further, claims were made on behalf of the nation as a whole, or in the context of communal, caste, or regional politics (Uberoi 1996: xi–xii).

Educational initiatives were an important aspect of the reformist discourse of the nineteenth and early twentieth centuries. They were also a central means by which reformers actively constructed and defined gender. This chapter analyses the educational enterprise of the Singh Sabha movement. Sikh reformers elucidated and, in some cases, modified the prevailing understandings of gender during the nineteenth and twentieth centuries; these changes were significant for reformist needs and designs. As noted earlier, the distinct minority status of the Sikhs vis-à-vis other religious communities in Punjab is of particular importance in this discussion of gender construction. The tendency to present gender relations between Sikh women and men as distinctive became a major aspect of the reform process. However, there were a myriad dissensions among the reformers and factions among the Sikhs were themselves intensely vying for prestige and power in the newly developing political arena under the Raj. Reforms in terms of gender came to be pivotal to the discourse surrounding the power dynamics of the period.

Ultimately then, the task of analysing the construction of gender during the Singh Sabha period is a formidable one; the variance of gender reforms among the Sikhs and the rationale bolstering those differences must be central to the discussion. Clearly, however, given the intense communal rivalry between the religious groups, particularly in the early twentieth century, identity formation was critical. Preconceived British notions played no small part in this process. The effeminate Indian, the effete though defiant Bengali, the somewhat manly though excessively conceited Muslim, and the masculine and loyal Sikh were characterizations heartily subscribed to by the authorities. These notions continued far into the twentieth century. In a lecture at the Royal Central Asian Society as late as 1961, Major J. Short, who was with the 47th Sikh Regiment, noted:

To come to grips with Anglicanism, you must come to grips with the mere English. To come to grips with Sikhism, you must grasp the significance of the Manja Jut Sikh.... Be that as it may, what is certain is that while these Jats of Juts generally are more or less Indianized, the Punjabi Jut who is a Sikh is not only strikingly unlike the Punjabi Jat who is not one, but the Jut Sikh, very specially the Manja Jut Sikh, is the most strikingly un-Indian of all Indians (1981: 367–8).

Further, referring to the feminine character of the average Indian, Short asserted that Jut Sikh, on the other hand, is 'an out-and-out male'. More significantly, these classifications, along with their feminine counterparts, were conveniently endorsed by certain reformist groups in the early twentieth century and vehemently protested by others. In all cases, these increasingly essentialized gender constructs were important to the communal consciousness-raising carried out by the powerful new elite. The Tat Khalsa, as the Singh Sabha reformers identified themselves, took on the role of representatives of the Sikh community and of a refined, 'pure' Sikhism that was in direct contrast with Sanatan Sikhism. The latter, largely represented by traditional structures of orthodoxy among the Sikhs, supported a version of Sikhism that was more at ease within the Hindu milieu. The Tat Khalsa vigorously opposed any joining of Hinduism and Sikhism, insisting instead that Sikhism in the past, as in contemporary times, was an entirely separate religion. 'Tat Khalsa' and 'Singh Sabha' will be used synonymously throughout the volume.

THE SIKHS AND FEMALE EDUCATION—THE MISSIONARY ENDEAVOUR, SIKH ORTHODOX TRADITION AND REFORM INITIATIVES: AN OVERVIEW

The educational advancement of all the communities vying for representation in the administrative bureaucracy of the Raj figured greatly in the process of identity formation. For the Sikhs, educational progress, particularly the education of females, became the common goal uniting the various factions. The American Presbyterian Mission in Ludhiana set up its first elementary school for females in 1836. The Punjab administration patrorized these efforts to the extent that they closed one of their own schools and bequeathed the building at Rawalpindi to the missionary effort. Further, zenana instruction within the homes of prominent Indians was carried out almost exclusively by missionary women, both European and Indian. Less than fifteen years after its annexation there were more than thirty European women educating the 'natives' in Punjab (Punjab Education Report, 1861–2, cited in Sidhu 1985: 131–2). In time, a new emphasis was laid on the indigenous education of Punjab's youth. According to Baba Khem Singh Bedi, '[t]he appointment of teachers should rest with the people, for they only can best know what kind of teachers they require. Unless the teacher possesses the confidence of the people, these latter will not send their girls to schools.' With regard to the missionary efforts, he noted that '[t]he disinterested and unselfish efforts they make in this direction lose almost all their value when people consider that all this is done for the sake of the Christian religion' (Leitner 1971: 109). Bedi, the main representative of the Amritsar Singh Sabha, though widely vilified by the powerful Lahore group, was nonetheless considered highly instrumental in the establishment and funding of female education. He is credited with having established 108 schools for girls and women by 1882. Other members of the guru lineage also facilitated Sikh education, particularly the women of these groups. The religious establishment's involvement in the education of both males and females was part of a long-standing tradition. Udasi and Nirmala Sikhs had often held classes in their respective *deras* or *dharamsalas*. The wives and mothers of the *bhais* of the Sikh religious establishment had run Gurmukhi schools. Their husbands helped these women attain an elementary level of literacy; the women then instructed children in reading and religious duties. Under the judicial auspices of the education department, these 'mysterious institutions', perceived as lacking the requisite means, form, and substance to properly educate Sikh girls, were closed. G.W. Leitner, the newly appointed Director of Instruction in Punjab was very apprehensive of this action, noting that '[a]fter all the agitation that had taken place regarding "female education", it was certainly inconsistent to sweep away at one blow 108 schools.' Leitner believed that government intervention and innovation in the form of inspected and monitored schools was unrealistic and injurious to the very cause of female education. He was well aware of the notions of honour that formed the basis of Sikh society and insisted that a more effective course of action would necessarily involve the religious establishment. 'That the wives of priests should visit females of their community and teach them is right and proper, but that girls especially of a marriageable age, should cross bazars in order to assemble in a school, is, I think, objectionable.' In defence of these notions of honour he claimed that the 'better classes' held their women in 'respect and a religious affection of which we have not even the outward profession in Europe.' He also advised authorities to return to and support indigenous traditions of learning. '[D]omestic happiness and purity will be furthered by abolishing the present Female Schools, except wherever the local priesthood wish for their continuance, or where the management can be made over entirely to men like Baba Khem Singh and his relatives.' Leitner, upon his appointment as director, revived fifty of these indigenous schools (ibid.: 102–4).

With the establishment of the Singh Sabha movement, Leitner foresaw an effective vehicle for the promotion of education, particularly for Sikh girls and women. Indeed, the education of Sikh females was cause for great concern among the upwardly mobile, newly educated Sikh males. While they had gained greatly through the educational opportunities offered by the missionary establishment, they were exceedingly threatened by Christian influences upon their women and girls. But they were also wary of the intentions and educational approach of the traditional religious elite, which was historically connected to the increasingly denigrated Amritsar Sabha; this became especially significant as the animosity between the Amritsar and Lahore factions amplified. Lakshman Singh gives a detailed account of the acrimony between the two groups. In one small town named Sukho, Lakshman Singh opened the Sukho Khalsa School in 1898. Within a year it was faltering due to lack of funds. Its rival, the Sanatan Khalsa School, also in Sukho, was inaugurated a short while later and ran successfully through support from Baba Khem Singh Bedi and other moneyed people. Bedi was eventually persuaded to support both schools, which allowed the former to remain functional (see Singh, G. 1965: 145–53). In this particular incident, the rivalry between the two groups was curtailed due to intervention by both Baba Khem Singh Bedi and Lakshman Singh; generally, however, such a cooperative approach did not mark the relations between the Sabhas. The Lahore Sabha in particular was confronted with a good deal of opposition from within the Sikh community and a number of a gurudwaras banned its members from meeting on their premises;

by and large, gurdwara officials, as part of the Sikh orthodoxy, rejected many Lahore Sabha designs. The latter was thus forced to establish its own gurdwaras served by officials who were in line with the Lahore Singh Sabha ideology (Jones 1994: 111). The battle lines between the two groups were drawn until well into the twentieth century, despite a ceasefire between them with the formation in 1902 of an umbrella organization of the Singh Sabhas, the Chief Khalsa Diwan. According to the *Khalsa Advocate* in September 1908, 'the problem of educating the masses, difficult though it apparently seems, would have erelong been solved to the satisfaction of every body, if our aristocracy had only cared to lend a sympathetic ear to the advocates of education.'[2] Because the aristocracy was still closely tied to the ideology of the Amritsar Singh Sabha, representatives of the Lahore faction were well aware that continued animosity towards this group would only lessen opportunities for monetary support for their educational ventures. Notwithstanding their increasing hegemony, the Lahore Sabha had few arrangements in place to financially sustain their grand educational schemes.

The Tat Khalsa and its Educational Ideals

Sikh literati expounded on their ideals of education through the various mediums at their disposal; tracts and newspapers were especially utilized to spread their objectives. Women, it was acknowledged, were sinned against as infants, in their youth, as wives and daughters-in-law, and as widows. Education came to be intricately entwined with the upliftment of women and with the notion of nation-building. Without educated mothers, the Sikhs would continue to be mired in superstition, ignorance, and immoral practices; they would also be unable to compete in the milieu offered by their new rulers. British notions of the Jat Sikhs as remnants of the Aryan race were appropriated to call for a return to their glorious heritage where both women and men had been educated. While their Western counterparts had flourished as a result of education, reformers insisted that the Sikhs, inspite of their distinguished past, had degenerated to a point of arrant illiteracy; the situation, particularly with regard to women, was a far cry from the lofty ideals of Sikhism. 'Among the Sikhs, the women have always been entitled to receive education as men.

Our Rahit-namas enjoin clearly that both boys and girls should be sent to school' (*Khalsa Advocate* 4 April, 2 May 1908; 15 August 1904). The rahit referred to was *Prem Sumarg*; following in the footsteps of the Namdharis, Singh Sabha reformers increasingly accorded it authoritative status in their rallying call for girls' education. According to the Singh Sabha, there had indeed been a resplendent time in their history when women had not been influenced by the degenerate customs that defined Sikhism in the early twentieth century.

While the Sikh reformers were aware of the need for female education, the form, content, and end of that endeavour was not nearly as clear. Particularly during the early years of the twentieth century, in an attempt to sway education-wary public opinion, the reasoning behind promoting female education was promoted through newspapers of the day and through speeches and tracts. However, convincing the bulk of the Sikh population of the benefits of female education was no small feat. But what was increasingly apparent, at least to the small group of Sikh reformers, was the need to protect their young women from the educational advances of the Arya Samajists, as well as from Christian missionaries. For the most part, however, these were issues of importance only for the educated elite; the bulk of the population was largely unaffected by the fervent debates being carried on in the cities. For instance, the number of girls and women educated at the principal educational institution of Ferozepur, the Sikh Kanya Maha Vidyalaya are relatively insignificant. Between 1908 and 1914 the school educated 1,608 girls; by 1915, 315 girls were on the school's rolls. These girls and women were largely drawn from the families of the educated elite. The number of girls and women in residence in 1907 was 115. While a majority hailed from Punjab, a number were sent to the school from the United Provinces as well as from Burma. The breakdown was as follows: Amritsar District, 19; Ferozepur, 17; Patiala State, 15; Ludhiana, 13; Montgomery, 9; Nabha State, 8; Lahore, 5; Jhind, Kapurthala States, Lyallpur, Jhelum, Agra Districts, and Burma, 3 each. Of the number from Patiala, 8 girls belonged to the Rajinder Pratap orphanage. Of the total number of students, 97 were girls, 5 were widows, and 19 were married women. Of those married, 11 had children, a number of whom were cared for at the boarding house. Also, 27 of the female students were from Hindu families. As late as 1915, the boarding house had not been completed and the school itself had been in danger of closing due to a paucity of funding (Singh, S. 1915). While the educational enterprise largely revolved around the children of leading Singh Sabha families, the need to raise the consciousness of the wider Sikh populace was taken seriously by the new leaders.

THE POLITICS OF GENDER: THE HOME AND THE WORLD

Popularized Victorian notions of woman as helpmate to man became increasingly central in the discussion of women and education. Meredith Borthwick has explicated on the popularization of this notion in the context of Bengal. The educated elite had direct experience of Englishwomen in positions of social companionship with their menfolk at gatherings that included Indians and British. She recounts the story of Krishna Mohan Banerjea attending 'conversational parties' where the host's family was present. Banerjea was impressed with what he saw and recommended that the Europeans give all Hindus an opportunity to see what female education had accomplished. Indian men were fascinated with this open interaction between the sexes—for men to be in the company of women without the 'uncivilized' element of sexuality usually associated with social contact with women outside of the family unit, namely, with prostitutes or nautch girls. However, the 'united front of self-righteousness adopted by the British in India at this stage, did not provide the *bhadralok* [the educated Indian male] with any material that may have challenged the superiority of British civilization...' Hence, at this early stage of the British-Indian encounter, Bengalis were simply not aware of the position of women in England, and their view of the British helpmate was highly idealized. For Bengalis, the restraints of purdah as well as the lack of female education among their own womenfolk became indicative of their own unenlightened position viz-á-viz the British; ensuing criticism of the position of Indian women forced the newly educated elite to confront the women's question with singular ardour (Borthwick 1984: 33–7).

Given the relatively late annexation of Punjab into the Raj, the notion of the helpmate had undergone significant transformation. Conscious of the deeply ingrained work ethic of the Jat Sikhs, Singh Sabha leaders fused Victorian notions of the helpmate with the traditional Punjabi work ethic, hastening to assure the sceptical populace that education in and of itself would not diminish women's abilities to work. According to the *Khalsa Advocate* of 15 February 1905,

They say that domestic economy requires that women should not be educated. If they are educated they will refuse to do the work which they usually do at home and chaos and disorder will take the place of order and tranquility. Is this objection of theirs well founded? ... But happily it is only based on the superficial observation which our countrymen make of the habits and the ways of the English women living here.

Benefiting from the information and experiences of the Bengalis who had been educated in England, as well as a small number of their own who had travelled to Britain, Sikhs were far more aware of the different circumstances between women in England and the *memsahibs* in India. Concurring with the hard-working peasantry, these reformers did *not* want their womenfolk to emulate the practices of their rulers, or at least their British female counterparts. Laziness, associated by them with the memsahibs, was to have no place in Sikh society. But, the reformers adroitly noted, *without* education women were wont to be less thrifty and more prone to idleness. Well aware and equally critical of the suffragette movement in Britain, Sikh reformers insisted they could look forward to no such 'nightmare of feminine frivolity'. Their reasoning for female education and appropriated notions of the helpmate had nothing to do with women having access to polling stations or occupations outside of the home. Rather, the 'true' helpmate was to maintain her proper position at the fireplace (*Khalsa Advocate* 25 April, 11 July 1908; 16 January 1909).

For the new social elite, novel dichotomies such as the spheres of home and the world, and the woman's function within the realm of the home became pivotal in the ensuing discourse. In the case of rural Sikh Jats, women's roles had been strikingly similar to those of men; both worked the fields and both men and women had had varied roles. In essence, the means of subsistence and production had been commonly held. The large number of court cases instigated by women over ownership of land was indicative of the centrality of women's roles within the rural populace. In sharp contrast, the new urban elite endorsed a differentiation of domestic and social orders. With this separation came an accentuated understanding of the private being subordinated to the public. As

Joan Kelly has pointed out, with this separation came an accentuated loss of control over property and production for women; as surpluses increased and the notion of private property developed, the communal household became a private economic unity, a family (extended or nuclear) represented by the oldest male of the household. The family itself was in turn subordinated to a broader social or public order, one governed by the state. This too tended to be the domain of men (Stimpson 1984: 10–15). It is precisely the differential construction of the private and public spheres in the colonial period that underlay the class character of the new Indian elite. Victorian notions of purity, education, and the 'home-bound nature' of womanhood were an integral aspect of the very *formation* of the middle class (Sangari and Vaid 1990: 10). While the husband toiled 'in the world', only the wife in her appropriate position and with sufficient education could make the house a 'home'. Education of girls and women was expected to lead to a situation where the true helpmate could discharge her duties in the home properly.

Home in its true sense is that sacred place where the troubles and anxieties of the world cannot enter, where a man after his daily work and struggles can find that rest and bliss which under the present circumstances falls to the lot of a few happy mortals.... Who can then make a true home? It is only a true and noble wife that can do so.... In order to achieve this object, education must be physical, intellectual, moral, as well as religious.... They must also be trained for the performance of those little household duties such as cooking and sewing, other similar things which contribute so very largely in the comforts of a family (*Khalsa Advocate*, 15 February 1905).

Proper duties in the home included above all the education of children; women who were not educated could hardly contribute to the process of nation-building so ardently sought by the reformers. Significantly, the reform initiatives on female education inaugurated a hitherto unheard of stipulation in matrimonial notices appearing in the newspapers; education increasingly became a prerequisite for marriage possibilities and a 'modern' home. Uneducated women found it more and more difficult to secure educated husbands (Darling 1934: 299). According to the prevailing view,

In the first place, and on the first rank stand the mothers of the country, the great army of patient, unknown, unrewarded workers whose best years of strength, intelligence and knowledge, are devoted to the perfecting of the future generation.... Every young woman has a chance to do her share of the work. If she is self-respecting and inspires in young men that meet her a high idea of womanhood, she is helping to push along the development of humanity in her little corner of life. Incidentally, she is preparing herself for a wise marriage and that most useful of all work, the addition of really good children to the population.

Conversely, in the rural tracts, the reformers noted contemptuously that it was the ability to recite 'in a sonorous tone the love story of *Hir and Ranja*' that was considered to be a sign of high breeding (*Khalsa Advocate*, 29 April 1905).

The increased use of Western medicines labelled in English gave rise to an additional concern. The illiterate condition of the female population could lead to appalling blunders in the home, particularly in the proper treatment of children. According to one observer,

I know of a family... where turpentine oil was given to a boy instead of the dose of medicine simply because the lady in charge of the house could not distinguish between the label of a bottle of turpentine and the medicine, placed in the cupboard. In these days of hard struggle when the men are so busy in the worldly affairs in their businesses—we have to depend upon our ladies, and, such mishaps do occur and will continue to occur as long as their condition remains such.

Reformed attitudes toward the position of the 'fair sex' as gentle helpmate to her husband translated into a not-so-subtle critique of women who did not conform to this ideal. The Victorian ethos informing the English-educated reformers allowed for little space for independent women; even worse, some men even followed the counsel of their women. Well aware of British notions of the 'manly' nature of the peasant female Jat, men ruled over by women were derided. In the case of the peasantry, reformers posited that the 'weaker' sex was prone to rule, as opposed to attending to, her husband (*Khalsa Advocate*, 15 April 1990). And with this despicable state of affairs came the reason for the degenerate condition of Sikhism, fallen from its once pristine state of purity. Accordingly, it was difficult to encounter a 'true' Sikh; women raising children and passing on superstitious attitudes and practices to them accounted for the lack of genuine religiosity. For women are the most conservative, they make the customs and custom derives its force mainly from women.... How often do we hear of men meeting... and passing resolutions to do certain things and not to do others, and how often directly do they go home, get their tail twisted and walk on quietly and meekly in the beauty path, never moving an inch this side or that.

True men, however, were able to counter the un-Sikh practices that had crept into Sikh social and religious life. Indeed, well versed in British allocations of manliness and femininity, as well as in their own traditional hypermasculine values, Sikh reformers ingeniously reversed the acclaimed notion of the 'manly' peasant Jat female into the precise opposite. Only men who were able to move away from the debased sway of their womenfolk, namely, the reformed and the educated, were *truly* manly. Consequently, the Jat peasant, mired in the superstitious ways of women, was unmanly. Still, even those few workers within Tat Khalsa circles were in danger of falling from their lofty heights of manliness; 'for the smallest things they begin to quarrel like women' (*Khalsa Advocate*, 15 April 1904).

The decidedly offensive attacks on the Jat peasantry in the *Khalsa Advocate* must be placed a larger perspective. In 1901, the British enacted the Land Alienation Bill to protect the interests of the rural population from the encroaching urbanites who had the surplus capital to buy up land. This policy was interpreted by those living in cities as being anti-urban and too beneficent toward the favoured Jat peasant. An attack therefore on the traditional manliness of the rural Jats is understandable, particularly since many of the English language newspapers were read by the same British officials who were responsible for the Land Alienation Act. The remarks made were double-edged though highly subtle (Kumar 1976: 154–9). Sexual inversions, in this case, the displacement and replacement of the foolish and unmanly with the sophisticated and truly manly, according to Michel Foucault, have less to do 'with a negative mechanism of exclusion as with the operation of a subtle network of discourses, special knowledges, pleasures, and powers' (1990: 72). Given that the reformers increasingly assumed positions of authority as a result of their educational opportunities, their circumstances allowed for a judicious construction of distinctions between truly masculine behaviour and attitude and that which merely paraded as manly.

The revisions of masculinity put forth by the new elite must also be understood as an attempt to counter popular reaction to the reform enterprise. For the most part, the attitude of the peasantry was marked by contempt towards the Singh Sabha reformers. Significantly, this disdain had everything to do with deeply ingrained notions of masculinity. The hard physical work ethic of the Jat peasantry, along with traditional aversions to the 'softening' effect of education, led to a popular taunt among the peasantry, especially among women: 'They become Singh Sabhas, when they cannot provide'.[3]

The taunt has been closely associated with Punjab's womenfolk. Given that historical writings have tended to focus on male pursuits, it is difficult to point to women's voices and women's agency in history. It thus becomes important to listen for even oblique dissent or criticism in the absence of overt insubordination vis-à-vis existing dominant systems. In Sikh history, although barely perceptible, the taunt has tended to survive time as well as the layers of the male bias of history. It has been utilized by the powerless and by the voiceless to protest the manoeuvrings of hegemonic discourse (see Anand 1978 for an overview of taunts in Punjabi folklore). In the case of Sikh history, women's taunts are sexualized; women taunt men for not being true men (Fenech 1996: 181). Taunts pointing to the effeminacy of males, given the hypermasculine ethos prevalent since the formation of the soldier-saint ideal, were doubly effective. In the colonial milieu, provision for family in the form of tilling the land and filling graineries, according to the rural masses, were the true measures of masculinity. From the rural Jat perspective, as the taunt attests, urbanites, particularly Jats who rejected their ancestral peasant mooring, could fulfil few of the requirements of true manliness. Educated Sikhs were thus increasingly necessitated to construct a formula of masculinity that corresponded with their hard won positions of prestige as the leaders of the Sikh community.

Nonetheless, there were repeated concerns that Sikh men attending institutions of higher learning were in danger of losing their manly carriage. Insisting that Sikhs had distinct needs, being of a different breed from other Indians, calls were made to address this dilemma:

It is a matter of great concern for every Sikh, every government on the Indian soil and every apostle of peace to see any deterioration in the

physique and hardiness of these sons of Mars. Handsome, brawny youth....
come out of our school or college rooms with haggard looks, sunken
eyes, tottering frame and pale faces.... Hence for the Sikhs at least, the
culture of intellect and development of brain and enrichment of mind
alone are meaningless, absurd, and detrimental to the true interests of
the community as well as of the country. It is therefore the duty of the
men of light and leading to insist upon adequate arrangements being
made for the revival of our old national games like gatka, riding, *chacker*
throwing, wrestling and others.... The question is a common place one,
on the surface, but a little thought will disclose its immense gravity and
far-reaching consequences, for the decay of physical vigour is the first
sign of the death of a nation (from the *Khalsa Advocate*, 13 September
1913).

In all likelihood the oblique comparison made between Sikhs
and other Indians is a reference to the Bengalis. Stereotypical
notions of the Bengalis as over-educated, effeminate, and weak were
commonplace in the nineteenth and twentieth centuries,
particularly given the British penchant for comparing the manly
Punjabi and the effeminate Bengali. The fears expressed were
indicative of widely held Victorian notions of excessive education
without adequate physical exercise leading to unmanly behaviour.
These notions were heartily appropriated by Lakshman Singh. In a
series of pamphlets published in 1918, he responded to some
observations made by Sir Rabindranath Tagore on Sikhism. In these
Singh referred to Bengalis as 'quill drivers, penny-a-liners or throat-
renders', who

indulge in so much cant on the pulpit and on the platform, or newspaper
scribblers or writers of brochures, whose patriotic instincts act only within
the precincts of temples or lecturing places, or glow on the pages of books
and periodicals. It is nothing short of impertinence for Bengali Babus,
however literate or high placed, to pose as critics of men whom they are
constituted to understand.

Bengal had not yet produced soldiers 'to protect the honour of
its hearths and homes'. This state of affairs Singh compared with
the Sikh soldiery of Punjab, 'the beau ideal of the people', who
though unlettered and untaught were 'more susceptible to noble
impulses' than the highly educated Bengalis (Singh, S.B.L. 1918:
9–19). Similar to the contemporary golden age of athleticism in
Britain, the Sikh reform endeavour incorporated the fear that without

the necessary element of physical exertion, education would lead only to moral depravity and unmanly behaviour (Hyam 1990: 73). With great ingenuity they insisted that the 'manly' pursuits posited as essential for the wholesome progress of the Sikh nation were integral aspects of their glorious Sikh heritage.

As already noted, the newly crafted understanding of true masculinity was paired with the novel construct of the feminine. For the Singh Sabha reformers, crucial indicators of the lack of true femininity came to the fore with the annual report of the Excise Department in 1905. While reformers were aware that drink was the bane of the Sikh peasant of the Punjab, the Excise Commissioner's report indicated that women too were given to drinking. Nonetheless, while taking care to respect the Commissioner's observations, the reformed mindset found this reproof difficult to accept. The reformers did, however, acquiesce that it was 'possible to find, here and there, a stray woman of easy-going habits belonging to the unfortunate class of fallen women' who had come to 'imbibe some of the more objectionable masculine vices' and had thus 'unsexed themselves'. For the Excise Commissioner to have formed such an opinion, however misplaced, of the average Sikh peasant woman was indicative of the alarming extent that drink and its influence was 'sure to be the ruination of the manhood of the country' (in the *Khalsa Advocate*, 17 June 1905). The need for the unsexed of their society, those who were no longer true females due to their unwomanly practices, to receive a proper education on true femininity became urgent. If these masculine ways were not altered, the effects on the manhood of the Sikhs would be devastating. In essence, the men could become effeminate. The Singh Sabha reformers were well aware of the contempt of the British towards the effeminate Bengali; to suffer similar revulsion from their esteemed rulers, given the high esteem that had come with the purported masculinity of the Sikhs, could not be tolerated. Indeed, only through proper educational initiatives, now more imperative than ever before, could Sikh women become worthy of their highest calling—gentle helpmates to their husbands. Needless to say, the power dynamics are palpable; the actual wording points to an active process of sexual inversion. The reformers, armed as they were with the artillery of modern methods of communications, were well equipped to actively maintain this ideal construct.

In routine objections by the 'half educated and the ignorant masses' to female education based on fears of the subsequent irreligion of women, reformers found their greatest incentive *for* the cause of female education. It must be remembered that the education offered by the traditional religious leaders, the granthis, and their womenfolk would have largely catered to the peasant population. These educators were held suspect by those educated by the missionary enterprise; their students were thus maligned as 'half educated'. And if Sikhism was in a state of degeneracy, it was precisely because the traditional religious orthodoxy supported degenerate customs observed by Sikh womenfolk. This had long been the opinion of the Christian missionaries who earlier had noted that 'the religion of the Indian women chiefly consists in adhering to superstitious rites and observances' (ibid., 15 February 1905). The Reverend C.B. Newton also furthered this perspective, insisting that the 'strong point of Indian heathenism today, is in the fact that the women are still its devoted adherents...' (1883: 35). Thus the reformers found a triple adversary: Hinduism, aligned with heathenism and superstition, the traditional Sikh orthodoxy who represented the Sanatan mindset, and women, who were responsible for the degenerate state of affairs in Sikhism. A major key to the alleviation of this state of affairs was in a *proper* education of Sikh girls. Only education would lead to a proper judgement of 'the right and the wrong, the true and the false, the beautiful and the ugly, and the noble and the ignoble.' Religious education, above and beyond all else, was to become

the life blood of our educational movements.... Thank God that our girl schools.... are very particular in this respect. Religious instruction is a primary function there and secular education but a secondary thing. In a short time we may expect to have in our midst a set of pious sisters to give shoulders to the clogged wheel of the female portion of our community.

The 'clogged wheel' became the favourite euphemism utilized by the Singh Sabha reformers to refer to their *own* situation vis-á-vis their women. Progress could never be achieved if that wheel was not aligned with the other, the quickly moving wheel of the reformers. For 'an uneducated and therefore *uncivilized* wife is a standing nuisance for her advanced husband' [italics mine]. The consequences of this state of affairs were far-reaching. 'Just image the future capabilities of a child developing under the steady control of its scholarly mamma and those of one frisking around an idiot mother. Brethren, all the intellectual shortcomings are due to this deplorable state' (*Khalsa Advocate*, 14 April 1908).

This state of affairs was intricately intertwined with the notion of Sikh 'national progress', which, from the reformed perspective, formed the crux of the Singh Sabha agenda.

The husband, out of love with his community, wishes to join in all its undertakings whereas the imprudent wife thoughtlessly stands in his way to do this. You might often have heard of such and such person's wishing to help propaganda but failing to fulfil his wish on account of his selfish wife's protest. What a pity then if alive to all these defects and disadvantages, we should suffer this sorry state to continue.

And there was but one remedy to support the initiatives of the Singh Sabha reformers as well as address the ills of Sikh society. Education was to start as early as possible while girls were still 'beautiful and delicate flowers'. Younger girls, according to Bhai Thakat Singh of the Singh Sabha girls' school in Ferozepur, were far more pliable than older females; girls 'on the wrong side of twenty' shirked work and rebelled against the school's discipline (see Caveeshar 1984: 117–18). The form that education was to take was also of great concern to the reformers. Care was to be taken in 'selecting books for a young girl. They should not be heaped into their laps just as they come from the circulating library fresh with everything that springs from the font of folly. Their education should be deeply religious and moral.' Only learning based on Sikh religious principles could once again return the fallen Sikh populace to a position worthy of their calling as the true representatives of their gurus. Jat Sikhs, females in particular, with their 'pitiable want of education' were most severely in need of the reforming influence of Singh Sabha-initiated schools (*Khalsa Advocate*, 15 February 1905; 15 July 1904).

The town of Ferozepur became the site of increasing competition between the various reform groups with regard to the issue of female education. By 1910, Ferozepur had girls' schools founded not only by the Singh Sabha and the Arya Samaj, but also by Muslims, Christians, the Dev Samaj, and the government. The small district was thus a locality of intense vying for students. It was the earliest site of Arya Samaj attempts to educate their females; in 1877, their girls' school was initiated as an adjunct to the Samaj's orphanage.

The Arya Samaj, though initiated *after* the birth of the Singh Sabha movement, had moved decisively in the arena of female education. Largely motivated by fear of Christian influences, a number of highly influential Arya leaders began an active campaign for the education of their young girls (Jones 1988: 46–7). By the 1880s, a more aggressive sector of the Arya Samaj became the effective catalyst for increased female education. As early as 1892, the divisive issue of starting a girls' high school came to the fore, despite warning calls regarding costs of the project. It was feared that the expenses of this proposed facility would compete with badly needed contributions for the Dayanand Anglo-Vedic College for males. By 1894, the Managing Committee of the Anglo-Vedic College made a well-publicized break with the champions of the women's educational movement. Still, despite fears of the 'unsexing' of their girls through the effects of higher education, a number of Samaj groups supported the latter campaign and pushed ahead with their goal of upgrading the Kanya Maha Vidyalaya in Jullundhur to a high school, inaugurated in 1896, and eventually developing into a women's college. By 1906, the school had on its rolls 203 females— unmarried, married, and widowed. It became the centre of a new movement, as its alumnae themselves opened other girls' schools. In an attempt to meet the need caused by the paucity of literature suitable for women, the *Panchal Pandita*, a Hindi monthly propagating female education, was inaugurated in 1898. Further, the Mahavidyala started to publish readers and texts for the moral uplifting of Arya females (Jones 1989: 216–17).

THE SIKH KANYA MAHAVIDYALA

While the Arya Samaj was forging ahead with plans for a girls' high school in the 1890s, the Sikhs were more wary of this directive. According to one observation in the *Khalsa Advocate* on 15 April 1904, 'higher education for females cannot be made to succeed on a large scale, but we can expect to have Primary and Secondary education.'[4] The champion for girls' education was Thakat Singh. While still a student in Lahore, he had become convinced of the need for female education. The pioneer of the Lahore Sabha and professor of Oriental College, Gurmukh Singh, had expounded on the topic of Sikh womanhood; characterizing the women as *abla* or helpless, he had bemoaned the condition of contemporary women. Thakat Singh had then stood up and declared that he would dedicate his life to championing the cause of the 'helpless'.[5] He began an elementary programme of education for girls in Ferozepur in the 1890s—the inauguration of Singh Sabha educational endeavours for females. The Sikh Kanya Mahavidyala, the school started in 1892 by Bhai Thakat Singh and his spouse Harnam Kaur, came to embody the ideals and hopes of the Sikh reformers. While the Singh Sabha leadership lauded the efforts of the founders, the education-wary bulk of the Sikh population gave little financial support to the school. It was only in 1904 that the Sikh Kanya Mahavidyala acquired a boarding house to allow for girls from outside the Ferozepur locality to receive an education based on Sikh principles. According to her biographer, Harnam Kaur was the first to suggest the idea of a boarding house; Thakat Singh, however, aware of Sikh attitudes towards female education rejected the idea, convinced that the Sikh community would not contribute the necessary finances for this new venture. However, in time Singh became an active crusader for the necessity of accommodating and educating girls from far and wide. It was Harnam Kaur, however, who took the initial steps for the boarding house; she rented a spacious building near the school as the first abode for female students. By Baisakhi Day, 1904, handbills were distributed among a gathering in Amritsar, appealing to Sikhs to donate funds (see Singh, B.S. 1908: 42–51).[6] The controversies that accompanied this venture were substantial, and indicative of the anti-female-education ethos facing the reformers. While there was some support for the girls' school, there was also a backlash against the efforts of the crusading couple, particularly during the early years of boarding opportunities at the school. Given the notions of protective honour among the Sikhs, to allow females to leave the confines of gentle family homes to live elsewhere was inconceivable. To calm the fears of parents of prospective boarders, another handbill was distributed, which explained in detail the objectives of the boarding house. This took place at the annual celebrations initiated by the Khalsa Diwan, which by 1905 included separate 'Ladies Diwans'. The main event was held in Amritsar, on Baisakhi Day, and the *Khalsa Advocate* (22 April) reported:

Married couples and ladies were only permitted to enter the place selected for this meeting. The usual program of singing Shabads from the Sikh

Scriptures was carried out solely by the women. Several of them delivered speeches at the occasion, which, according to reports was exceptionally large; it included the respectable Sikh women from the leading families of Amritsar and of the Province in general.

Given that the Diwan was composed of leading members of the reform movement, the opposition to the boarding house is indeed surprising. Even amongst this elite gathering, traditional attitudes toward women held fast. The fact that the event was closely monitored, only women and married couples being allowed onto the premises, was indicative of the highly protective stance of Sikhs towards their women. That the defensive posture was in little danger of abating as late as 1916 was demonstrated by a scandalized appeal to the Sikh populace; apparently love poems were being read by students at the institution. Observers remonstrated against these reports, insisting that this was an outrage to their sisters (*Khalsa Advocate*, 16 September).

The objectives of the Sikh Kanya Mahavidyala were indicative not only of the attitudes of the educated elite, but also of the cultural values of the larger Sikh populace. Deeply ingrained notions of modesty, a well-defined work ethic, and above all, the religious instruction of the students were the watchwords of the school. Visitors noted that particular attention was paid to 'inculcating modesty, meekness and devotion', the 'peculiar traits of Indian womanhood' (Singh, S. 1915: 48). Further, given popular fears that laziness and pride would ultimately be the outcome of female education, the school employed no servants; the students themselves cooked and cleaned the premises. Accordingly,

the chief feature of the institution is the simplicity and the modesty of the girls, which strike the visitors very much. These are the virtues which are the real ornaments of Indian women and which we would be very much the worse for losing. Self help is taught to the girls in a very practical manner, *viz*, by requiring them to do all that work by themselves.... This alone will stand them in good stead, when they leave the school to join the worldly life with its attendant duties and responsibilities (ibid.: 49).

The general ideals in full force at the Ferozepur institution were not unique to the reform initiatives of the Sikhs. For the most part the institution was run along the widely accepted premises of female education put forth by Swami Dayanand. Harnam Kaur was a product of the Arya system. Her biography is rife both with the values inculcated by the Arya Samaj and the objectives of the Singh Sabha movement. Education, according to Kaur, was as essential for girls as it was for boys. Moreover, the education of females had more far-reaching effects than that of males; through the education of females, entire families could receive the benefits of learning. Espousing popular views on the advancement of European nations due to their attitudes toward female education, Harnam Kaur, like Dayanand, hearkened back to the golden days of Draupadi and Sita when women, due to the egalitarian ethos of the day, contributed greatly to society. According to Kaur, the overriding state of illiteracy among the Sikhs had led to the humiliating position of contemporary Sikh womanhood. The responsibility for this state of affairs was placed squarely at the feet of women. 'Chains of slavery shackle your feet, oh women, because of your refusal to accept the jewels of learning.' For the biographer it was clear who was responsible for this predicament—*they* refused to be unshackled. While acknowledging that the jewels of learning would not lead to the same ends as for males in terms of occupation, Bibi Harnam Kaur insisted that the effects were nonetheless important. It was only a proper education that could illuminate the minds and morals of women. Education would also lead to happier conjugal relations and peace in the home (Singh, B.S. 1908: 88–97). These sentiments were remarkably similar to Dayanand's vision. In *Satyartha Prakash*, Dayanand insisted that not educating women would lead to a situation of 'constant warfare between the gods and demons and there would be no happiness.... Household affairs, conjugal happiness, and home-keeping are the things which can never be satisfactorily accomplished unless women are well educated' (Upadhyaya 1960: 112). For both Harnam Kaur and her mentor, the responsibility for her husband's contentment could easily be traced to the housewife's heeding the educational call. Her biography tells of one occasion where a married student complained about the marital misdeeds of her husband. In response, Harnam Kaur told her student a similar story about the daughter-in-law of the ruler Shiv Nath coming to Guru Nanak for advice about her oppressive husband. Guru Nanak, said Kaur, brought a koel to the attention of the distraught wife. The bird, despite its unpretentious black coat had an enchanting voice. Shiv Nath's daughter-in-law could succeed in changing her husband only by her modest demeanour and the sweetness of her tongue. Accordingly,

Harnam Kaur advised the young student to be properly humble and accept her situation; only thus, along with pleasing words to her husband, could she fulfil her duty as a wife and perhaps even change the troublesome ways of her spouse (Singh, B.S. 1908: 66–71). Perhaps not surprisingly, Harnam Kaur's own lessons on correct behaviour towards her husband came from none other than Bhai Vir Singh. In a letter to Kaur he noted that the three most important words in a woman's vocabulary were to be 'I made a mistake', 'whatever you say', 'I accept things as destined by God' ('bhul gai, bhala ji, bhana rab da') (ibid.: 125). These three *bha*'s, the first letter common to all words, as they were known, came to be quoted and requoted by other reformers, particularly within the pages of the *Punjabi Bhain*, a Sikh journal for women (Malhotra 2002: 131).

THE POLITICS OF LANGUAGE: A GENDERED PERSPECTIVE

While the objectives of the Singh Sabha educational endeavour were in most ways identical to those of the Arya Samaj, there were pivotal differences between the two. One increasingly important issue was that of language. With the establishment of Punjab University and the appointment of the Hunter Commission on Education in 1882, education had become intricately tied to communal identity based on religious affiliation. The Anjuman-i-Islamia in Lahore demanded Urdu, the Arya Samaj and Brahmo Samaj agitated for Hindi. The Punjab administration only fuelled the debate with its sanctioning of Urdu as the official language. Punjabi was rejected by all save Leitner and the Singh Sabhas; language was seen as a 'vehicle of communal solidarity at the intra-communal level' (Singh, N. 1992: 66–7). By the early twentieth century, the language controversy had only intensified. For while the Arya Samaj and the Singh Sabha movements were closely aligned until the late nineteenth century, the twentieth century witnessed an increased focus on the distinct religious identities of Sikhs and Hindus. With this distinction came a novel understanding of a separate linguistic identity. Moreover, with the increased focus on female education by the Singh Sabha movement, the issue of language acquired renewed force. For the Tat Khalsa, given its objectives of female religious instruction in the schools that necessarily included recitation from the Granth, the singing of *shabads*, and general moral instruction, the Punjabi language in the Gurmukhi script was essential. It was thus, with the ever-present threat of the Arya Samaj to the educational endeavour of the Sikhs, that Punjabi, as opposed to Hindi, was ardently championed by the Sikh reformers.

Both the Arya Samaj and the Singh Sabha were united in their criticism of Urdu as the official government language. The *Khalsa Advocate* gave considerable space to the issue. Increasingly, it became intricately tied to the situation of Sikh womanhood. Given the traditional custom prohibiting women from uttering the names of their husbands aloud, official procedure carried out in the Urdu language was cause for great concern. With regard to postal services, these

poor ladies, when writing to their husbands who are... in military service... had to request an Urdu knowing man to write the address of her husband on the envelope... the lady, being charm-bound not to give out the name of her husband, could not get the address written by any other person. So, in some cases, the letters had to lie over a few days before they could be posted (15 October 1904).

While the official usage of Urdu was problematic for most of the Sikh peasantry, the issue when combined with the image of the helpless Punjabi female took on an added significance. For Sikh females to approach males in postal offices would have been a source of aversion to the honour-bound Sikhs. Subsequently, the Post Master General of Punjab issued a circular ordering all officials and clerks of his department to learn Gurmukhi by the following year. With Gurmukhi as the official language, women would be in a better position to observe their 'charm-bound' customs. Given the small percentage of Sikh females who were literate, the language problem was less an issue for Sikhs than were notions of honour.

Another incident involving a Sikh woman on a train was also highly publicized and served to unite Sikhs on this contentious issue. Travellers on a train were being re-routed due to a railway accident. The Sikh woman was asked the name of her husband, which, 'she considered as a sacrilege to express, which in writing she was at a loss...' (*Khalsa Advocate*, 4 April 1908). Using this incident as a case in point, the Chief Khalsa Diwan carried out a regular campaign appealing to the government in favour of the Punjabi language. The promoters of Punjabi were further rewarded when the railway authorities agreed to write the names of stations in Gurmukhi script (see Bhatia 1987: 163). Needless to say, while supposedly motivated by concern for women, in reality, women became the backdrop to the political agenda of the Tat Khalsa. As was so often the case, women became the 'currency', so to speak, in a complex set of exchanges in which several competing projects intersect' (Mani 1990: 119).

THE SIKH EDUCATIONAL CONFERENCE—ENLARGING FEMALE SPACE

The 'cause' of the Punjabi language and female education became the main concerns of the Sikh Education Conference, inaugurated in 1908 in Gujranwala. The impetus for the conference came from a similar endeavour amongst the Muslims of Punjab. By 1905, the Mahomedan Educational Conference had received a good deal of publicity through various Sikh mediums. In the intervening years, the *Khalsa Advocate* had started calling for a similar venture among the Sikhs. Delegates to the conference were elected through four mediums—the Khalsa Diwan, the various Singh Sabhas, public meetings where no Singh Sabha existed, and through the various Sikh educational institutions. However, the wives of the educated elite, many of whom were forerunners in the education of females through their gratuitous teaching efforts in Sikh schools, were not elected to the Conference. Ultimately, while notions of reform regarding the women's question were loudly extolled by the Singh Sabha reformers, the proclamations simply did not translate into palpable and public representation at this most consequential event in the Sikh reform movement. This limitation becomes highly significant in the light of women's election as delegates to the Indian National Congress in Bombay as early as in 1889. The lack of women representatives at the Sikh Educational Conference nearly twenty years later was indeed indicative of the resolutely held attitudes of the Sikhs towards women's place in the home front. While it was necessary to extol women as essential to the 'private' order, it was a completely different matter for women to participate in the 'higher', public realm.

Nonetheless, well-wishers of the conference criticized the omission of women delegates. For, 'if we are to progress we must not leave our womenfolk behind.' By the second Educational

Conference held in Lahore in 1909, the reception committee resolved to admit women to the proceedings. Apparently stung by the criticism, the *Khalsa Advocate* took great pains to increase the number of female delegates, insisting that even those women visiting the conference be officially called delegates. It duly notified all readers that women as well as men were welcomed to the common langar meal. Also, while special seating arrangements were made for Sikh women at the conference, a separate 'Ladies Diwan' was also planned for this second gathering. Following closely the injunctions specified in the earliest of the rahit-namas, women were permitted to read the Sikh sacred scriptures and sing shabads, but only among themselves. The seating arrangement referred to by the *Khalsa Advocate* was a curtained area behind which women sat at the conference (6 February, 20 March 1909; 16 November 1907). The separation of women and men at gatherings sponsored by the reformers was of course not unique to the Singh Sabha movement. J.C. Oman, visiting an anniversary celebration of the Arya Samaj in 1886 noted that a woman, Mai Bhagwati, was one of the lecturers at the gathering. Well aware of traditional attitudes towards women in public, Oman sarcastically noted: 'A woman lecturing in public! This was a real attraction; an opportunity not to be neglected.' He continued that Mai Bhagwati 'stood behind a screen, and poured forth, from her place of concealment, a long discourse in Hindi on women's rights' (1908: 164–6).

Of particular interest is Oman's observation that the educational opportunities and the subsequent birth of the new middle class led invariably to *new* restrictions being placed on the women associated with the new elite, particularly their wives.

The purdah is now looked upon as a mark of gentility, and will not easily be lifted, even by the reforming spirit of the age. One might think that the spread of education will soon release women from their present seclusion, but in some cases it produces the very opposite effect. The cheap education now available in most parts of India raises a great many persons out of their natural humble sphere of life. The wives of such men, who once enjoyed the privilege of moving about freely in their own village, are converted into *purdah nasheens*, the seclusion of the women being an indication of superior rank (ibid.: 165).

Certainly, the elevation of the reformers' social standing placed their wives in a difficult position. Class limitations became increasingly pronounced with their superior standing in the community; the social confines of purdah represented their rise along the hierarchical ladder. Yet reform rhetoric invariably decried the custom as utterly foreign to Sikhism and chastised the practice as indicative of the Hindu elements that had inadvertently crept into their society. Ultimately however, social recognition was highly compelling. Yet there were those among the educated elite, not necessarily Sikhs, who disregarded the outward manifestations of prestige as they pertained to women. An observer in Lahore (quoted in the *Khalsa Advocate*, 16 November 1907) noted that 'a great change has come over a section of the native population of Lahore.... Certain bold men have begun to take out their wives in the evening for a drive in open vehicles. A week ago we saw the daughter of a man of position walking with her father on the railroad platform at Lahore.... Her face was quite uncovered....' Despite the winds of change, the observer's astonishment was indicative of the rigidity of traditional attitudes towards women. By 1913, however, rumblings could be heard against the observance of purdah among the elite who were gathering for the Educational Conference. The *Khalsa Advocate* insisted that the injunctions against purdah by Sikh gurus should be upheld; instead, women were instructed to sit with their husbands; whether the delegates to the conference heeded these calls is not clear. The fact that a woman, Bibi Savitri Devi, was invited as one of the presenters at the seventh Sikh Educational Conference would point to the possibilities of purdah restrictions having been at least partially lifted (13 December 1913; 11 April 1914).

Papers presented at these educational conferences made due reference to the glorious legacy of female education among the Sikhs. One lecturer, aptly reversing earlier reformed attitudes toward Sikh education carried out by the orthodox religious elite, instead lauded these traditional methods; British intervention through the official sanctioning of Urdu was instead identified as responsible for the defective state of education among the Sikhs:

The first, and the only attempts at popular education was made by our Gurus, when every Sikh, man and woman, was expected to know the teachings of the Guru Granth Sahib. For the first time the power, the potentiality of the mother-tongue was recognized and a system of popular education started.... The popular education was gaining in strength and was extending its borders till the British Government, with its love of uniformity conceived the strange idea of teaching the Punjabi villagers through the difficult medium of Urdu.... The result has been disastrous.... It is round the language learned at the mother's knee that the whole life of feelings, emotions and thought gathers, and we have in the Punjabi language a religious literature which has no rival. The pastoral poetry, the rural folklore and women's songs are full of soulful humanity, throbbing with the heart's joys and sorrows and is unsurpassed for the sweetness and true spirit of poetry (*Khalsa Advocate*, 10 April 1909).

Women, as the bearers of children and the traditional mainstay of folk culture, had the most to lose from this state of affairs. Indeed, the language issue became a central one at the second Sikh Education Conference. Given that a number of the presenters had spoken in English in 1908, it was suggested that only papers in Punjabi be read at the second gathering. This was expected to allow all, including the newly appointed women delegates, to understand and follow the proceedings (ibid., 6 February 1909). Thus the reformers ingeniously whetted the language issue by adding a focus on Punjab's womenfolk. Women's issues inevitably brought with them the notion of honour, or *izzat*, and few things were dearer to the Sikh male than his izzat.

SIKH ROLE MODELS AND THE TAT KHALSA—CRISIS OF AUTHORITY[7]

Another important difference between the Arya Samaj women's educational endeavour and that of the Tat Khalsa was the authority upon which the two based their claims in support of female learning. For the Arya Samaj, both the Vedas and Swami Dayanand's vision were paramount; Singh Sabha reformers instead turned to the contributions of their gurus. If the Aryas considered female education to originate with Swami Dayanand, they were sadly mistaken. Guru Nanak's legacy of equality for women long preceded Dayanand's efforts. The oft-quoted passage by the first guru, 'Why call her inferior of whom kings are born?' was interpreted by reformers as indicative of the absolute equality of women within Sikhism. If women were thus upheld, did it not follow that the Singh Sabha reformers were directly in line with Guru Nanak's intentions? On the other hand, Dayanand's educational methods left much to be desired. Reformers noted in *Khalsa Advocate*, 18 February 1910:

We cannot regard the Arya Samaj as having been the pioneer of female education in this province without restricting the meaning of 'education' to a close imitation of the Western manner of living, a few words of English and an imperfect knowledge of an embroidery for which the bulk of the Punjabis can hardly think of any use....

Similar to reform efforts across India and across communal divides attempting to conclusively illustrate that the prevalent 'malignant' social practices were anathema to the pure and ancient Indian practices, especially those pertaining to India's women, Sikh reformers increasingly turned to scripture to substantiate their claims. Without doubt, many of the Sikh gurus had criticized the denigration of women and empty ritualism. But as Cybelle Shattuck (1999: 94) has pointed out, medieval poet-saints were levelling their complaints at problems within the sphere of religious life. They 'were not trying to reform the social order beyond the realm of devotional practices.' Yet ancient texts, including the Vedas, the Upanishads, and the *Adi Granth*, became sources of 'pure' religion and ethics which were used to condemn social practices. Gradually, the medieval poet-saints came to be seen as the forerunners of the nineteenth- and twentieth-century reformers and their criticisms of religious institutions were extended to the larger social order.' It was thus that for Singh Sabha reformers, female education came to be intricately tied to newly forged versions of Sikh history. A Tat Khalsa writer (in *Khalsa Advocate*, 15 April 1910) warmly noted that among 'his numerous reforms of society, my Guru put the raising of womankind on a high pedestal. He told us that women, the mothers of heroes, saints, and prophets, [were] not to be despised, and that her education should precede and not follow that of man. The influence of his teaching was remarkable.' The gurus' wives, Bibi Bhani, Mata Gangaji, and Mata Gujriji, the 'makers of Sikh history' whose names could 'not be taken without sending a thrill of pleasant and reverent sensation through our beings', were able to contribute to this glorious legacy because they were educated. Bibi Bhani, the daughter of Guru Amar Das was 'due the highest credit that can be claimed by any one woman in the world', for she sacrificed five generations of men for her motherland. He continued, 'Can any one say that all this was not the effect of home education which this noble lady received from her parents and imparted to her children? Raise the position of your women and you raise yourselves.' Another maintained that opening the pages of virtually any segment of Sikh history would lead readers to see 'men and women—sitting... in congregations at the feet of the Guru and engaged in theological and spiritual discourses' (18 February 1910).

Ultimately, Sikh reformers were in need of role models—Sikh role models—and devising these became central to the reform endeavour. Given the paucity of information about Sikh women in scripture and history, the reformers began to specify that a systematic study on the position of women in both areas be formulated. In the light of their objectives to conclusively distinguish Sikhism from Hinduism, new models to serve as female archetypes and novel paradigms within which Sikh womanhood could be rooted, were essential. The names of Sikh women who had contributed greatly to their glorious heritage began to be uplifted. Sundri, Sharn Kaur, Rani Sahib Kaur—these came to be examples of true womanhood. The reformers were aided in their efforts to promote Sikh womanhood by British writers who were also gathering stories on Indian women.[8] According to the reformers, Sikh women, in contrast to contemporary British suffragettes whose incentive was purely selfish, had imbibed fully their gurus' essential doctrine of service. 'Service is the root of Sikhism; service is the middle (means) of Sikhism and service is the end of Sikhism.' One only had to look to the 'many discontented malcontents', the 'selfish agitators and lawless scenes' of the West to see the effects of education without this central Sikh doctrine, upon women (*Khalsa Advocate*, 15 April 1910). In fact, Sikh educational institutions took great pains to shield their girls from what they considered the harmful elements of Western education. Thakat Singh insisted that 'I am against *parda* but I am also against too much freedom of the western type. I have heard from many of my European friends about the evils of the new feminine movement in England and on the Continent.' He also believed there was little worry about the girls in his care becoming too liberal in their outlook, since they were 'too mild to play that role' (Caveeshar 1984: 118).

The notion of service along with that of duty increasingly became the slogan of the Singh Sabha reformers in their transformational endeavour of Sikh women. The inauguration of Sikh girls' schools had opened a novel occupational option for Sikh women—to serve as honorary teachers at the various girls' schools. Bengali women had long served in provinces that were desperate for teachers. Sikh institutions were, however, discouraged from employing them, despite the great paucity of female teaching staff.[9] A novel Sikh feminine ideal came to be instituted: one who gave her services to the fledgling educational enterprise. Deeply-held Sikh values stressing service, *gratuitous* service in the case of women teachers, came to be embodied by those who were willing to cast off the traditional shackles of honour. Here is the comment of one observer (in *Khalsa Advocate*, 25 January 1908) writing about two such women, Bibi Mohan Kaur and Srimati Bibi Jawala Kaur:

What graceful names these.... The grace consists neither in the earthly bodies of the above Bibis, nor in their positions in life or the quantity of gold and silver they may have on their persons but it lies in the spirit they are animated with.... I wish my daughters had the same spirit.... How could this be done? Why by the simple process of utilizing their services in honorary positions as mistresses or Head mistresses in Sikh Schools where they might not only improve their souls by the teachings of Guru Nanak and secular education, but might also enlighten their sisters.... Let S. Atma Singh set them a noble example by allowing his daughter to serve as an Honorary Mistress.

The greatest praise was reserved for the husbands and fathers of these women who moved beyond their honour-bound customs.

Duty became another watchword with regard to women and education, particularly in the light of an added financial burden. For, given the gratuitous nature of teaching (by women) among the Sikhs, education for females came with no economic rewards. Further, the previously unpaid labour of female family members would have to be done by additional hired servants in the home (see Borthwick 1984: 61 for an outline of the financial costs of gratuitous teaching in Bengal). The dearth of teachers continued to be one of the most pressing issues facing the girls' schools. By 1908, the call for teachers filled almost every edition of the weekly medium, the *Khalsa Advocate*. The lack of female teachers threatened the successful continuation of girls' education. The new ideal in turn took on an additional aspect, one of reproach; if schools were not furnished with the honorary services of teachers, the onus was on the women who did not fulfil their duty toward the Sikh community. Ultimately, however, despite these varied attempts at rectifying the desperate need for female teachers, obstacles remained firmly in place. Malcolm Darling, addressing the lack of teachers as late as in 1934 wrote,

Most of the available teachers are of urban origin, and in nine cases out of ten it is useless to send a town-bred to live and work in the village... [for] her heart will not be in her work, her teaching will have an urban bias, and she will be regarded as an alien. Even if a sufficient number of qualified village teachers could be found, there remains the immense difficulty of their accommodation and protection under conditions which in no way allow for women living alone (299–300).

Reformers turned to the memory of Harnam Kaur, the first spouse of Bhai Thakat Singh of Ferozepur, as a noble inspiration to the ideal of service. The first edition of her biography published in 1908, two years after her death, was sold out in four months. Harnam Kaur's service to the community became intricately intertwined with that of another ideal, martyrdom. The apathy of the Sikh community towards female education was presented as ultimately responsible for her untimely death. Bhai Thakat Singh was the living martyr, having offered his wife's life and services to the school. Thus the Ferozepur school was founded at the cost of her life. Martyrdom in the name of service was the highest honour that could be accorded to any individual attempting to further the Sikh cause (*Khalsa Advocate*, 30 January 1909).

An earthquake in the Kangra Valley in 1905 presented another fortuitous opportunity for Sikh women to show their true mettle in the form of service to the suffering victims. Stories of yore when women had accompanied the Khalsa army into battle, had cooked food and supplied it to the warriors and nursed the wounded and had taken care of them were lifted high as models for contemporary women. According to an article originally published in *The Tribune* that underwent frequent reprints in the *Khalsa Advocate*, the degraded position of Sikh women was finally being attended to by reformers, resulting in women volunteering to 'minister unto the sufferers from the Earthquake as they did during the days of the Khalsa wars.' The catastrophe in the Kangra Valley was presented as an ideal opportunity for women to return to the position of pre-eminence accorded them by the sublime teachings of the gurus. And a number of Sikh women rose to the occasion. Along with their ministration efforts in the Kangra Valley, several women in Amritsar began a campaign of door-to-door collection of funds for the relief effort. Observers noted that the Sikh guru's teachings as well as the reform efforts were beginning to make their mark on the debased position of Indian womanhood. Repeated calls were made to other women to follow the example of the Amritsar Sikhs (27 May 1905).

By and large, however, traditional Sikh codes of honour continued to reign supreme, most particularly among the leaders of the reform initiative. According to one critic, 'the things have come to such a pass that if a Sikh comes to see another Sikh at the latter's home, he is made to wait at the door till the female of the house manages to hide herself in some corner' (Gujranwala, cited in Dhillon 1972: 169). The well-known couplet 'The woman who lives indoors is worth lakhs, one who moves about it worthless', attested to the venerable position given existing notions of honour among the Sikhs. Yet the newly constructed paradigms of service and duty, the dual watchwords of the movement's march towards reform, allowed for a limited dismantling of the traditional codes that were designed to maintain both women's position at the hearth and the family honour.

The necessity of proper role models for Sikh women led to a critique of the lack of writings, beyond scripture, on them. Calls were made to the Khalsa Diwan to supply the public with such stories. And Sikh writers began heeding the appeal. Accordingly, '[m]easures of reform are being taken in certain quarters. Lives of Sikh ladies... have recently been written and published. With their study the tide of reformation has set in' (in *Khalsa Advocate* 1904, 1905). The form these writings took as well as their content was varied; novels, dramas, poetic works, instructional treatises, tracts, and stories focussing on women soon began to dot the Sikh literary horizon. Journals dedicated solely to the need for female education as well as other concerns of Sikh women came to be published; they also fulfilled the need for 'proper' reading material for Sikh females. The best known journal, *Punjabi Bhain*, was published through the Ferozepur Sikh Kanya Mahavidyala and edited by the school master. *Punjabi Bhain* contained articles on the Sikh religion, stressed the need for 'pure' Sikh rites for females, and focussed especially on family and household duties. Above all, the journal was singularly non-political in nature. The journal ran issues from 1908 to 1930. Another periodical for women was *Istri Satsang*, published in Amritsar from 1904 to 1908 (Barrier 1970: 75–88).

Tracts expounding on the benefits of female education in conjunction with particularly pious or productive lives were also written. Instruction booklets for women's daily activities, condemning the social evils prevalent among women, included directives on proper Sikh women's rituals, knowledge befitting Sikh women, and appropriate attitudes for women. Suitable family relationships were expounded upon; so too was the victimization of women in the context of 'un-Sikh' behaviour such as the effects of drink, the negative consequences of unions between Sikhs and non-Sikhs, early marriage, and gambling. Loyalty to their British rulers also became an important aspect of the attitudes Sikh reformers attempted to inculcate in the women-focused writings. All were placed in the context of a newly organized, carefully crafted understanding of 'true' Sikh womanhood (see Appendix A for an overview of the women-centred literature of the time).

Heroism and piety were traits that were especially promoted through the various genres utilized; some were fictional representations and a number were vaguely based on historical fact. Death as the ultimate sacrifice by women was another important subject matter for the world view that the Singh Sabha reformers were attempting to construct; martyrdom increasingly came to be presented as a particularly 'Sikh' ideal. Sikh martyrs in the context of brutal Mughal rule in particular caught the imagination of numerous writers. Stories of women who persevered in their faith despite atrocities committed by the Muslim barbarians were held high; their recounting was to serve as inspiration for contemporary Sikh women. Further, Sikh distinctiveness as well as Sikh nationhood became inextricably entwined with this Sikh ideal. As one writer claimed,

Blessed above every other nation, however, are the people whose women can lay claim to martyrdom equally with the men and have sacrificed their holy and precious lives for the sake of their country. Our mothers, who could outrival even their Spartan sisters, gave us no cause for shame even when the Sikhs were being subjected to the bitterest persecutions by those who wielded authority at the time.... It is, however, to be regretted that the stories of these women are enveloped in obscurity. This pamphlet is an attempt at removing that obscurity, and will contain the stories of the bravery and contempt of life displayed by a band of Sikh women and children.

The selfless deeds of Sikh women of yore were elucidated in graphic detail. In one such example, when executioners carried out the orders of the Mughal governor Mir Mannu (1748–53) and killed the infants of the captured Sikh women, their 'gory corpses were thrown into the laps of the latter or suspended from their necks.' Instead of buckling under the governor's brutal pressure, these women were grateful for the opportunity they had been given.

What recked it if their darling babes, who were the very light of their eyes, had been killed in a most merciless manner? The poor things had met their death in the cause of the Sikh religion, and they were glad of this. They thanked God that their children had no chance of ever being called unworthy, and had tasted of the cup of martyrdom in their very infancy (Singh, B.A. 1906: 6, 15).

Persistence in the Sikh faith, in spite of husbands being tortured and children dying of starvation, chastity and honour upheld despite tyrannical threats, hard labour in the face of hunger—this was the substance of true Sikh womanhood. These virtues were held up ultimately as distinguishing Sikh women from their Hindu and Muslim counterparts.

BHAI VIR SINGH AND THE INVENTION OF TRADITION[10]

The prolific writer, Bhai Vir Singh (1872–1957) deserves particular mention for his concerted efforts to create role models for Sikh women. Educated at the Missionary High School in Amritsar and well aware of the ways and means of the Christian missionary endeavour, he gleaned a good deal of information about successful proselytising activity. Missionaries utilized the vernacular in their proselytising tactics as opposed to the official language, Urdu, so that they could reach the masses. Missionary example became the initial impetus for reformers to also champion Punjabi in the Gurmukhi script. Bhai Vir Singh remained the foremost proponent of Punjabi. He was also responsible for a great proportion of literature stemming from the late nineteenth and early twentieth centuries. Following the example of the influential Ludhiana Mission Press, he set up Wazir Hind Press in 1892 for the express purpose of publishing Sikh texts. By 1894, Bhai Vir Singh had inaugurated the Sikh Tract Society along the lines of the American Tract Society (Singh, A. 1997: 547). He became the most important spokesperson for the Singh Sabha movement and produced a monumental volume of literary works that gave voice to the movement's concerns. Anonymously, Vir Singh wrote a great number of tracts on the proper status, behaviour, and attitude of Sikh women. Further, he dedicated four of his best known works to the piety and heroism of Sikh womanhood. The novel *Sundri*, written in 1898, depicted the life of a brave young Sikh heroine; *Bijai Singh* delineated the process whereby a young woman, through her pious example, impelled her Hindu husband to convert to Sikhism. *Satwant Kaur*, the writer's third novel, told the story of an ideal Sikh girl who was captured and then served as a slave in a Muslim household in Kabul. Through the force of her piety Satwant Kaur won over the lady of the house, Fatima, and then escaped and returned to India in the guise of a young man. *Rana Surat Singh* was an epic poem describing the immense devotion and love of Rani Raj Kaur for her husband Rana Surat Singh.

Bhai Vir Singh's first novel, *Sundri,* remains his most successful work. While the volume has been hailed as the original Punjabi novel, others have maintained that the earliest novel in the Punjabi language was instead *Jyotirudae*, an anonymous work published at the Punjab Text Book Committee by the Ludhiana Mission in 1882. Though written in Punjabi, the novel appears to be a translation from Bengali. It is very likely that *Jyotirudae* was the model for Vir Singh's creations.[11] *Jyotirudae* was an attempt to show the superiority of both the West, including Western ideological thought, institutions, and family structures, and Christianity; the latter was sharply and negatively contrasted to religions of the East. The book's primary attack was upon Indian womanhood; the central character of the novel was a woman named Basant. Indian women, according to the author, were dually subjugated—by the patterns of extreme male domination of society, and by the general backwardness of India. Child marriage was especially censured by the writer, who took great pains to contrast negatively the situation of Indian brides with that of their British counterparts. The English were characterized as marrying at a much later age. Further, while British women were enabled to choose their life partners, Indian women had no such choices. The novel suggested that the British came to India to 'free' Indians from their permanent state of lawlessness, and Indian women in particular from servility and backwardness. The writer especially pointed to the educational opportunities offered to Indians by the British government and Christian missionaries. Perhaps surprisingly, the author did not portray the main protagonists as converting to Christianity. They were, however, presented as enlightened characters, having imbibed the essential, liberating aspects of Western thought.[12]

Sundri was essentially a counter-attack on many of the major points propounded in *Jyotirudae*. Bhai Vir Singh's main protagonist too was a woman. Sundri, who was about to be married, ultimately chose to remain single; it would appear that Singh was countering *Jyotirudae*'s contention that Indian women had no choices in terms of marriage options. Sundri was an avid horsewoman; she rode free and without the constraints of purdah. In sharp contrast, Hindu and Muslim women remained hidden. Further, *Jyotirudae* presented Christian thought in particular and Western influences in general as transforming positively the 'lawlessness' of Indian society. For Bhai Vir Singh, it was instead Sikhism that produced truly moral and exemplary women and men. The ideal of service was for Bhai Vir Singh utterly integral to Sikhism; it was the notion of service that was lacking in the self-centred individuality inherent in Western thought. Further, while the intent of the earlier novel was doubtlessly to proselytise, it did so indirectly and somewhat subtly; the protagonists maintained their Hindu identity. Bhai Vir Singh's objective on the other hand was unmistakable and bluntly rendered; Muslims and Hindus were being called to the superior tenets of Sikhism. Finally, while *Jyotirudae* proposed that English was the ideal medium for the liberation and moral enlightenment of Indian society, Vir Singh strongly advocated Punjabi as crucial to the reformation of Sikh society.[13]

As with numerous other women-focused writings of the period, *Sundri* was situated during the times of Mughal persecution of the Sikhs. According to its author, the 'purpose kept in view for writing this book is to educate the Sikhs about their history and to inspire them to become true adherents of their religion' (quoted in Kohli 1973: 148). The novel was based on a popular folk song about a young and newly married Hindu woman who was abducted by a Mughal chieftain. The heroine, in attempting to save her honour, decided instead to kill herself on her funeral pyre, but at the last moment, her brother reached the flames and saved his sister. Vir Singh ingeniously adapted this tale and forged a new version of the story within a decidedly reformed Sikh outlook. The heroine, Surasti, though of a Hindu household, was secretly a devoted Sikh; while on the funeral pyre, she was determined to die reciting Sikh scripture (see Guleria 1988: viii–ix). Her brother and saviour, Balwant Singh, was also a Sikh; he was the only 'true' man in the family who exhibited utmost bravery in the face of danger. It was not uncommon practice for Hindu families to commit their eldest male progeny to Sikhism.[14] Thus, Bhai Vir Singh reproduced in fiction a common custom in Punjab. Balwant Singh, whilst expounding on the grave sin of sati, pulled his sister to safety and took her back to her ancestral home. The family however was horrified, and frightened of Moghul wrath. Balwant Singh, insulted at his Hindu family's cowardice, instead retreated into the jungle with Surasti; there they were met with carnage. His Sikh brothers had been overtaken by a bloodthirsty band of Turks. Viewing the bloody remains, Surasti was

fired by a religious zeal and felt that there was nothing better for her to do than serving the Sikh soldiers whom [sic] had risked their lives for their faith. She felt convinced that her brother had acquired the courage of his conviction and noble demeanour because of his Sikh faith and living with the Sikhs. He had grown into a noble person. Why could not she be as brave as her brother.... She began to reflect on the role of women—Why should not women participate in the struggle for the defence of morality and religion? If all women could not do so, at least she could set an example of courage by following her worthy brother (*Sundri*: 9–10).

And thus began Surasti's life with the roving band of Khalsa men. Surasti was formally initiated into the Khalsa and renamed Sundri Kaur. After her initiation into the Khalsa fold, Sundri dedicated her life to caring for the men surrounding her. On occasion she too, 'Durga-like', took up the sword in the defence of her faith. Her attitude of mercy toward any wounded person, however, led to her downfall. For stopping to help a wounded Pathan, Sundri was wounded by a stroke of his sword. Sundri eventually died a martyr for her faith, prostrated before the Sikh holy scriptures. Vir Singh continued with a word for Sundri's contemporary sisters:

O Sikh maidens of today, born with a silver spoon in your mouth and living in luxury and comfort! The daughters, sisters and mothers of the poor and rich Sikhs! Look at the faith and the plight of your forerunner Sundri. She never loses her faith. She takes a risk with her life, but does not give up her virtue. In times of trouble and calamity, she remains firm and sticks to the doctrines of Sikh religions. Just look at yourselves and find out for yourself if you are damaging the Sikh community or not!... Be brave and truthful Sikh ladies like Sundri; be virtuous like her and make yourself and children true Sikhs, otherwise you will prove to be, for your husband, the pernicious creeper which dries up the plant and then itself perishes (Sundri: 99–100).

Easily breaking the continuity of the historical narrative, Vir Singh paused to address the contemporary situation of Sikh womanhood and impress on his readers the need to follow the example of his imaginary but 'truly Sikh' model. In other words, Sundri in the hands of Vir Singh became the site of Sikh women's identity construction and hence symbolic of a recovered and purified Sikh tradition. Sundri and the other Sikh protagonists were flawless paragons of virtue and bravery, even supernatural. The protagonists were not transformed, they were the conduits of transformation. As such they came to serve as archetypal figures, a fundamental requirement in the world view the Tat Khalsa was in the process of creating. Vir Singh, as the foremost proponent of the Tat Khalsa mindset, was the decided master of this invented tradition.

Singh Sabha reformers knew that they were caught in a 'crisis of authority'. Hindu ideals in the form of archetypal figures had traditionally sustained the imagination of the Sikhs, serving both as authority and as fundamental bond between the two communities. The creation of alternate Sikh heroes and heroines was thus necessary to fulfil the elementary needs of a world view intent on the creation of Sikh distinctiveness. For their creator, Sundri, Balwant Singh, and the other figures became the necessary surrogates for the pantheon of models offered by Hinduism. The Hindu image of the warrior-goddess Durga was no longer necessary for the Sikhs; in fact, she only served in the deterioration of Sikhism. As a role model, the supreme warrior Sundri was sufficient. The transformation of her name from Surasti to Sundri is also significant in this regard for Surasti, as derivative of the Vedic goddess Sarasvati, bestower of knowledge and learning, was far too intimately connected to the very pantheon Bhai Vir Singh was in the process of rejecting (Kohli 1973: 149–51).[15] However, in the very rejection and subsequent equation of Durga with Sundri and Sarasvati with Surasti, the latter became perpetually idolized. Vir Singh's other volume, *Rana Surat Singh,* contained a literal rendition of this process. The saintly Sikh hero who died a martyr's death, Rana Surat Singh, came to be installed as a statue in his widow's garden. To the statue Rani Raj Kaur pleaded,'Pray, will you bend your head, my husband darling, and let me put these garlands around your neck? High is your turban, and tall you stand, out of reach of this feeble woman.' The illusion however could not be maintained. 'Something inside her snapped. And dazed she fell to the ground, cold like stone. A lifeless image lay in front of a lifeless image—A statue prostrate in homage before a statue' (cited in Khosla 130–1).

Victor Turner describes the passage from traditional archetype to a novel inception, or from conventional paradigm to its alternative, as fraught with difficulty. 'The danger is, of course, that the more persuasive the root metaphor or archetype, the more chance it has of becoming a self-certifying myth, sealed off from empirical disproof. It remains as a fascinating metaphysics' (Turner 1974: 29). While Vir Singh attempted to address the profound vacuum of Sikh female role models, in the case of Sundri, a new goddess, a natural extension of the old paradigm that was supposedly being displaced was born. Accordingly, Sundri was described as 'not an ordinary woman; you are a goddess'. The passage continues however, 'But you must always have the courage of a man to face this kind of hard life (Sundri: 24–5).' With the displacement of the traditional with a novel interpretation came an added and significant twist; elevation to the level of goddess included an additional element of that which was essentialized as 'manly' behaviour, namely, courage. Simone de Beauvoir has aptly summed up this process of the divinization of women: 'Man wishes her to be carnal, but he would also have her smooth, hard, changeless as a pebble' (1968: 179). Lost in the process was the humanity of Sundri as a potential figure of relationality, of an ordinary human role model. In other words, Sundri was transformed from a feasible, useful model to an archetype, a goddess. Yet 'in-the-flesh' role models are essential in that 'much of the fascination in reading novels and autobiographies or biographies lies in the models they provide for the most central of human tasks, the discovery of self-identity.' The feminist theologian Sallie McFague further notes that role models, 'unlike discrete metaphors, are systematising, organising grids or screens, offering complex and detailed possibilities for analogical transfer to another life' (McFague 1982: 67–8). Role models are important to the process of identity construction. According to one critic, (Kohli 1973), Bhai Vir Singh's protagonists are devoid of this self-identifying possibility. They are

ideal characters who look like 'types' and on whom the circumstances have no effect.... Such things do not happen in the ordinary course of life.... On the other hand the writer is forced, by his urge to propagate the Sikh ideals, to bring in such incidents, acts and speeches as seem unnatural, incredible and deliberately interspersed in order to suit the plot and characters.[15]

Ostensibly speaking from a feminist perspective, Nikki-Guninder Kaur Singh extensively analyses the writings of Bhai Vir Singh; in particular she examines his contributions to female emancipation in the light of modern feminist thought.

The identification of the poet [Bhai Vir Singh] with the female and the creation of female protagonists as the paradigms of morality, courage, spirituality, and philosophical quest manifest not only the tenderness of Bhai Vir Singh's poetic perception but also his, that is to say, the Sikh, worldview in which women enjoy great esteem. These characters are not abstractions of an 'eternal feminine'. *Each is a living and breathing individual. They are not fairyland characters, but human beings of flesh and blood* [italics mine]. Each in her own and separate way is a model worthy of emulation by women as well as men (Singh, N.K. 1993: 155).

For Nikki Singh, the choice of Sundri as principal character points to Bhai Vir Singh's radical break with popular attitudes toward the inequality of womanhood. Sundri, according to Singh, 'is the incarnation of all that is best in Sikh life and tradition, yet she does not remain a paragon of excellence or a distant goddess to be worshipped on a pedestal.' Sundri, 'on the contrary, is a living person, living in actual life truths and morals enjoined by the Sikh faith. She is a person in flesh and blood who gallops freely with men.' Needless to say, Sikh women during Mughal rule, or for that matter during the time of Vir Singh, did not 'gallop freely with men'; neither did women 'choose' between living at home and roving the countryside alongside their male companions. Further, Singh maintains that Sundri, and her creator, were directly in line with modern feminist thought seeking to provide holistic models for both women and men, 'opening up new avenues for self-empowerment and transcendence'. Yet these characters were flights of fiction, mere figments of the reformed male imagination. Given the Tat Khalsa's singularly derisive attitudes towards Sikh women at the time, Vir Singh created unattainable and untenable representations to aid in Singh Sabha constructions of 'true' Sikh womanhood. Yet Nikki Singh insists that his *Weltanschauung*, essentially that of the Singh Sabha movement, maintained that

women were the protagonists who alone could bring about the much-desired change and transformation of their society. Physically very beautiful, spiritually highly refined, existentially deeply intense, ethically most noble, and mystically so exalted, the women in his vast array of literary creations... live palpably and energetically. They search for their own identities, and discover their selves through their own individual journeys without any male instructors.... Without a male to validate her, she exists harmoniously in a constellation of relationships... *she* in all her roles is equally important in her connection with the Divine (ibid.: 248).

Focusing on rather facile, scrupulously chosen aspects of Vir Singh's writings, without addressing the larger patriarchal structures of the day, Nikki Singh presents a singularly one-sided literary and historical perspective. Needless to say, one is left with the impression that hers is but an additional appeal to traditional Sikh apologetics, neatly aligned with the principle of negation, though cloaked in the jargon of Western feminist thought. Aligned with traditional hypermasculine Sikh values as well as appropriated Victorian sentiments such as that of the helpmate, the Singh Sabha and its spokesperson, Bhai Vir Singh, consistently maintained the 'proper' place of their womenfolk at the hearth. Thus the characters and the circumstances prescribed by Vir Singh were essentially untenable, for the most part only adding to the antithetical nature of the reform endeavour. For, the creation of the various protagonists as archetypal, in essence, the inception of *new* goddesses, flew in the face of precisely what the Singh Sabha reformers sought so actively to expunge in Sikh society—the existing heterogeneity in the female population.

The Political Milieu: Agitation and Allegiance

As noted earlier, the Singh Sabha reform endeavour, while similar in most respects to that of the Arya Samaj, differed from it in a number of aspects. Along with the language issue, Punjabi versus Hindi, and the creation of new, alternative role models, Singh Sabha reformers on the whole were distinct from their Arya counterparts in terms of their conspicuous efforts to inculcate categorical loyalty to their British rulers into their educational schemes. For increasingly, though far removed from the highly developed nationalism lending ferment to the political milieu in Bengal, British rule was being assailed in Punjab too. A number of factors gave rise to this new development. As already noted, due to massive increases in agricultural prices and land values, the indebtedness of Punjab agriculturists intensified. Taking advantage of the situation, urban moneylenders furnished the landowners with easy credit in return for land pledges. The Punjab Alienation of Land Act of 1901 was put in place by the government to effectively halt the increased land holdings of the urban populace and thereby stabilise the holdings of the peasantry. The official stance maintained that only through government intervention could rural satisfaction and support for the Raj be sustained.

To secure the contentment of the masses is our first duty in India: in it lies our safety. As long as they are loyal to and contented with their rulers, the internal peace of the country is secure, and the professional agitator powerless. And most of all is the loyalty and contentment of the sturdy yeomanry from whose ranks we draw our native soldiers, the safe foundation upon which our rule can rest secure (1895, cited in Barrier 1966: 37–8).

Through the Act the population was divided into what were called agriculturist and non-agriculturist tribes. Jats, Rajputs, Arains, and Gujars, as well as Muslim religious elites, were placed into the first category. Non-agriculturists were forbidden from acquiring permanent land in the rural areas. This 'measure not only halted the increasing expropriation of impoverished landowners but encouraged inter-communal political co-operation by giving concrete expression to the Muslim, Hindu and Sikh cultivators' common economic interests' (Talbot 1988: 56). However, while the Land Alienation Act halted the passing of land into the hands of moneylenders, it failed to solve the root problems leading to rural indebtedness. Malcolm Darling cites a description of the massive indebtedness of the agriculturists: 'Nearly half the mortgages were made by sonless proprietors who were often gamblers and spendthrifts, and that, excluding loans for the repayment of old debt... of the amount borrowed was spent of wine, opium and gambling (39.5 per cent), marriage (18 per cent), and litigation (4.5 per cent)' (1928: 51). High marriage costs were a direct result of the radical disparity between males and females in the state. The difficulty, according to Darling, was 'that out of a population of less than 21 million there are two million more males than females. Even in more advanced surroundings the result of this would be demoralizing, but in a country where the village woman is regarded as little better than a chattel, the purchase of brides is inevitable.' This was particularly the case for the Sikh Jat. A Muslim, Darling said, would pay four or five hundred rupees in bride price but the Sikh Jat had 'to pay one or two thousand... [for] the shortage of girls is greater with him that with any one else'. On the other hand, litigation in the western districts, also an important factor in the massive debt burden of the agriculturists, 'practically turn[s] on the question whether the mother or the uncle of a fatherless girl is entitled to the profits of mating her' (ibid.: 52–5).

What the Land Alienation Act did successfully was open the controversy between agriculturists and non-agriculturists. For the solidarity along communal lines in the rural areas was in radical contrast with the intense rivalries between religious communities in the cities; there, the various reform groups were striving to fortify communal identities. Darling noted that the Land Alienation Act added to this fortification, for the 'townsman is inclined to convert it into a political grievance' (ibid.: 186). Though not completely successful, the Act also began sowing seeds of communal dissent among the rural populace. It subdivided members of the Jat caste or tribe by their religious affiliation; land transfers between Hindu Jats and Muslim Jats came to be restricted. According to Sir Harnam Singh, the Council Member representing Punjab, 'the erroneous division of these agriculturists would eventually turn brother against brother and intensify communal unrest' (Barrier 1966: 73–4).

In February 1907, the Punjab Legislative Council passed the Colonization of Lands Bill. Through this Bill, the Punjab government transformed the extensive but barren crown land in western Punjab by digging canals and thereby allowing it to be irrigated. The new landowning peasant, enticed to the canal colonies from central Punjab was the means by which this transformation was made possible. These new proprietors had either been given land by the Punjab administration, or had paid a nominal fee for the landholdings. Cattle, implements, and building materials were also advanced to these new cultivators at very low interest rates. Water was initially supplied without cost and subsequently at moderate rates.

However, a large number of stipulations accompanied the land holdings; these were carefully monitored by the specially appointed canal officers. The officers, to maintain control over the colonies, put an informal system of penalties for infractions of these regulations in place. By 1903, the colonizers had successfully challenged the legality of this system through the courts; they had also founded a newspaper to express their dissatisfaction with the system. The Punjab Colonization Bill was an attempt to legalise the fine system and thereby strengthen the control of the canal officers over the colonizer.[16] Contrary to the principles of peasant proprietorship heretofore upheld, the Colonization Bill was based on the assumption that land was ultimately the property of the government; the agriculturist thus was demoted from owner to tenant. The government also proposed to modify the canal colonies' tenures and increased the water rate in the Bari Doab. The increase in November 1906 was as high as 50 per cent in some instances, affecting landowners throughout the districts of Lahore, Amritsar, and Gurdaspur (Jones 1989, Rai 1973). Needless to say, disaffection with these government decisions increased rapidly through the colonies.

At the same time there were rumours of further legislation to protect the landowners from exploitation by the moneylending urban classes. Urban Hindus in particular saw this as another unfair attempt by the administration to limit their economic base. In an effort to protect their interests, the urban classes began to mobilize. The Indian National Congress saw the Land Alienation Act controversy as a fortunate opportunity to enlarge its membership base among rural communities. In January 1907, 139 Punjabis attended the Congress meeting in Calcutta—the largest delegation ever sent from Punjab.

Moreover, a new wave of consciousness was overtaking the country. Educated Indians, particularly the growing number of nationalists, viewed the Japanese victory over Russia in 1904 as a victory of the Asiatic over the white man. Further, by August 1905, news of the proposed partition of Bengal reached Punjab. In an effort to agitate against partition, Swadeshi Sabhas sprang up in nearly every Punjabi town and city. The Swadeshi movement was not novel to the twentieth century; before the surge of Swadeshi in Bengal, the call for indigenous products over those imported from Europe had been inaugurated by a small portion of the Punjabi middle class in the 1880s. As noted earlier, the Namdhari Sikh movement also rejected imported British cloth. However, the movement was revived and grew substantially in 1905 as a means of political insurrection against the British government. This new consciousness along with the Colonization of Lands Bill, the increase of water rates in the Bari Doab, and the Amendment to the Land Alienation Act proved to be the combined stimulus that united rural and urban Punjabis in an effective anti-government stance (Jones 1989: 269–70).

A number of protest meetings were also held; students in schools and colleges took part in the political outcry. The nationalist press called on Punjabis to join the growing Swadeshi movement as part of the larger, national agenda (Sharma 1971: 311–12). Urban groups, already dissatisfied with the Raj, also took advantage of the situation; The *Tribune* and *Punjabee* were sued for libel by English officers and the editors of *Hindustan* and *India* were arrested for their part in the unrest. The dynamic leadership of Lajpat Rai and Ajit Singh began to mobilize the masses; Ajit Singh in particular called on the peasants, as the 'real' rulers of the country, to unite. *Pagri-Sambhal O'Jatta*, 'O Peasant, guard your turban, your honour', became his rallying call.

It was the mobilization of the rural classes, particularly the Sikhs, who formed the bulk of the Indian Army and had hitherto professed their steadfast loyalty to the Raj, which greatly perturbed the British government. Sir Denzil Ibbetson (cited in Rai 1973: 137–8), surveying the increasingly volatile situation noted that

One striking and exceedingly dangerous feature which has been observable everywhere is that special attention has been paid to the Sikhs and in the case of Lyallpur, to the military pensioners and that special efforts have been made to procure their attendance at meetings, to enlist their sympathies and to inflame their passions... The very sturdiness of the Punjabi, which makes him more difficult to move than the Bengali, makes the matter far more serious when he is moved and if the loyalty of the Jat Sikhs of the Punjab is ever materially shaken, the danger will be greater than any which could possibly arise in Bengal.

Also alarming to the authorities was a demonstration by students at Khalsa College in Amritsar, the stronghold of the Sikh middle class. Ultimately, the Arya Samaj was blamed for the political turmoil. Ibbetson had earlier warned his officials against the employment of Aryas because of their seditious nature and had urged them to dismiss Arya employees 'at the least sign of disloyalty' (cited in Jones 1989: 273). Attempting to deal with the increasing instability, the authorities banned meetings and public speeches. Further, officials arrested leaders such as Lajpat Rai and Ajit Singh, among others; some were subsequently deported to Burma. The arrests only led to calls for an all-India agitation. Finally, paying scant attention to imperial honour, Governor-General Lord Minto vetoed the Land Colonization Bill and postponed water rate increases on the Bari Doab canal. Calm was re-established almost immediately in the rural areas, followed by a surge of appreciation for the Raj. In the cities, members of the Arya Samaj were left with the full weight of government apprehension about them as the apparent organisers of the disturbances. According to Ibbetson, 'wherever there was an Arya Samaj it was the centre of seditious talk....' Leaders of the Samaj hastened to make amends; the hostile world of British mistrust and discrimination was simply too problematical. A delegation met with Denzil Ibbetson acknowledging that while some 'extremists' had taken part in the agitation 'the Arya Samajists as a body had nothing to do with the later disturbances, that the Samaj was an organisation which had for its sole object the religious educational advancement of its members...' (cited in Jones 1989: 275).

THE RHETORIC OF REFORM, EDUCATION, AND THE POLITICS OF PATRIOTISM

In sharp contrast to other urban elites taking part in anti-government agitation, Singh Sabha leaders for the most part stayed outside the fray. While other news organs were actively censured for inflaming the masses, the *Khalsa Advocate* was merely warned in June of 1907 about possible ramifications of contributing to the political turmoil, particularly with regard to Sikh sepoys (Bhatia 1987: 331).[17] Nonetheless, while Singh Sabha leaders on the whole did not officially support the anti-government events of 1907, a number of Sikhs did so wholeheartedly. Ajit Singh, the revolutionary leader of the movement was a Jat Sikh; two Sikh periodicals, *Panth* and *Punjab,* were used to criticize government actions. Even Bhai Vir Singh, as editor of the *Khalsa Samachar,* obliquely criticized the Government through his imaging of Guru Gobind Singh as the expeller of tyranny and injustice and in his asking Sikhs to be ready to rise and dispel the trouble from the country (Singh, J. 1991: 340–2). Nonetheless, on the whole, only a few Sikh reformers took part in the agitations, particularly those associated with the Chief Khalsa Diwan.

Distancing the urban Sikhs from the rural population that took part in the 1907 upheaval, one writer disclaimed the Sikh masses as 'an ignorant and idle people. There are comparatively few among them who take any real interest in the welfare of their community.' Well aware of their favoured position in the eyes of the British and the need to stay in that position of predominance so the Sikh community could progress, reformers loudly insisted that the 'educated classes owe their very existence to British rule and would literally go to rack... [if] the protection of the British *raj* was withdrawn' (in *Khalsa Advocate* 23 November 1907; 12 September 1908). Carefully taking their cues from their rulers and playing their communal cards remarkably well, the Singh Sabha placed full blame for the upheaval on the Arya Samaj. Within a few years, the *Khalsa Advocate* had distanced the Sikhs completely from those events, insisting that they had taken no part whatever in the unrest and 'improper' agitation of 1907 and loudly condemning those who had caused the British to suspect Sikh loyalty. To further show Sikh allegiance to the Crown, the few 'dastardly actions of those misguided youths' of Khalsa College who had taken part in the commotion of 1907 were severely censured (27 January 1911).

Loyalty to the Raj was central to female education as well; to beget loyal children, mothers first needed to be loyal. Education would lead to children imbibed with patriotic zeal making them honourable members of society. The uneducated, on the other hand, were 'many weltering sores' retarding 'social progress and weakening... national strength (*Khalsa Advocate,* 2 May 1908). Interestingly, the victory of Japan over Russia constituted an oft-repeated example of how the upliftment of womanhood could lead to astounding results. Japan's educational methods were fastidiously reported in the press, particularly with regard to female education.

Given the uprisings of 1907, British authorities kept a watchful eye on the development of education in Punjab. Lieutenant-Governor Louis Dane, in a stirring appeal to Sikh girls at the Ferozepur school, noted that education was the key to problems facing the Jat population and their continuing loyalty to the Crown. For the most part, the government was well satisfied with the growing educational movement among the Sikhs, particularly the direction taken by the Ferozepur school. The officials heartily supported the primarily religious and domestic, non-political training given to the girls. They were not nearly as appreciative of Arya Samaj's advances in female education. The Samaj's leadership in the 1907 disturbances did little to further British support of their educational ventures. Punjab authorities, aware that the Swadeshi movement in Bengal had acted as a major catalyst for women's involvement in the nationalist struggle, were especially apprehensive of the renewal of Swadeshi in Punjab. In Bengal, courage, heroism, and physical fitness came to be accepted as female virtues if they served a political, nationalistic purpose (Borthwick 1984: 347–8). It was believed that these problematic qualities were also being inculcated by the Arya Samaj. One official remarked that if 'the government is not quick, it will find the women of India educated by the Arya Samajists. Our position in the country will be almost hopeless if the women are trained up in hostility to us' (Gilbert 1966: 97). Annie Besant, on the other hand, appreciative of nationalist concerns, noted, 'I know only of one body which is energetic in this field [of female education] and that is the Arya Samaj' (1917: 220). Clearly, while government policy attempted to promote female education in its 'civilizing mission', in reality what was pivotal for British officials was not education of women per se, but a particular *type* of education that was to produce a *specific type* of woman. Because of its strained loyalties towards the Crown, Punjab authorities were increasingly suspicious of the Arya Samaj; its female educational endeavours were perceived as anti-British and thus closely monitored by the authorities.

The Sikhs had a great deal to lose if they displayed the least sign of opposition to the government. The middle class in particular, given its distinct minority status and the increasingly anti-urban tone of a number of government decisions, did not wish to lose their traditionally favoured position with the British. Nonetheless, as early as 1911, cracks appeared in the unmitigated support of the British for the Sikhs. D. Petrie, the Assistant Director of Criminal Intelligence for the British government compiled a secret memorandum on the developments in the Sikh political arena. His conclusions were ultimately damning of the Sikhs and issued as a forewarning to the government. The Sikhs and most particularly what he termed the 'neo-Sikh' party, namely the Tat Khalsa reformers, because of their preferential treatment under the Raj were suffering from 'wind in the head'. Petrie warned that while *ostensibly* a movement solely devoted to religious reform, 'the cloven hoof of politics has too frequently been shown' among the reformers. Under favourable conditions, the Sikh reform movement could easily identify and even merge with the overtly political Arya Samaj movement, the differences between the two being 'at best superficial and artificial' (Petrie 1920: 319–43).

The possibility of urban Sikhs and Hindus consolidating forces was not confined to Petrie; Baba Gurbakhsh Singh, the successor to Baba Khem Singh Bedi of the revered Bedi lineage, when elected to preside at the Punjab Hindu Conference of 1910 also advocated a unification of the two bodies. According to him, true reform in Punjab would be possible only if energies were not squandered by ongoing disputes between Hindus and Sikhs. Needless to say, as the voice of Sanatan Sikhism, Gurbakhsh Singh's perspective was intensely opposed by Tat Khalsa leaders. The Director of Criminal Intelligence, while acknowledging the contributions of his assistant, also played down Petrie's apprehensions about the Sikhs. Without doubt, it was of immense importance that the picture of Sikh loyalty hitherto upheld by the British be maintained; to admit otherwise would be to admit a historic blunder. From the perspective of the majority of Sikh reformers as well, the safety of Sikh communal interest lay not in participation in measures of agitation but in closer collaboration with the colonial masters.

The pro-British stance taken by the Tat Khalsa leadership over the events of 1907 did little to enhance their reputation among the peasantry. In standing fast with the government throughout the agitation, Singh Sabha leaders effectively turned their backs on the very real issues facing the rural populace. The Singh Sabha thus jettisoned the opportunity to induce the peasantry to support Tat

Khalsa-sponsored reforms, particularly with regard to initiatives for females. According to Takht Singh, reforms in practices such as child marriages were by and large confined to educated families. Moreover, the urban elite held a great number of negative assumptions about the rural populace. Thakat Singh alleged that girls from the rural districts 'are rather dull of understanding'. Only after being polished by more elite attitudes could these girls attain necessary Singh Sabha standards (Caveeshar 1984: 117, 120).

Negative portrayals of the urban elite also abounded among the peasantry. By and large, peasants had little use for an abstract ideology that could not translate into practical measures during times of adversity. As early as the turn of the century, Singh Sabha activities and ideology had already been characterized by the peasantry as 'Singh *safa*', safa being a pointed reference to the rampant destruction caused by the plague epidemic of 1902 (Singh, H. 1996: 281). In comparison, while the stronghold of the Arya Samaj remained in the cities, the influence of Dayanand's creed did extend into rural areas. This was especially the case in the canal colonies after the events of 1907, given the anti-government stance taken by the Arya Samaj. Yet, because of the predominance of Sikhs in the colonies, Singh Sabha reformers cried foul, warning their 'guileless brethren' to be wary of 'the net which... is being woven for them'. Ultimately, Tat Khalsa failure to make common cause with their rural Sikh base only paved the way for the educational and ideological advance of the Arya Samaj. Sikh colonists chose to send their offspring to a new Arya school inaugurated in Chenab colony rather than to the Singh Sabha institution in Lyallpur (*Khalsa Advocate*, 14 April 1908).

In line with Sikh reformers' vested interests, loyalty to the Crown had become the novel measure of true faithfulness to Sikh ideals. Similar to British Evangelical ideals combining patriotism, hypermasculinity, and godliness, Sikh reformers' carefully formulated expressions of loyalty to the Crown were closely inter-twined with highly specific allocations of true manliness and femininity.[18] Communal progress was couched in the language of patriotism and a novel construction of unadulterated Sikhism. Through the training of young Sikhs, both males and females, who were taking part in the Tat Khalsa educational initiatives, Sikh reformers spared little effort to devise ways and means to formulate these ideals. Given the heightened communal awareness already distancing the various reform groups from one another,

Singh Sabha leaders sought additional, concrete measures by which Sikhs were to be distinguishable from the wider Hindu populace. A thorough rejection in some cases, or an ingenious restructuring of popular customs and religious rites in others, was essential to reform efforts. A newly forged historical and theological framework gave credence to the reformers' claims of radical distinction between Hindu and Sikh communities.

NOTES

1. One recent exception, though not focusing specifically on Sikhs, is Malhotra 2002.
2. The *Khalsa Advocate* was the mouthpiece of the Chief Khalsa Diwan, especially put in place to propagate its ideals to the Sikh intelligentsia and to its British readership.
3. '*Bun gai Singh Sabhiay, jaddon muk gai arrey dey daney*'. I am grateful, both for the translation and the insight into the sexual innuendo of this proverb, to Surjit Singh Hans of Punjabi University, Patiala.
4. By 1907, Sikh reformers had started to criticize the Ferozepur institution for not advancing to the status of the girls' high school.
5. Private interview with Thakat Singh's daughter, Paranpal Singh on 25 April 1997.
6. I am grateful for P.K. Sharma's efforts, who spared considerable time and energy translating the biography *Sri Mata Bibi Harnam Kaur* into English. While the book claims to be an accurate biography of Harnam Kaur, it was written after her death by a contemporary and active member of the Singh Sabha movement, Suraj Singh; the values and actual words attributed to Harnam Kaur must be seen from this perspective. The volume, composed entirely in verse, was written specifically within the context of the Sikh reform movement. Clearly, the purpose of the book was to further the objectives of the movement with regard to education and women.
7. Johann Metz uses the phrase in his discussion of the church, authority, and modernity. See Metz 1974: 179.
8. One such imported anecdote appeared in the pages of the *Khalsa Advocate*, 15 May 1904, namely, John J. Poole's focus on Rani Sahib Kaur. See Poole 1892: 234–41.
9. Women in Bengal were by far the most educated in India. They were admitted to the University of Calcutta as early as in 1878, far before their British counterparts. See Chakravarti 1990: 62.

10. The phrase 'inventing tradition' is taken from Eric Hobsbawm 1983.

11. According to Joginder Singh Rahi, in a private interview in April 1997, Amritsar, there is no trace of the original Bengali version. However, Rahi has analysed the document in great detail and maintains that Bhai Vir Singh must have been aware of the Punjabi version.

12. Besides the obvious pro-Christian, pro-British content of the novel, almost nothing is known of its origins. It remains a work deserving detailed analysis.

13. I am indebted to Dr Rahi for his insights into the comparison between *Jyotirudae* and *Sundri*.

14. The practice of devout Hindus claiming the Sikh tradition for their eldest sons is well documented. These sons were brought up as *keshdhari* Sikhs, who observed the outwards forms of the tradition, the 5 Ks. In Anup Chand Kapur's family, which was orthodox Hindu, his father, grandfather, and great-grandfather had followed the Sikh tradition, as had his eldest brother. See Kapur 1985: iii.

15. Kohli's critical assessment is one of the rare instances of substantive criticism of Bhai Vir Singh's writings by a Sikh scholar. Volumes that indiscriminately champion all of Vir Singh's writings abound. See especially, Guleria 1984. The reader finds evidence of extreme veneration in epithets such as 'The Universal Man', 'Bhai Vir Singh was not an Individual but an Institution', 'The Poet-Saint', 'A River of Culture and Learning', 'A Legend', and 'Surgeon of Souls'.

16. The Chenab Colony, started in 1887, was considered a particular ideal of Punjab's administration and of the paternalism which guided the designs of the government. See Jones 1989.

17. For an excellent summary of the involvement of the British government and the publications in Punjab, as well as specific publishing laws during the early and mid-twentieth century, see Barrier 1975: 45–84.

18. Similar to the YMCA inaugurated in England in 1844, a group of Sikh students initiated the Sikh Young Men's Association modelled after the Lahore chapter of the YMCA. Comparable to the latter's objectives, the Sikh association wished not only to promote a new understanding on true, educated masculinity, but also to encourage patriotic zeal in its members. The Arya Samaj also had its own men's association called the Young Men's Arya Association. See Farquhar 1924: 120–9.

SIX

EXTENDING MALE CONTROL
The Gentrified Imagination and Popular Female Traditions

Alongside Singh Sabha educational objectives came an equally important and perhaps even more far-reaching goal. This was the displacement and reorganization of tradition, particularly women's traditions, including rituals, identity markers, and rites pertaining to notions of sacred space and time. In particular, colossal efforts were made to define that which represented 'Sikh', and that which constituted 'un-Sikh' and corrupted tradition. At times this included the actual *production* of novel Sikh identity markers and rituals. One important example of this process was the passing of the Anand Marriage Act of 1909, itself standing as a *rite de passage* of Sikhism in the early twentieth century. The name of the marriage rite was taken from 'Anand', the 'song of joy' composed by Guru Amar Das at the birth of his grandson. Anand marriages were mainly associated with Namdhari and Nirankari Sikhs; both were well outside of the Tat Khalsa realm. In time, however, the Anand Marriage Act came to represent Sikhism's distinction from the wider Hindu culture more than any other single entity during the reform endeavour of the Singh Sabha movement. This chapter focuses the lens of ritual transformation during the Singh Sabha period on the gender politics that came to reign supreme in the larger social, political, and discursive structures in the process of defining the 'ritual drama' of the Sikhs in colonial Punjab.[1]

THE ANAND MARRIAGE BILL: GENDER POLITICS, RHETORIC, AND REASON

The Anand Marriage Bill was introduced in the Legislative Council of the Viceroy by Tikka Sahib of Nabha, the appointed Sikh Member of the Imperial Legislative Council, in October 1908.[2] Earlier, Tikka Sahib had composed a letter along with a draft bill outlining the reasons for the necessity of the Bill; the letter was in turn forwarded to the Home Department. The provincial government was clearly not interested in furthering the cause of the Honourable Tikka Sahib, questioning his motives and maintaining that 'in the absence of any established necessity for legislation, the Lieutenant Governor, would be adverse to the adoption of any such action' (cited in Talwar 1968: 405). The issue was subsequently brought up again under Sir Louis Dane, the succeeding Lieutenant-Governor, who took a different view of the proposed legislation from that put forward by his predecessor. The reasons given by Dane pertained to challenges put forth by the Arya Samaj in the courts regarding the validity of Sikh marriages in accordance with the Anand ceremony. Alarm began reverberating among the Sikhs. These 'very people have not hesitated to call the issues of Sikhs who have united themselves in wed-lock in accordance with the ceremony of Anand, bastards and thus barred from inheriting the property of their progenitors.' Their offspring were called *haramzadas* (illegitimate progeny because the form lacked legislative recognition, *Khalsa Advocate*, 7 November 1908). However, the controversy surrounding Anand marriages did not originate in the early twentieth century; in 1899, the *Arya Gazette* queried its readership: 'Is it not time for the believers in the Vedic Faith to consider whether such marriages should be regarded lawful by the society, as also whether we should be present at marriages at which instead of the Divine knowledge poetry of human composition is sung' (*The Khalsa*, 20 September 1899).' Needless to say, the number of Sikhs who married according to Anand rites was small; most Sikhs were married according to Brahminic prescriptions. Nonetheless, these minute numbers spurred the controversial stance taken by the Arya Samaj.

Couched in the polarized and increasingly vehement communal politics of the day, as well as highly publicized calls alarming the public with regard to costly litigation possibilities if the Bill was not passed, proponents initially found ready support for the Anand Marriage Bill among the populace. The acclamation, however, quickly dissipated as the actual wording of the Bill came to be analysed and as the varied and vested interests of the different parties came to the fore. The *Panjabee*, an organ of the more militant sector of the Arya Samaj, took an ardent stance against the Bill. It argued that 'Sikhs and

Hindus are so mixed up in family and in social relations that the
attempt of those who wanted to make out two communities has
miserably failed' (reproduced in *Khalsa Advocate*, 5 June 1909). Most
especially, opponents reacted to claims of the rite's antiquity made by
proponents of the Bill. Sikh supporters insisted that the marriage
tradition dated back to the time of Guru Amar Das. The custom then
'continued to be observed slowly but steadily by the followers of the
Gurus. No doubt it did not make much noise in the world, but it
soon became an established custom among the Sikhs and all true
believers in the Gurus would not celebrate marriages in any other
form than this' (ibid., 7 November 1908). For corroboration, they
turned to Max Arthur Macauliffe and his recently published *The Sikh
Religion*. With regard to the actual practice of Anand, he noted that it
'is now repeated on occasions of marriages and rejoicings, also
before large feasts, and at the preparation of sacred food.' But he also
made reference to Gobind Singh's marriage to Sahib Devan by Anand
rites; for according to Sikh accounts, the guru never intended to
consummate his marriage with Devan (Macauliffe 1990: 108–9).
Proponents also insisted that there was an unbroken line of those
celebrating their marriages by this rite. These included Nirankaris,
Namdharis, Bandeis (followers of Banda Bahadur), and Bihangams
(Nihang Singhs). Similar to the Namdharis, Tat Khalsa reformers also
turned to the *Prem Sumarg* as supportive of Sikh claims of the rite's
antiquity (see Chapter Four). Yet, the inclusion of the Namdharis as
significant members of the Sikh community was ridiculed by the
Panjabee, given the earlier, well-publicized denouncements of Kuka
theology and practice. Critics of the Anand Marriage Bill charged
that the ceremony had *originated* with these fringe groups and was
being borrowed from them by the Tat Khalsa (replicated in *Khalsa
Advocate*, 5 June 1909). They insisted that there was simply no
evidence of the Sikh gurus having initiated or followed the Anand
marriage order, given the lack of references to Anand marriage in
classical Sikh texts. The fact that the Anand Bill did not specify the
form of the marriage ceremony also caused opponents to question
the Bill. Namdhari wedding practices were strikingly similar to
traditional Vedic rites in that they included the ritual fire in the
ceremony. Still others insisted that a 'very large number of Sikhs do
not approve of the Bill which is supported only by a few individuals
of the new School. The orthodox Sikhs not only do not look upon it
with any favour, but regard it as harmful to their best interests' (*The

Tribune, 16 September 1909). The *Panjabee* (cited in *Khalsa Advocate,* 13 April 1909) further charged that the Anand ceremony had hitherto been confined to individuals who had less-than-honourable reasons for getting married; legislation thereof would only lead to a proliferation of such unions. Well aware of the benefits of couching its arguments in the volatile question of inheritance, it warned: '[I]f the Bill is introduced in the Council, becomes law, any Chief, Sirdar, Jagirdar or any other Sikh may marry a foreign or a Muhammadan girl... and the offspring born of such unions will be considered legitimate. The States, Jagirs, and the landed property of the Sikhs, will, by influx of time, pass into the hands of those who will not naturally remain Sikhs.' For,

[t]he undefined term 'Sikh' however, enables them to call themselves Sikhs. They go through the so-called Anand ceremony to which the Bill gives legal sanction. This ceremony does not lay down that the couple will have to make a declaration that they belong to no other faith or that they believe in certain well-known dogmas peculiar to the Sikhs. The Bill will, therefore, encourage people to achieve their object by unfair means without making them the units of a social organism to which the Sikh belong (*Khalsa Advocate,* 9 October 1909).

Bhai Lakshman Singh countered this observation, insisting that only with the passing of the Bill, which would sanction unions between Sikhs alone, would a new state of affairs come into being. 'The woman, being duly baptized, will feel a natural interest in the safeguarding of the state of property. Lewdness and debauch will receive a check.... In a word, the new Sikh law will have made it impossible for a Sikh young man to take a non-Sikh woman to wife.' Yet the Bill made no stipulation of initiation as mandatory for Sikh identity; the clause 'any marriage between persons not professing the Sikh religion will not be legal' was considered sufficient for its purposes. Certainly the ceremony continued to be utilized by different groups for various reasons. They included Arya Samaj inter-caste marriages, which as a result of these unions were rejected by the Brahminical order. Tat Khalsa reformers in this case insisted that upholding the tenets of the Arya Samaj was no bar to being a Sikh. Other 'dishonourable' unions solemnized by Anand; included the marriage between a teacher and his younger student (ibid., 12 July 1913; 20 September 1913).

The opponents also pointed to the inappropriate motives of Tikka Ripudaman Singh of the princely Nabha family as having been 'actuated... by a desire on his part or that of his brother Sikh Princes and notables to contract "honourable alliances with European and Eurasian girls".' Early *support* for the Anand Marriage Bill also referred to these unions. It was noted that 'it is preposterous that the punishment of an enlightened native chief for obeying the dictates of his heart should be a red stain of bastardy on his progeny.' Other examples included 'foreign' unions by the late Maharajah of Patiala, the Maharajah of Jind, who had married a Eurasian woman, and the Maharajah of Kapurthala, wedded to a Spaniard. These 'Chiefs are very much in love with their foreign wives and are naturally anxious that no suggestion of the bar sinister should smirch the escutcheons of their children.'[3] Despite calls upon enlightened Sikhs to accept these alliances, some Tat Khalsa members, taken aback by these charges of 'un-patriotic motives', distanced themselves from the Honourable Member. The public was duly notified that the Bill itself only came to the notice of Singh Sabha leaders *after* its introduction to the Council. Still, Lakshman Singh maintained that 'even supposing the insinuation to be a correct one I can say that the majority of the Singh Sabhas have accepted the Bill in good faith' (*Khalsa Advocate*, 2, 16, 23 October 1909).

Some supporters of the Bill urged that the name be changed from Anand Marriage Bill to Sikh Marriage Bill. This led to a proliferation of attempts to classify what constituted 'Sikh'. Proponents insisted that the term be defined as one who followed the baptismal injunctions of Guru Gobind Singh, namely, to exclude all but *Kesdhari* Sikhs. For

by widening the connotation of the word Sikh we would be throwing the gates wide open to so many weaklings who dare not take Amrit. It is much better that we should be few but Sikhs through and through than many drifting straws. Social purity in every respect is the bedrock on which the communal fabric may be permanently built. No one should in my opinion, be allowed to marry in Sikh form unless by accepting Amrit he outwardly manifest by his intention of abiding by the rules of the community whose form he has adopted on the most solemn occasion (*Khalsa Advocate*, October 1909).

This caused an outcry from the traditional Sikh orthodoxy. Bhai Avtar Singh, long associated with the late Sir Khem Singh Bedi as his secretary, argued against the change because of its utilization by a very small minority in the Sikh community. The question of Sikh identity became increasingly urgent. According to one contributor to the *Khalsa Advocate* (25 September 1909), 'there is a large section of Sikhs called *Sahjdhari* Sikhs who are quite indistinguishable in their appearance from, and yet are a very important section of Sikhs quite distinct in their religious beliefs and practices from, the Hindus, whether Arya Samaj or Sanatanists, Vaishnavites or others.' Rifts began to make themselves known within the Singh Sabha community as well. The Khalsa Diwan, Lahore, calling upon its historical significance as the oldest registered Sikh association and the founder of Khalsa College, began to call for the Bill to be dropped in its entirety. The Diwan insisted that the Bill 'does not yet meet the actual requirements of the case and will always be found a source of unnecessary and sometimes ruinous litigation.' It pointed to the 'great irritation' among different sections of the Sikh community as indicative of the ineffectiveness of the Bill. Further, the Lahore faction insisted that

it is not apparent that the Bill has been introduced by the so-called Reform party among the Sikhs; for there is no clause providing against the pernicious practices of infant marriage and polygamy among the Sikhs. But alas, our reformers have no desire for mitigating those evils which are sucking into the very vitals of the community (*Khalsa Advocate*, 16 October 1909).

Others outside of the Sikh community insisted on amendments to the Bill in the spirit of reform. The *Pioneer* charged on 6 February 1909 that '[h]ere is an opportunity for the Sikh leaders to put their heads together and to have the Anand Marriage Bill so broadened and modified that it may give equal rights to women and raise her to that position which she occupies in all the civilized nations of the world, and thus establish social equality among themselves which is a keynote of Sikhism.' It continued to champion for clauses that stipulated monogamy, legalization of customary divorce, consent of the parties, and registration of marriages. This would 'prevent useless litigation which often leads to murders and injuries'. The *Panjabee* concurred, adding that 'it is your duty to say that your community is prepared to take one step at least forward in advancement of social reform which may tend to secure the rights of the weaker sex.... Then indeed this legislation will be worthy of your professions and worthy of the mighty Sarkar whose aid you are seeking' (cited in *Khalsa Advocate*, 23 October 1909).

To these charges as well as to criticism that the Bill was becoming instead of a Marriage Bill, a 'Muddle Bill', Lakshman Singh ingeniously responded:

I repeat, it is too much to expect that the Anand Marriage Act will serve the purpose of a Sikh marriage Act even if so named.... A *Sikh Marriage Act* ought to be of such a nature as to be worthy of the intelligence and good name and fame of a community which has had such noble and high minded leaders as our great Gurus and whose Scriptures are full of lofty ideals. It ought to provide for a) Inter-marriage b) Monogamy c) Remarriage of widows and d) Divorce in certain well-defined cases. It ought also to guard against early marriage and late marriage. It may be even necessary to include therein some rules on inheritance.... If the effort of the Sikh reformers in this direction fail and the Bill becomes law in its present shape, I do not think it will deserve to be called a 'Muddle Bill'. As I have said elsewhere in this letter it will be a decided gain to our cause and will be a step in advance (*Khalsa Advocate*, 23 October 1909).

The Khalsa Diwan, Lahore, in turn was vehemently ridiculed and characterized in the *Khalsa Advocate* as 'the Sikh god in Lahore' and a 'mere bubble by proponents of the Bill'. Certainly, the rift in the Singh Sabha caused extraordinary alliances. Both representatives of the Viceroy's Legislative Council, Tikka Ripudaman Singh and his successor Sirdar Sundar Majithia, at the forefront of the Bill, had close affiliations with the once powerful Amritsar Singh Sabha; it had of course earlier come under vitriolic fire from the Tat Khalsa of Lahore as being damaging to true Sikh interests. Lakshman Singh, adjusting his own judgment of the Amritsar group, pointed to the historic tensions between the two groups: 'I am glad time should have shown how mistaken I was in my estimate of the Hon'ble Sirdar Sundar Majithia and his following whose strength it was my aim to break' (16, 30, October 1909).

After a full year of deliberation and minute changes made by the Select Committee in charge of the Bill, Sunder Singh Majithia moved that the Bill be made law. Changes to the wording of the Bill had included an alteration of Clause 5 of the Bill which had read: 'Nothing in this Act shall be deemed to validate any marriage between persons who are related to each other in any degree of consanguinity or affinity which would, according to the personal law of the Sikhs render a marriage between them illegal.' The term 'personal law' was instead changed to 'customary law', given the precedent set by the well known Majithia Will case.[4] In his speech to the Imperial Legislative Council, the Honourable Sardar Majithia pointed out:

I am sure Your Excellency and my Hon'ble Colleagues will agree that a proselytising religion like that of the Sikhs which draws converts from all castes and creeds cannot be ruled for ever by the Shastric Laws.... The explanation of the sacred and solemn import of marriage and of the duties of married life and the personal and spiritually solemn contract between the parties made in the presence of the Guru Granth Sahib ji which generally forms part of the Anand ceremony of marriage raises it far above the level of other ceremonies which have degenerated into empty rituals and unmeaning recitations so far as the persons principally affected are concerned. The reduction of the marriage expenses and the simplification of the whole ceremony is a moral gain which I venture to say is no small value.

He also addressed the concerns of another member of the Select Committee, Justice Nair of the Madras High Court, who had strongly objected to the exclusion of clauses relating to the protection of females—those pertaining to age limit, the prohibition of polygamy, divorce proceedings, and marriage registration. To this Majithia responded:

The opinion.... is worthy of all respect and is probably shared by a large number of enlightened members of the Sikh community. But social reform among the Sikhs is not confined to an educated few; it affects the entire mass of the Sikh population and as long as there is not a general desire on the part of the whole Sikh community for such social legislation as is indicated by the Hon'ble Justice Nair it will not be right for us to ask for social legislation of the kind. Reforms like these are certainly dear to our heart but these ought to be carried for a sufficient length of time before their recognition can be sought for at the hands of the Government. It would not do to force reforms which may be considered as mere innovations by those for whose benefit they may have been intended. Let us hope that with the expansion of female education amongst the Sikhs the desire for a higher kind of marriage law will grow and express itself and the present Act may serve as a frame work for building up a marriage law worthy of a god-fearing and progressive community like that of the Sikhs.

To objections with regard to the actual rendering of the marriage rite, Sir Herbert Risley, also of the Select Committee, noted that

Sikh and Hindu marriages were far too fluid and variable, and moved that the Bill be accepted without a precise delineation of the ceremony. Sir Louis Dane, Lieutenant-Governor of Punjab then gave his final pronouncements. Aware of the dissenting voices within the Sikh community, Dane noted:

[The] experience gained in the controversy which has arisen over the measure shows how careful we must be not to take public utterances of a reforming party as opinions of the whole of the community.... At the same time, I must admit that my sympathies are largely with the promoters of the Bill, for the reason that it marks an important step in social reform and that it may bring about a possible, nay a probable decrease in marriage expenditure which is one of the main causes of the indebtedness in this province. I join Sardar Sundar Singh in regretting that it was not possible in this measure to raise the age of marriage under the Anand ceremony, and to provide a system of marriage registration.... In conclusion... the Tikka Sahib's Bill, with such minor amendments as have been suggested above, has behind it the popular support of the vast majority of the Sikh community, that it in no way infringes the civil, social or religious rights of the minority who are opposed to it, that it affords the basis for a valuable social reform in the direction of the reduction of marriage expenses... and may prevent very costly and widespread litigation... (the Anand Marriage Bill Proceedings in *Khalsa Advocate*, 30 October 1909).

The Bill was passed. These legislative statements have been quoted at length because they provide a valuable insight into the forces at work behind the passing of the Bill into law. The discourse is of pivotal importance in the discussion of the women's question, an issue loudly proclaimed by both the British government and the Tat Khalsa as central to their reform initiatives. Here was a propitious opportunity to address precisely those forces that sustained the precariousness of the position of women in Sikh society, yet it was not taken. Further, why did the government pass a Bill that was so clearly problematic to large numbers of Sikhs and Hindus? Indeed, an understanding of the transformation of the Anand Marriage Bill into the Anand Marriage Act necessitates its contextualization within the wider framework of Punjab politics, both communal and administrative. Events that had transpired a year before the introduction of the Bill—the rumblings of discontent among the rural Jat population—played no small part in this judicial decision. As already noted, the blame for the previous altercations between the rural populace and the government had been placed squarely at the doorstep of the Arya Samaj. British apprehension towards the Samaj coloured their response to any activity undertaken by the body, including its sustained attack of the Anand Marriage Bill. Thus, while forwarding sound reasons for amendments to the Bill on the one hand, and calls for dropping it outright on the other, the government paid scant attention to any suggestions that even resembled those of the Arya Samaj. Ultimately, the acrimonious remarks ostensibly made by a member of the Samaj hailing the progeny of Anand unions as haramzadas brought about the initial, positive change in the Punjab government's stance toward Tikka Sahib's Bill. Further, well aware of the inroads made by the Arya Samaj against which the Singh Sabha movement was reacting but also upon which according to British reports, the Sikh reform movement was modelled, was indeed cause for worry. The similarities between the two groups, aside from abstention from tobacco and the wearing of the five Ks by the Tat Khalsa reformers, were well known to the authorities. These were viewed as 'at best superficial and artificial differences'. According to Petrie, Assistant Director of Criminal Intelligence who closely monitored the activities of the Tat Khalsa, a 'union between the two is by no means unthinkable' (1970: 307, 319). The British had little desire for the military prowess of the Sikhs and the remonstrative, political acumen of the Arya Samaj to mobilize together and be pitted against them. It was thus of primary importance to ensure that the Tat Khalsa Sikhs remained autonomous from the Samaj. The passing of the Anand Marriage Bill, despite legitimate claims and objections, was an advantageous measure taken to safeguard both British and Sikh interests through the deepening of the communal rivalry between the Arya Samaj and the Singh Sabha movement.

Second, for the British, a 'purified' Sikh identity was pivotal in checking the absorption of Sikhism into the wider Hindu fold. As noted earlier, the need to foster this Sikh identity began initially through the regulations put forth in the Indian Army; each recruit and soldier was required to be initiated according to the prescriptions of Guru Gobind Singh. Accordingly, 'Sikhs in the Indian Army have been studiously "nationalised" or encouraged to regard themselves as a totally distinct and separate nation; their national pride has been fostered by every available means....' A relapse into Hinduism and 're-adoption of its superstitious and vicious social customs' could lead only to the loss of Sikh martial instincts and his ability as a fighting machine (Petrie 1970: 309).

Macauliffe noted that the Hinduization of the Sikhs had another, even more ominous result. Upon meeting with several young Sikhs of the Guru lineage, Macauliffe noted that loyalty towards the British, so clearly associated with 'true' Sikhs, had all but disappeared. They were 'ignorant of the Sikh religion, and of its prophecies in favour of the English', they referred to the British as *malechhas*, or persons of impure desires, and demonstrated 'disgust for the customs and habits of Christians' (Macauliffe Vol. I, 1990: xxiii–xxiv). The magical effect of initiation in the making of a purified Sikh identity and consequently, its effectiveness in producing the Sikh military machine loyal to the Crown, was widely accepted by the authorities. It was thus that the Tat Khalsa movement's objectives were closely aligned with those of the British; both strove for the crystallization of a distinct Sikh identity. Petrie continued that 'in so far as the movement [Singh Sabha] tends to consolidate the Sikh nation and to enable it to present a solid front to external aggression, it must command the most unqualified approval, for it has already been shown that Government cannot view with indifference the disappearance of the Sikhs as a distinct national identity' (Petrie 1970: 321).

For the Tat Khalsa, neither insinuations of impropriety regarding the very rationale for the Bill nor the threat of increasing rifts in the Sikh community could outweigh its benefits vis-à-vis the legislation of Sikh identity as distinct from the wider Hindu community. A few short years earlier the highly publicized Majithia Will case, after years before the courts, had proved to be a massive blow to the efforts of reformers to distinguish Sikhs from Hindus. The philanthropist Dyal Singh Majithia of the Brahmo Samaj had willed the majority of his wealth to the Samaj, including his English newspaper *The Tribune*, Dyal Singh College, and the Dyal Singh Library. His wife, Bhagwan Kaur, and his closest agnatic relative had challenged Dyal Singh's last testament on the grounds of Majithia's Sikh background; as such, they believed, Hindu inheritance laws could not apply to his estate. Yet the Privy Council disagreed, thus ensuring that Hindu law continued to cover the Sikhs (Gopal 1992). The Anand Marriage Bill in the ensuing rhetoric came repeatedly to be pitted against the Majithia case and became for the reformers, a legislative battle to be won at all costs. For it proved, beyond the grand orations of the Tat Khalsa reformers and beyond the claims of those who opposed the sanctioning of this distinction, that Sikhs were *not* Hindus and that Hindu laws did *not* apply to Sikhs, particularly in a rite as central as that of marriage. The courts finally recognized Sikhs as having a legitimate and distinct identity through the passing of the Anand Marriage Bill.

Needless to say, the Sikh identity consolidated with added political clout. Direct proportionality of representation and power to numerical strength had become a central concern for the elite in Punjab. The effects were far-reaching. For example, in an effort to balance admission to centres of higher learning, the government regulated access according to communal representation. Sikhs thus had an advantage over other groups in gaining admission to colleges and medical schools. *The Akali* noted that in an effort to secure admission, even *patits* (apostates) declared themselves to be Sikhs (see Kaur, A. 1992: 267). Further, Sikhs were aided in their endeavours to augment their numbers by the British government whose census officials were instructed to demarcate those who claimed *both* Sikh and Hindu affiliation, as Sikhs. The Anand Marriage Bill, although in many ways widening the rifts in the Sikh community, did manage as a cooperative effort between the government and a segment of the Singh Sabha reformers, to bring the distinct identity of the Sikhs to a more substantial level through the legislative process.

As regards the government, a third pivotal reason for passing the controversial Bill was the maintenance of political stability among the powerful Sikh elite. Objections to the passing of the Anand Marriage Act were minimized as the court followed the bidding of the majority voice within the Tat Khalsa. Dane's regret at the actual introduction of the Bill is evident in his closing remarks (quoted in *Khalsa Advocate*, 30 October 1909).

It is perhaps unfortunate that Tikka Ripudaman Singh should have raised the question at all, but as he has done so, and as he is supported by the great body of his co-religionists and as it would probably cause serious popular discontent if no action is taken in the matter of the Bill, the Lieutenant Governor considers that it should be passed into law.

The fear of the Tat Khalsa mobilizing against the government was central to the government's acquiescence to the demands of this powerful elite. The proponents of the Bill were highly organized and remarkably effective in their zeal to mobilize public opinion in its favour. 'The word goes forth and petitions, practically identical in substance, pour in from all parts of the world.' Those who opposed the Bill, delineated by Dane as conservative, responded at a much more ineffectual pace and manner. Even important questions of litigation and marriage costs were subsumed, at least for the government, by the larger issue of political stability. For as Louis Dane himself noted, since the 'Anand ceremony is not necessarily proceeded by a formal betrothal, it is more difficult to prove such marriage than an ordinary Hindu marriage of orthodox type.' Precisely because these marriages could *not* be proved, it was likely that litigation procedures could increase among the Sikhs. Nonetheless, its proponents repeatedly alluded to the alleviation of high marriage costs through the Bill and litigation patterns among the Sikhs. The argument was, the Anand Marriage ceremony could be conducted without the services of Brahmins; Brahmins were responsible for escalating marriage costs among the Sikhs. Yet, in reality, many Anand marriages continued to be conducted by Brahmins (*Khalsa Advocate*, 21 June 1913). Further, the rhetoric surrounding the Bill was based on the notion that the Act would also provide the necessary mechanism to alleviate the problem of indebtedness. But Malcolm Darling, writing almost twenty years after the passing of the Act, noted that wedding costs and general indebtedness had only *increased* among the Sikhs. Weddings had become more costly for the Sikhs since they had become major feasts that continued for days. Litigation had also not subsided, given that there were far fewer females than males, and this led to increased bride prices and inheritance concerns, especially among the Sikhs. Accordingly, 'a large number of lawsuits, civil and criminal, practically turn on the question whether the mother or the uncle of a fatherless girl is entitled to the profits of mating her' (Darling 1928: 54).

One of the critical issues ignored by the legislative process surrounding the Act was the actual *form* of the Anand marriage ceremony. Parry, writing well after the passing of the Bill, describes a Sikh marriage conducted by a Sikh Granthi, which however still revolved around the sacred fire pit (1921: 33). As noted earlier, many marriages continued to be conducted by Brahmins. Further, important aspects such as age limits, polygamy restrictions, divorce regulations, and forced marriages, became relegated by both the British government and the Tat Khalsa reformers to the sidelines. These were significant issues, given that historically among the 'better class of Sikh betrothals took place at very young ages (Falcon 1896: 51). Further, the Census of 1910 indicated that high rates of polygamy continued among the Sikhs. Forced widow remarriages to maintain family land rights were also common practice. Certainly, when critics of the Bill were proclaiming its shortcomings, many did so for legitimate reasons. Tat Khalsa reformers however continued to insist that 'by deliberations, the community can be educated in a better way in social reforms than by putting down the social evils through legislative measures' (*Khalsa Advocate*, 12 December 1914). For the British government, the widening of the gulf between the Tat Khalsa and the Arya Samaj, the continued purification of Sikh identity, and fears of political instability through the instigation of the Tat Khalsa, subsumed any concerns for the alleviation of detrimental customs affecting Sikh women. For Sikh reformers, the women's question was deemed insignificant in the light of the larger cause—the recognition by the courts of the distinctive, national identity of the Sikhs.

R. Radhakrishnan (1992: 78) has posed important questions as to the subordination of women's politics to the politics of nationalism in India.

Why does the politics of the 'one' typically overwhelm the politics of the other? Why could the two not be coordinated within an equal and dialogic relationship of mutual accountability? What factors constituted the normative criteria by which a question or issue is deemed 'political'? Why is it that nationalism achieves the ideological effect of an inclusive and putatively macropolitical discourse, whereas the women's question—unable to achieve its own autonomous macropolitical identity—remains ghettoized within its specific and regional space? In other words, by what natural or ideological imperative or historical exigency does the politics of nationalism become the binding and overarching umbrella that subsumes other and different political temporalities?

The discourse around the Anand Marriage Bill is significant precisely because Singh Sabha reformers so loudly proclaimed the amelioration of females as central to their reform mission. Here was the opportune moment to make significant changes to deeply ingrained social attitudes and practices that had negative consequences for women in Sikh society. But the opportunity was not taken, in spite of repeated calls for amendments to the Bill, both from inside and outside of the Sikh community. To understand the motives spurring on the Singh Sabha reformers, questions pertaining to Sikh women must necessarily be contextualized within the overarching question of national identity—the Sikh national identity. To return to Radhakrishnan, 'the women's question... is constrained to take on a nationalist expression as a prerequisite for being considered "political"' (ibid.). For the Tat Khalsa reformers, women's politics became an issue only as an added bulwark when larger questions such as Sikh religious identity came to the fore. Even Tat Khalsa education initiatives ultimately had the same intent vis-à-vis Sikh identity concerns: they were intent on producing 'true' Sikh women who would take up their proper place in the home, and conduct their duties in the home in a proper manner befitting an educated Sikh woman who would then be enabled to raise proper Sikh children. For the Singh Sabha reformers, this was the very essence of reform for women. As the *Khalsa Advocate* noted on 30 June 1911:

> The softer and weaker sex rules over the stronger... call them ignorant and superstitious, or designate them with whatever bad name you like.... [I]f you wish to push on your cherished object you must bring your women to the same level of enlightenment in which you are environed.... When her education as required is finished she turns out a competent housewife, efficient teacher of her children and good counselor to her husband, relatives and friends. Her prejudices vanish and the task of social reform is facilitated and easily accomplished.

For Sikh reformers, widely publicized calls for alleviating the status of Sikh women thus ultimately remained in the realm of rhetoric. In an effort to promote Singh Sabha political designs, the amelioration of women in Sikh society became subsumed by outward and judicial distinctiveness between Hindus and Sikhs. Certainly this was not completely lost to British officials; Petrie had made note of the inter-communal jostling for recognition, saying that 'there is no community that is not fired with the idea of consolidating and improving itself to the utmost of power' (1970: 320).

Needless to say, intense communal rivalry and indicators of particularity did little to challenge attitudes towards women; nor did they have a transformative effect on those Sikh customs that were pivotal in circumscribing the status and situation of women in Sikh society, namely, the marriage practices of the Sikhs. As Bruce

Lawrence has aptly noted, the 'mindset of the modernist bias' generally perpetuated by indigenous elites in colonized countries and clearly at play during the process of the Anand Marriage Bill becoming Act, included notions of 'quantity over quality, change over continuity, commercial efficiency over human sympathy...' (1989: 97–8).

Extending Male Control: The 'New Patriarchy'

Ultimately, the private realm was to remain as it was, untouched by the foreign ideas that were viewed as encroaching upon Sikh womanhood. Although denouncing purdah as an un-Sikh evil custom, Tikka Sahib of Nabha insisted that there was a difference between purdah and the home as sacrosanct. 'That privacy in the home of course, must be kept sacred. No stranger, not even a relative, should be allowed to intrude upon her privacy except by a special sanction of herself and her guardians.... The sacred privacy of woman must be maintained' (*Khalsa Advocate*, 30 June 1911). Tikka Sahib's concern with privacy stemmed from Punjabi joint-family systems requiring women to cover themselves in the presence of an elder, a superior, or a stranger. This also included any intercourse between a daughter-in-law and a father-in-law and, in some cases, between a wife and her husband's elder brother. Darling related an anecdote with regard to the customary confines between members of Punjabi joint families: 'A Sikh Jat relates how one night his sister's father-in-law arrived at her house unexpectedly when her husband was away and after all the servants had gone to bed. Not a word was exchanged between them, and he could no more ask her for food than she could offer it: so he went supperless to bed...' (1934: 308–9). Darling noted, however, that the rigorousness of the custom was slowly loosening its hold on the Punjabi populace.[4] Not surprisingly, this unravelling of restrictions on women translated into no small measure of alarm for reformers. The customs that demarcated women's space from that of the wider society, as well as newly appropriated notions of the gentle helpmate, came increasingly to be rendered by what Partha Chatterjee calls the 'new patriarchy' into tighter control of women and their activities. The Indian middle-class male was sharply distinguished both from the social order of modern Western society *and* the patriarchy of indigenous tradition. Women and the home became the symbol of all that was considered spiritual in Indian society; the virtues associated with both necessitated guarding from excessive Westernization at all cost. While the new order also adopted elements of tradition as imprints of its indigenous cultural identity, it was a 'deliberately "classicized" tradition—reformed, reconstructed' (Chatterjee 1990: 243–5). According to Meredith Borthwick, travellers to Punjab, particularly the women of Bengal, had long been astonished by the apparent unconstraint of Punjabi women. The 'Brahmo puritanism' of a goodly number of the wives of professionals was acutely disturbed by Punjabi women bathing naked in the rivers and lakes; so too by the singing of obscene songs by women at festivals and weddings. (Borthwick 1984: 235). Lakshman Singh's autobiography attests to these unabashed bathing customs of women. Needless to say, women's nude bathing practices in Punjab's rivers came to be condemned as unequivocally immoral by the new patriarchy of Punjab society.

Increasingly, restrictions on women came to occupy a central place in the imagination of reformers. Accordingly, Neki Parcharak Committees, or Social Reform Committees, were set up in every village (*Khalsa Advocate*, 7 July 1911). To what extent and form this initial meeting of the committee continued beyond the first is unknown. However, the focus on women and women's activities was indicative of an increasing concern to do away with traditional women's customs. While ostensibly initiated to condemn acts such as the selling and purchasing of daughters, and female infanticide, these committees also included in their mandate a wide number of restrictions pertaining to the women's customs. These included: putting an end to ear piercing for boys and nose piercing for girls; women's ornamentation in general was to cease; drinking and nautch girls were to be eliminated from wedding celebrations; in the practice of singing 'immoral' songs the use of abusive language by women was to be unconditionally stopped.

The concerns with regard to ear and nose piercing did not originate with Neki Parcharak Committees. According to the reformers, time-honoured Sikh rahit, particularly *Prem Sumarg*, strictly prohibited the boring of ears and noses (15 August 1904). Harnam Kaur's biography also addressed this issue. It noted that adornment of jewellery was a device utilized by the male-dominated society to enslave women. *Sri Mati Bibi Harnam Kaur* also noted that women in advanced countries had no need to pompously display their jewels and justly ridiculed

Indian women for doing so; thus ornamentation was simply an indication of the 'backwardness' of Indian women in comparison to their Western counterparts. It continued that jewels could not ultimately lead to true happiness in a marriage; only true inner ornamentation would lead to true conjugal satisfaction. Influenced by Kaur's admonitions, several women took off their jewellery and donated them to the coffers of the boarding house (Singh, S.B. 1908: 132–5).

The discourse surrounding women's ornamentation is significant in the context of the larger cause of reform. Women were called upon to contribute to the cause beyond their duty as honorary teachers, through donating their jewellery. Those who contributed in this manner were widely lauded as exemplary women whom other women were charged to emulate. Repeated requests for women to follow the new regulations put in place by the reformers with regard to abandoning jewellery became increasingly regulated; by 1917, at the Tenth Sikh Education Conference, Sikh females were strictly prohibited from coming 'laden in ornaments' and dressed in 'showy' suits (*Khalsa Advocate*, 24 March 1917).

Though the issue appears to be easily relegated to immaterial and superficial regulations, the discourse takes on significance when the *role* of jewellery for women in early twentieth-century Punjab is added to the equation. Parry noted in 1921 that Sikh women were generally 'heavily decorated with silver bangles of all sizes and shapes. The nose is always pierced and contains some ornament. The ears and neck are covered with heavy silver bangles and chains. The ankles are generally hidden by heavy silver anklets' (pg. 24). According to another observer:

A woman's social standing, unless she is a widow, is largely determined by her jewels.... And it is not only her social but also her material position that is affected. In a country in which women are bought and sold it can be understood that her position is highly insecure. A quarrel may lead to separation, or her husband's death may leave her in unprotected and penniless anxiety, therefore, it is always to have something that may be retained in her personal possession against the uncertainties of fortune, and nothing serves this purpose so well as jewellery (Darling 1928: 62).

Given the sacrosanct position of the male over that of the female in terms of inheritance laws in Punjab, the ownership of jewellery imbued women with both a tangible and intangible form of material wealth, power, and status. In some cases, jewellery served as collateral in exerting power over and manipulating male family members. In fact, sometimes 'women would not agree to a smaller allowance of jewellery unless their bibulous husbands consented to a smaller allowance of drink' (Darling 1934: 296). Tat Khalsa initiatives in essence began to curtail any economic agency that women may have had.

Eventually, Singh Sabha concerns with women's outward appearances also came to include prohibitions against wearing make-up and on the thickness of the cloth used in women's clothing—clothes were to be in no way see-through. The veil, according to Darling, was undergoing a subtle change. 'Once so thick that nothing could be seen through it, and so full that it could envelop the whole head, it is becoming semi-transparent and, if it is long enough to be drawn across the face, it is sufficient' (1934: 309). Certainly the concern for women's clothing was not restricted to the Sikh reform endeavour. S.C. Bose, loudly condemning late nineteenth-century Bengali men for their imitation of European dress, also insisted that well-covered female bodies went 'hand in hand with religious, moral and intellectual improvement. The one is essential to the elevation and dignity of female character as the other is to the advancement of the nation in the scale of civilization' (1881: 194, 195). Farquhar also made reference to this newly emerging male control over women's clothing among the Bengali elite, noting that 'they invented a new and becoming dress, more suited for outdoor wear and social intercourse than the rather scanty clothing of the stay-at-home Bengali wife' (1924: 48). While pointing out the similarities with regard to Indian male reformers across India, it must be stressed that Sikh women in Punjab did not generally wear saris. Falcon described the dress of Punjabi women: 'Musalman women wear trousers of striped stuff of dark blue or green, loose at the top and tight at the ankle. Hindu Jat women, when married, wear the same style of trousers with a petticoat (ghagra) generally of red or madder brown, over the trousers' (1896: 47, 59). Sikh women were so closely aligned with Hindu women that Falcon makes no distinction between them in terms of their dress. Blue cloth however, was strictly prohibited for Sikh women as it had long been associated with the order of the Khalsa. While Punjabi women ostensibly could not be accused of sporting the 'scanty clothing' of Bengali women's homewear, reformers did take issue with the weight and cloth of Punjabi women's clothing, most particularly, their veils.

With regard to the issue of nautch girls, dancing girls were an important aspect of celebration and performance in Punjab. They were common in the court of Maharajah Ranjit Singh; during festivals he encouraged them to dress in military garb, ride on horses, and form his bodyguard, and they were endearingly described by observers as Amazons. Soltykoff, who toured Punjab in the mid-nineteenth century, noted that courtesans and dancing girls walked freely in the court of Maharajah Sher Singh while his wives lived in strict accordance to the rules of purdah (Garrett 1971: 54, 104). The institution of nautch girls had thrived well into the twentieth century. They were professional musicians who were paid to perform at weddings; they wore seductive clothing, danced provocatively, and sang ribald songs to their audience. They were entitled to a great deal of autonomy and subsequent immunity from the traditional restrictions placed upon female Punjabis. Understandably, for the educated and gentrified new patriarchy at the helm of Sikh reform, the independence of these women could not be condoned. While nautch girls at wedding celebrations had long provided an element of boisterousness and abandonment to these rites of passage, Tat Khalsa reformers insisted that they were instead to be carried out in solemnity and austerity.

According to Judy Whitehead (1996: 187–8), control of the body, particularly women's bodies, is indicative of another, wider agenda:

Since the human body is simultaneously a physical, symbolic and emotional phenomenon, a measure of control over it is a crucial adjunct to any assertion of authority. Forms of bodily discipline connect the individual body to the wider body politic, allowing for a constant interchange of meanings between the social world and the 'natural' world of the body. Discussions over changing forms of bodily regulation can reveal the class distinctions underlying the ongoing formation of nationalist gender identities.

In this light, the largely male reform movement's attempts to restrict both women's bodies and actions is illustrative of their initiatives to carve out a distinct Sikh identity within the wider political and religious milieu. Maintaining that stronghold necessitated an increased control over elements that were traditionally outside of their domain of authority. This included an appropriation of the power to name, order, and classify while also defining the rules by which women were to live. In essence, the conversion of women's bodies into 'semiological markers' reached new levels with the ascendancy of the reformed mindset (Malhotra 2002: 34). Accordingly, the feminine identity sought was not a symbol of women's making in the way that masculinity was a symbol of men's making. Perhaps even more importantly, the persistent calls for maintaining the sanctity of the home combined with a newly forged agenda of regulating women's behaviour points to a selective move *beyond* mere rhetoric to an active structuring and management of class identity. Indeed, to return to the Anand Marriage Bill in this regard, *despite* the avid opposition to its passage and precisely *because* of its ensuing passage, the most vocal, the 'true' Tat Khalsa, were proven to have attained the position of the new powerbrokers of Sikh society. This position necessitated safeguarding; the arrangements put in place to ensure the preservation of social and political control translated into an elaborate strategy that included bodily and sexual restrictions of females. Indeed, within the context of the nationalist movement, ever encroaching controls over women were essential; the focus on the 'inner' world, the home, and womanhood was a selective coping mechanism in coming to terms with the West. 'In the fight against the enemy from the outside, something within gets even more repressed and "woman" becomes the mute but necessary allegorical ground for the transactions of nationalist history' (Radhakrishnan 1992: 84). Stallybrass and White (1986: 89–90) also throw light on this strategy, delineating it as a form of identity construction—identity created through a process of negation of threatening domains.

Manners, regulations of the body thus become the site of a profound interconnection of ideology and subjectivity, a zone of transcoding at once astonishingly trivial and microscopically important. Traversed by regulative forces quite beyond its conscious control, the body is territorialized in accordance with hierarchies and topographical rules... which come from elsewhere and make it a point of intersection and flow within the elaborate symbolic systems of the socius.

For Singh Sabha reformers, the 'threatening domain' of female space was traditionally outside the spectrum of male authority, but the perceived need to consolidate their hard- won position of power necessitated an attenuation of male control. This included, above all, the removal of traditional women's customs that inconvenienced the 'new' honour of Sikh men in general and the Tat Khalsa reformers in particular; it also attended to those elements of feminine tradition that diminished the authority and status of the husband (Jones 1988: 54).

The restrictions were largely confined within the Singh Sabha reformers' own social parameters, particularly the notions of home and privacy that were posited by the leaders of the Tat Khalsa. They did not attempt to include the peasantry; in rural areas the public field of work for a woman from the cultivating classes was in fact an extension of her private area (Chowdhry 1994: 385). For the female peasant, the field itself, as well as the freedom to work on the field, was as essential to her identity as was the home. Moreover, aside from their occasional maligning of the 'simple' peasantry, reformers had little desire to tamper with them. The sturdy female Jat was by and large considered to be outside the pale of the refined urban ethos; moreover, she necessitated safeguarding as she contributed so well to the economic well being of Punjab. On the other hand, the by-now securely positioned elite took great pains to forge and thereby control a concrete, physical identity for *their* womenfolk, those largely confined to urban areas and associated with male members of the Tat Khalsa. Restrictions placed on women's festivals, rituals, and habits were largely limited to women of the educated class, both in the nineteenth as well as the twentieth centuries (Jones 1988: 53). Partha Chatterjee's observation relating to the construct of the 'new' womanhood by Bengali nationalists is similar to Singh Sabha objectives:

The new woman defined in this way was subjected to a new patriarchy. In fact, the social order connecting the home and the world in which nationalists placed the new woman was contrasted not only with that of modern Western society; it was explicitly distinguished from the patriarchy of indigenous tradition, the same tradition that had been put on the dock by colonial interrogators.... The new patriarchy was also sharply distinguished from the immediate social and cultural condition in which the majority of the people lived, for the 'new' woman was quite the reverse of the 'common' woman, who was coarse, vulgar, loud, quarrelsome, devoid of superior moral sense, sexually promiscuous, subjected to brutal physical oppression by males (Chatterjee 1989: 627).

The legacy of colonial rule to create classes conducive to its rule, which in turn developed officially sanctioned ideologies, led for the most part to an extension of already existing unequal relations within the various sections of Punjabi society. Nowhere was this more in evidence than in the palpable distancing between the Sikh urban, educated elite and the rural peasantry.

Douglas Haynes' analysis of what he calls 'negotiated hegemony' is particularly helpful in understanding the political and rhetorical shifts in power dynamics, especially with regard to ascendancy into positions of power. Negotiated hegemony allows for explanations of these shifts beyond the processes of Westernization and modernization; it moves beyond ambiguous assumptions of Western superiority and allows for a more applicable explication of the revisions in both value and power systems. He notes that since viable access to the political language of both the imperial rulers and the native population at large remained confined to a select few, mediators, the educated elite with knowledge of *both* kinds of discourse, easily and quickly moved into positions of power and prestige. While British administrative policy was particularly attentive to and supportive of the aspirations of the Sikh peasantry, ultimately those who had 'shaped their values and self-images in reference to political languages derived from their rulers' culture', and had made recourse to a vocabulary and symbols that had meaning to their rulers became hegemonic in the political arenas of the day. Despite overt British policy in Punjab to advocate the cause of the sturdy Jat peasantry, the position of authority acquired by the educated elite was both necessary and inevitable. Haynes thus notes that proficiency in the language of the rulers' became perhaps the most important aspect of the educated elite's rise to power. For

language tends to define the bounds of potential debate and conflict. Specific kinds of political discourse have built-in assumptions about the nature of power and justice. Language furbishes conventions which govern the performance of political acts; it supplies the categories, grammar, and principles through which political assertions are articulated and perceived; it provides yardsticks by which claims to authority and justice are measured and disputed. It defines the terrain of political debate, including some matters as legitimate points of discussion and excluding others (Haynes 1991: 7–11, 22–5).

The educated elite among the Sikhs, by virtue of their proficiency in the language of their erstwhile conquerors, took advantage of their position, claiming full authority to translate, elucidate, and define new parameters, particularly for those who were closest and most subordinate to them, their womenfolk. Indeed, gender politics must be acknowledged as pivotal to this very process of differentiation, since defining gender is crucial to the formation of classes and dominant ideologies. Restrictions on women served to bolster the shift in their class identity. In other words, novel patterns of control over Sikh womanhood, particularly those closely aligned with male reformers, constituted an important aspect of the hegemonic position coveted by the Tat Khalsa. It is within this context that the restrictions on women's dress and their activities can be understood, especially with the renewed focus on female customs such as singing immoral songs and using abusive language. As with the previous complaints of 'irrational' female activities voiced by the Amritsar Dharm Sabha, here too the honour of these new elites was at stake. Instead, Tat Khalsa reformers advocated ceremonies that were 'sober and solemn at once' with 'no exhibition of ornaments and clothes... no expensive conservative ceremony, no fireworks and nothing of the sort at all' (*Khalsa Advocate*, 4 September 1909). Assuredly, the concern for rigorous austerity at the time of weddings was not new to the twentieth century. An early critic had noted:

We notice that at the time of weddings all women, young and old, start singing such deplorable songs that they would put even the devil to shame. The Bhands [entertainers] who are notorious for using abuse and obscenities in their performances would find it hard to compete with the shameless language of these songs. What is amazing is that these lewd compositions are sung by women in the presence of their male kin and family patriarch, in front of whom they would normally go veiled. This despicable behaviour is most regrettable and reformers must take urgent steps to stop these bawdy songs (*Khalsa Akhbar*, 28 August 1886 cited in Oberoi 1994: 313).

According to Darling, repeated censure was beginning to take effect 'in a minor way.... At a marriage in the north-west, men and women used to sing them in antiphon, but now, if sung at all, it is mostly done by the men when no women are present' (1934: 302). Clearly, an important mode of expression conveying women's insubordination had here been appropriated by men. If there was to be any of this 'despicable behaviour' in public places, it could take place only in the company of males; females, were to have no part in these 'shameless' and 'bawdy' assemblages. Puritanism, asceticism, and restraint, characteristics that in time would become the hallmark of the Tat Khalsa were part of a strategic blueprint for a new culture that eventually sought to envelop private space beyond the regulation of public space.

POPULAR FEMALE TRADITIONS AND THE GENTRIFIED IMAGINATION

The vision of a new society came to be extended far beyond concerns regarding women's ornamentation, dress, taunts, and lewd singing at weddings. The gentrified elite attempted to dismantle virtually all forms of popular religious practices of the Sikh populace. Largely influenced by the reform ethos of their predecessors, the Namdhari and Nirankari Sikhs, as well as an enlightened, rationalized, and purified Sikhism infused with Western ideology, Tat Khalsa reformers began to advocate an *authentic* tradition, thereby 'for the first time label[ling] many of the current beliefs and practices among the Sikhs as acts of deviance and expressions of a superstitious mind' (Oberoi 1992: 365). Sikhism in the nineteenth and early twentieth centuries was teeming with life if one looks to the religious sensibilities of the peasantry. Heterogeneity reigned supreme in Sanatan Sikhism, which included a myriad of orthodox, popular, and village traditions; nature worship, witchcraft, spirits and spirit possession, miracle saints, goddess worship *as well as* devotion to the Sikh gurus, shaped the enchanted universe of the majority of rural Sikhs. Central to this cosmology was a complex and highly defined understanding of sacred time and place. For the rural populace, whose very existence was dependent on changing seasons and agricultural rhythms, calendrical festivals, pilgrimages, and rites that corresponded to nature's cycles were crucial signposts in time's sequence. Yet, while sustained by these notions of sacred time and space, this elusive universe went far beyond specific rites or mere localities to a larger, more generalized mode of understanding that included parodies, curses, oaths, abusive laughter, unconstrained dancing, and profanities. Mikhail Bakhtin (1968: 10) has circumscribed this as the amorphous 'world of the carnival'. It is

topsy-turvy, of heteroglot exuberance, of ceaseless overrunning and excess where all is mixed, hybrid, ritually degraded and defiled.... Carnival laughter, then, has a vulgar, 'earthy' quality to it. With its oaths and profanities, its abusive language and its mocking words it was profoundly

ambivalent. Whilst it humiliated and mortified it also revived and renewed (Stallybrass and White 1986: 8).

Needless to say, the world of the carnival was assailed by the Tat
Khalsa as diametrically opposed to Sikhism; rigorous attempts were
made to eradicate all aspects of the carnivalesque from the tradition
they were redefining. And understandably so, for this variable set
of symbolic practices, images, discourses, and imaginations was
employed by the disempowered in an ingenious enterprise of
'symbolic inversion and cultural negation'; according to Barbara
Babcock, this refers to 'any act of expressive behaviour which inverts,
contradicts, abrogates, or in some fashion presents an alternative
to commonly held cultural codes, values and norms be they
linguistic, literary or artistic, religious, social and political' (1978:
14). Thus, the world of the carnival can best be understood within
the context of the relativity of authority and truth. Only thus can
acts of inversion and negation be possible and relevant.

To contextualize the world of the carnival within 'great' or 'dominant' religious systems, one needs only to look to the traditions
alternately known as 'little', 'popular', or inimically, as 'superstitious',
to come to an understanding of this process of inversion. Robert
Redfield maintains that both traditions are interdependent and 'can
be thought of as two currents of thought and action, distinguishable,
yet ever flowing into and out of each other' (1960: 42). Popular
traditions fulfilled specific needs within societies that could not be
satisfied by the major religions. Women in particular claimed
calendrical festivals as their own; not only did they play important
ritual roles during the celebrations, they were also given the rare
opportunity to congregate with women from other localities (Lewis
1965: 237–8). Festivals also served to strengthen family ties, particularly the connections between female members. Further, festival
occasions marked the times when family members sent gifts to
daughters. Further, within the village cosmology, 'things mingle and
merge that are normally kept apart; things carefully regulated over-
flow their usual bounds. And on the level of symbolism pervading
these events it is perhaps above all the relations between what is
male and what is female that surge beyond all restrictions' (Brubaker
1983: 156). In this context, regulation and routine were ostensibly
turned head over heels: women taunted the very men before whom
they normally lived in servility; the goddess was dominant and male
deities were submissive to her wishes. Possibly reflective of an

ancient, pre-Vedic cult, Lewis' field research (1965: 238) in North
India's rural tracts indicates that the principal deities worshipped
by women are female. Moreover, stories told at women's celebrations focus on female deities; the deities most concerned with
matters of life, childbirth, sickness, and health are goddesses. While
females are typically subordinate to males, they gain sustenance in
the knowledge that their goddess, is all-powerful. The supreme goddess, Mahadevi, alternately known as Durga, Kali, Kalka, Mahesri,
or Bhiwani, was a particularly important aspect of Sikh religious
practices in the nineteenth century.[5] According to David Kinsley,
Durga, '[a]lthough she is created by the male gods and does their
bidding, and, although she is observed and applauded by them,
she (along with her female helpers and attendants) fights without
direct male support against male demons—and she always wins.'
In many ways then, Durga violates the Hindu ideal of womanhood.
'She is not submissive, she is not subordinated to a male deity, she
does not fulfill household duties, and she excels at what is traditionally a male function, fighting in battle. As an independent
warrior... she reverses the normal role for females and therefore
stands outside normal society.' Further, the goddess is also manifested
in lesser deities like Sitala Devi, Mansa Devi, and Naina Devi.
Kinsley (1986: 97, 201–2) notes that village goddesses are highly
ambivalent in nature, manifested in sudden outbursts of rage and
are relatively independent of male consorts. For the Sikhs of the
nineteenth century, and well into the twentieth, worship of the
goddess in her many manifestations most fully represented the
process of inversion and the element of the carnivalesque that flourished alongside the dominant tradition. An extension of this process
was also to be found in another aspect of women's practice, spirit
possession; possession allowed for a unique opportunity for the
powerless sector, especially women, to voice their dissent and to
articulate needs that were otherwise repressed; the encroachment
of normative social conventions could be transferred to supernatural
forces (Oberoi 1994: 61).

The poetics of inversion that was associated with the popular
religious realm was anathema to the male reformers of the upper
echelons of Sikh society—the learned, the distinguished, and, indubitably, the powerful.[6] It was, in essence, a finely tuned though
amorphous instrument utilized by those who could not find occasions for deviance, role reversal, and negotiation within traditional

religion. Those aspects of 'little' traditions allowed for the inversion of dominant structures were mechanisms of empowerment for the disempowered, a grasping of voice for the voiceless. Prem Chowdhry's analysis of popular cultural practices of women in Haryana is particularly helpful in this regard.

All these occasions provide opportunities for joyful gatherings of women, very often exclusive ones, to dance and sing songs drawing on the reservoir of their deeply felt and commonly experienced emotions.... In these women-centred activities women can most freely express themselves both physically and verbally and voice their criticisms as well as aspirations and self-awareness (Chowdhry 1994: 393).

Moreover, beyond offering women opportunity for dissent, they also allowed for temporary expressions of revenge against those who normally wielded power over them (Banerjee 1990: 127–79). Perhaps most significantly, many of these popular songs were specifically directed toward the sexual inadequacy of the male populace whose very self-image depended upon their virility and hyper-masculinity (Chowdhry 1994: 395).

Further, the unlettered had little awareness of or use for the communal rife increasingly shaping urban society; popular religious customs allowed for a glorious mingling of heterogeneity, fluidity, and tolerance. Fairs, festivals, visits to shrines, provided many peasants, particularly home-bound females, their initial glimpses into the wider world; pilgrimages took people outside of the village while other festive occasions brought outsiders into villages. But these gatherings also rendered another equally important service. According to Oberoi, their prime significance was the enhancement of a sense of solidarity among rural communities: 'By their very nature melas as a motley assemblage of people from different neighbourhoods, villages and regions, diluted the codes of class, caste and religious differences. In these an individual could not stand apart, he had to blend into the crowd' (1994: 189–90).

Obviously, the continuance of Tat Khalsa hegemony hinged precisely upon the suppression of the multifarious aspects of popular customs; these were referred to as superstitious, immoral, and, definitively outside the increasingly rigid boundaries of Sikhism. Yet these un-Sikh elements had a fast hold on their community. The barrage continued against 'Hindu-Sikhs' who were portrayed as fickle followers of Muslim Pirs, 'poor simple Hindu females...

with their babes and infants' to beg of the Pir to intercede for them and their children. Holi became another festival particularly maligned by the reformers. They not only condemned it as immoral, but also solicited considerations of sanitation in an attempt to curb the highly celebratory affair. Well aware of the persistence of the festivities among the masses, who had little use for the enlightened perspective of the educated elite, reformers instead turned to the British bureaucracy to officially rectify and legislate the matter (*Khalsa Advocate*, 30 September 1916; 21 March 1914).

Since women were pivotal participants in the various procedures undergirding many popular rites, they were expressly targeted in the Tat Khalsa reform endeavour. But the reformers were faced with no easy task. Particularly during marriage festivities, it was women who ensured that specific rites be carried out in an effort to thwart malevolent spirits; these interventions were perceived as crucial to conjugal happiness. Barstow described a number of these customs: the '*kangna*', a string band, in which various articles counteracted malevolent spirits, was prepared by seven women. It was then worn on the bridegroom's right wrist. A '*baddhi*' was a similarly prepared band that was tied to the groom's right ankle. Both were worn by the bride as well, but on the *left* wrist and right ankle. Another precaution taken was the wearing of a knife by the bridegroom, also believed to ward off evil spirits (Barstow 1984: 153–4).[7]

The targeting of these customs is best characterized by the moralistic writings of the day. Vir Singh's zealous attempts at reform took careful aim at the degenerate customs practised by women. Ultimately, Sikh women were responsible for the debasement of Sikhism from its original purity.

Look at yourself and see whether or not the decline of the Sikh nation is caused by your very own hands. Leaving your God and your true Gurus, you worship stones, trees, idols, tombs and saints. Forgetting Sikh religion, you rot in another religion. Turning your back on the true Gurus you teach someone else's religion to your offspring too. Your children will grow to be half baked like you—Sikh on the head, Brahmin around the neck and Muslim below the waist (cited in Oberoi 1994: 311).

Vir Singh continues with the warning: 'If you turn your face against Guru Gobind Singh and adopt devious ways of worshipping another deity, your children will be cowards like jackals, and evil will become a part of your character. You will lose all respect in the eyes of others and your honour will vanish.' Cowardice and unmanliness (Muslim below the waist...), certain outcomes of un-Sikh practices, were diametrically opposed to traditional values of manliness and courage; the recurrent themes of respect and honour on the other hand, had become the trademark catchwords with regard to the feminine ideal the Singh Sabha reformers were advocating.

The professionals responsible for the generation and transmission of the little traditions, including women, were also attacked. Fundamental to the objectives of the Tat Khalsa reformers was the displacement of the cultural mediators who instructed and performed in the myriad tasks, practices, and rites sustaining popular religion. Bards, genealogists, healers, shamans, storytellers, minstrels, and cultural bearers had been patronized throughout Punjab. Further, barbers, or *nais,* were essential players during marriage proceedings. They opened negotiations between the two families, played the role of messengers, and were seated at places of honour during wedding celebrations (Oberoi 1994: 265, 336–40). The role of the nai's wife was to accompany the newly married couple to the husband's home. These cultural transmitters, increasingly depicted as derelicts, cheats, and, ultimately, as culpable for the high costs and degenerate condition of ceremonies were to be dispensed with and replaced by properly regulated Sikh emissaries. Only 'foolish parents' entrusted marriage arrangements to 'greedy' nais, who 'affiance the poor girls to unsuitable matches'. The 'vagrant loafers in the garb of mendicants' frequenting festive occasions were also censured (*Khalsa Advocate,* 7 July 1911).

Significantly, in their attempts to intervene in the domain of the cultural mediators, Singh Sabha reformers called upon *women* to replace paid musical professionals; their gratuitous services were to be put to use during wedding, birth, and initiation celebrations. This would do away with the 'exorbitant remuneration' demanded by musicians. The replacement of musicians with properly trained females would also check the vulgarities associated with this class of professionals; music was to be restricted to the singing of sacred hymns. According to the reformed mindset, 'the teachings of our Gurus do not confine the singing of *shabads,* which are nothing other than prayers to the merciful Father, to any particular class of men. Hence, the [female] sex can also discharge this duty' (ibid., August 1910). The rising fortunes of the Singh Sabha and the decline of key mediators traditionally responsible for the transmission of culture were closely interconnected. Resolutely, Tat Khalsa initiatives continued to combat any manner and rite within the wider tradition that was deemed un-Sikh and contaminated by what they considered to be outsiders' customs. Girls' schools were called upon to train female students to render this divine service. By 1920, a necessary prerequisite to become a teacher included competence in harmonium playing, presumably to further the musical abilities of female students and thus to ensure the complete dissolution of the class of cultural mediators (*The Akali*, 18 November 1920).

Notes

1. Paul Radin uses the phrase 'ritual drama' to distinguish the performance of ritual in terms of individual admission to spheres of restricted membership. See Radin 1957: 289.
2. For the full text of the Anand Marriage Bill, see the *Khalsa Advocate*, 7 November 1908.
3. According to the Rajput princess, Brinda, who had married into the Jat Kapurthala dynasty, the five other wives of the rajah were highly incensed by this union, as were other Rajputs. The Kapurthala family, however, was elated by the match. See Brinda 1954: 112.
4. The Majithia Will case revolved around Bhagwan Kaur, the wife of the deceased Dyal Singh Majithia, challenging her late husband's will. She had claimed that Hindu laws could not apply to her husband's will. However, the Privy Council decided that 'Sikh personal law' did indeed refer to Hindu law.
5. For a discussion of the central, though highly ambivalent, position of Durga in Sikh tradition, see, Jakobsh 1986: 97, 201–2.
6. The attack on women's popular customs was certainly not confined to Sikh reformers. The Arya Samaj was also consistent in its attempts to eradicate the singing of 'indecent songs' at ceremonies and festivals. See Chowdhry 1994: 394–5.
7. The custom of the groom wearing a knife to ward off evil spirits may well be the predecessor to the current Sikh custom where the groom carries a long, ceremonial sword as he leads his bride around the sacred scripture. A paucity of historical sources dictates that this connection must remain conjecture for now. If it is at all true, it would be a most fascinating example of popular religiosity having been re-translated and rendered into 'proper' form.

SEVEN

REDEFINING THE RITUAL DRAMA
The Feminization of Ritual[1]

CREATION AND REVISION—THE FEMINIZATION OF RITUAL

In an attempt to divert women from customs that were avowedly contaminating the purity of Sikhism, Singh Sabha reformers introduced a novel agenda for including women within the heretofore exclusively male ordinances of the Tat Khalsa. The rite of initiation for males and the corresponding outward symbolism of the Khalsa had increasingly become the central signifier in the discourse around Sikh identity. For the British administration, particularly the military establishment, initiation into the Khalsa brotherhood was viewed as indispensable in the creation of the ideal Sikh fighting machine. For Tat Khalsa reformers, initiation by khande di pahul and its corresponding external signifiers were the foremost indicators of Sikh distinctiveness within the wider social and religious milieu. The Majithia Will court case along with the Anand Marriage Bill had produced a whirlwind of controversy precisely with regard to the question of Sikh identity. Traditional factions within the Sikh community became increasingly polarized with calls for delineating the definition of a true Sikh on the one hand, and equally determined appeals for the expansion of Sikh identity, on the other. The hegemonic Tat Khalsa position, benefitting greatly from the institutional support of the British Raj, asserted that only those initiated into the Khalsa in accordance with the injunctions of Guru Gobind Singh were true Sikhs. However, Udasis, Mahants, Nirankaris, and the guru lineages continued to play a significant and highly esteemed role within the Sikh tradition in the nineteenth and twentieth centuries, despite their consistent refusal to acquiesce to the dominion of the Khalsa order and its identity markers. Furthermore, a large segment of the

Sikh populace was simply indifferent to the symbolism of the Khalsa. Thus, both the rejection of the Khalsa ideal by certain segments of Sikh society as well as the indifference of others to it came to be combated by the mandate of the British army to enlist only initiated Sikhs, as well as by the agenda of the Singh Sabha reform movement. Yet many, particularly those most at ease with the amorphous nature of popular religion in Punjab continued to consider the external markers and initiation of the Khalsa as extraneous to their everyday existence.

But the Tat Khalsa struggle to promote a purified Sikh identity, patently spurred on by religious conviction but also by political considerations, hinged precisely upon the unique symbolic prescription furnished by the institution of the Khalsa. To advance their objectives, the Tat Khalsa utilized varied but highly effective methods of persuasion. Singh Sabha trained preachers, educational objectives, and literature produced under the aegis of the Tat Khalsa invoked the once glorious tradition of the Khalsa and directed public attention to the benefits of adherence to authentic Sikh rahit under the British. With regard to the advantages inherent in the wearing of long hair for males, reformers ingeniously turned to images of 'true manliness' borrowed from a startling variety of sources. Heroes of yore, including the invincible Solomon of Hebraic glory, were invoked in support of Guru Gobind Singh's injunctions for hair (*Khalsa Advocate*, 1 May 1915). Tat Khalsa reformers also attempted to challenge the sway of popular religious practices and superstitious customs that were deemed as alien to Sikhism in its true and unadulterated form. Having little effect on the wider populace, Singh Sabha reformers initially directed their attention towards the womenfolk within their own circles. In an attempt to distance the refined from the illiterate masses, popular rites were ridiculed as the foolishness of the ignorant and uneducated. Within the new patriarchy, the correspondent new woman was projected as the reverse of the common, vulgar, quarrelsome woman who was utterly deficient of superior moral sense (Chatterjee 1990: 244–5). For Sikh reformers, the regenerated, woman was contrasted with the bulk of the populace whose lives were ordered by attempts to align themselves with the natural world and the appeasement of malevolent gods and goddesses. Only with the eradication of irrational and what were presented as essentially absurd practices, at least among the educated elite, would the Sikhs as a nation ascend the steep slope of the civilizing enterprise.

Satisfied that Sikh males were well established within the social and religious milieu through traditional injunctions clearly directed towards them, the self-appointed guardians of the Khalsa ideal went to great lengths to delineate an appropriate place for women within the Khalsa order. Central to their objectives was the replacement of 'superstitious' women's rituals with proper Sikh rites. To achieve this end Singh Sabha reformers were assiduous in charting out new territory for Sikh women. Though citing selective examples of heroic women in Sikh history and the inherent equality of men and women within Sikh sacred scriptures as foundational to their efforts, Tat Khalsa reformers were nonetheless faced with an abstruse dilemma. For tradition was either conspicuously silent or overtly prohibitive with regard to the involvement of women within the Khalsa brotherhood. As already noted women were clearly not included in the normative injunctions for the Khalsa brotherhood outlined in the earliest Sikh texts. Most particularly, women were unequivocally excluded from the pivotal rite of khande di pahul. It is however conceivable that the rite of *charn-amrit*, the earliest symbol of devotion to the guru among the Sikhs that was later transformed into the ritual charan di pahul was viewed as an adequate vehicle of initiation for women's circumscribed entry into the Khalsa fold.[2] Nonetheless, it is clear that even if women were given partial entry into the order of the Khalsa, their status remained subordinate to the Khalsa ideal that required initiation by khande di pahul and the wearing of arms. For given that the highly acclaimed external signifiers of the Khalsa revolved around traditional male emblems, namely those of weaponry, females customarily excluded from martial associations were naturally affixed in an ancillary position within the Khalsa order. In essence, the ideal was inaccessible to women.

Needless to say, Tat Khalsa reformers were in a difficult position; the tradition that was so congenial to the male ideal was singularly unobliging with regard to females within the Khalsa order, at least in terms of identity markers and rituals. Conceptually, both women and men were to be embraced, yet tradition offered scant latitude for recognizing women as equal partners within the order. Novel interpretations of history and satisfactory references were thus pivotal in providing historicity and the rationale for female initiation. Fortuitously, Singh Sabha reformers were able to turn to *Prem Sumarg* with its claims of antiquity, also endorsed by the Namdhari movement. Initiation, according to the *Sumarg*, was *as* essential for women as it was for men (Singh, R. 1965: 25);[3] the rite was also to be identical for males and females (Grewal 1996: 170). However, the emphasis on women's initiation is one of the most significant indicators of the *Prem Sumarg*'s composition during the mid-to-late nineteenth century, as opposed to its claims of antiquity. Early sources were either troublingly silent on the issue or, in the case of the earliest text, the *Chaupa Singh Rahit-nama*, were unequivocal in insisting that women *not* be initiated by khande di pahul. Nonetheless, validated through the apparent antiquity of *Prem Sumarg*, Tat Khalsa reformers made pointed references to the 'fallen' state of Sikhism as ultimately responsible for the dearth of properly initiated women within their ranks. However, factions within the reform endeavour suspended the possibility of a unified resolution to the question of female initiation. As opposed to the highly uniform particularities of the rite for men, the specifics of the female rite remained indeterminate and open to a myriad interpretations and variations. The Bedi camp advocated the use of a single-edged sword in stirring the sweetened water for women, as opposed to the double-edged sword traditionally reserved for male initiation. Uttam Singh (1884: 68) recorded still other innovations, including a significantly shortened roster of scriptural readings in comparison to the prescribed readings for male initiates to accompany the preparation of amrit for the rite. While Uttam Singh did not specify which groups in particular advocated these revisions, they are similar to those espoused by Baba Khem Singh Bedi (Vahiria, cited in Falcon 1896: 58).[4]

Further, instead of the 5 Ks prescribed for male initiates, just a small kirpan (dagger) or an iron bangle was to be worn by females. However, both were to wear white clothes and the kachh (breeches). Nonetheless, there was little uniformity among the various groups advocating some form of initiation for women. Among the Nihangs, both women and men were initiated and required to maintain the full injunctions for weaponry prescribed by Guru Gobind Singh (Uttam Singh 1884: 68). By far the most radical voice, Babu Teja Singh Overseer, the leader of the Bhasaur Singh Sabha, insisted that not only were women to receive initiation, they were also to don saffron-coloured turbans—a significant injunction, given the connection of saffron to the Brahminical order and the decided aversion to it among Sikhs. Nonetheless, this became a pivotal mandate of the Babu; women who did not wear the traditional male headgear were refused initiation into the Khalsa (Barrier 1970: xvi–xxvii). Although not willing to fully endorse the radical initiatives of Babu Teja Singh Overseer, the *Khalsa Advocate* described the women of the Bhasaur group 'in their picturesque attire with turbans as their headgear.... Their distinctly manly carriage and unfeminine behaviour were so striking that they irresistibly carried the mind back to the times when Sikh ladies stood shoulder to shoulder with their brothers and husbands in the fields of battle' (29 April 1910). However, the traditional Sikh orthodoxy, represented by Sanatan Sikhs and Baba Khem Singh Bedi, were vehemently opposed to this development. They also carried considerable clout within the central holy sites of Punjab. Pujaris of the Golden Temple hindered female students of Bhasaur from performing kirtan at this most revered of shrines (*The Akali*, 11 June 1920).

The most authoritative voice of orthodoxy for the general Sikh populace was that of Baba Khem Singh Bedi in the late nineteenth century. According to Lakshman Singh, Khem Singh Bedi wielded such power over the populace that his followers, after the rupture between the Amritsar and Lahore Singh Sabhas and the ascension of the Lahore group, boycotted the movement in its entirety (Singh, G. 1965: 104). Similar to the Sanatan Sikhism espoused by Bedi, regulations outlining initiation allowed for varied and manifold interpretations of the rite. He conceded the need for women to be initiated into the Khalsa order but insisted that that there be significant divergence between the actual form of initiation for women and men. He advocated, for instance, the use of a different sword for females. If a double-edged sword *was* used for women's initiation, the handle, as opposed to the blade, was to be employed to stir the water. If the blade was used, distinctions were to be made between the back and the front of the weapon, the former applying to women. In addition, sugar, as opposed to the traditional ingredient of *patasia*, was to be used for the rite for women (Vihiria, cited in Falcon 1896: 58).

Certainly, Bedi's acknowledgement of the need for transforming female initiation rites was significant. Falcon had observed that the rite of charan di pahul had long been used for birth observances as a general initiation into the faith. When a child was born, the feet of the *manji*, or the stand upon which the Granth was kept, were to be washed. The water was to be caught in an iron cup, mixed with patasia for a boy child and sugar for the girl, and fed to the infant. For boys, specific shabads, or hymns, were to be read eleven times upon which the names of the ten gurus were to be recited. This was to be followed by the prayer 'O god, by thy will a man Sikh has been born; may he be a doer of good works, be healthy and skilled in arms, pious, maintaining the Khalsa religion; in all things worthy of his ancestors, and continue the worship of the Guru.' For a girl child, the following prayer was said: 'O God, by thy will a girl child has been born, may she be good, pious, free from all wicked deeds, chaste, modest, sensible and charitable.' The difference between girls' and boys' rites, not only in the actual form but also in the different invocations, points to the ingrained differentiation that was made between females and males. Prayers for boys included references to wearing arms; modesty, piety, sensibility, and charity were the attributes upheld for girls. Not surprisingly, the rahit accompanying women's initiation into the Khalsa order *also* reflected orthodox attitudes towards women. A woman, according to the *Sanskar Bagh* (Vihiria 1894, cited in Falcon 1896: 56–9), was

to consider her husband as her god and obey his orders, keep him cheerful, not to associate with other men, to pay respect to her father-in-law and mother-in-law, not to wear blue pajamas, not to join in the women's mourning ceremony (of beating the breast and wailing), to give alms, not to worship Muhammadan or Hindu shrines, etc., to be modest and worship one God.

The injunction against wearing blue stemmed from Guru Gobind Singh's earliest pronouncement that members of the Khalsa order (men) were to wear blue garb. Its continued emphasis for women is particularly fascinating given Falcon's observation that this custom for males had fallen into disuse, save with the Nihangs. As a direct indicator of the theology of difference between males and females since the inauguration of the Khalsa, it is significant that the insistence on this distinction for women continued well into the twentieth century.

Gilbert Lewis, an anthropologist, has attempted to explicate the parameters of that which constitutes ritual. According to him, ritual is exceedingly difficult to define in that its identification is inextricably bound not only to specific expressions and codes, but also to the ability to interpret what is being communicated. Ritual in essence can be likened to a form of language, art, performance, or a specific code of conduct. Yet not just any formula of communication, action, or behaviour can be construed as ritual; Lewis delineates what is essential to ritual:

To say the action is prescribed, that there is some ruling about the circumstances for its performance, moves closer to an answer.... What is always explicit about ritual, and recognized by those who perform it, is that aspect of it which states who should do what and when. It is practical. It guides action. And phrases like 'prescribed routine', 'standardized behaviour', 'behaviour with incongruous rigidity', which appear in most of the definitions given... refer to this.... The explanations for what is done may be clear, or complicated or uncertain, or multiple, or forgotten: but what to do is clear.

Further, Lewis notes that to conform to a particularized ritual is to acknowledge that one is part of the specific group for whom the ritual has meaning (1988: 6–8, 11–12). By implication then, the *lack* of conformity to a particularized ritual would attest to restrictions placed upon comprehensive membership within the specific group. The argument can be extended to a *segment* of the group as well as to individuals. It is useful in coming to an understanding of the mechanisms of gender-based inclusion and exclusion in the context of group formation and identity. In particular, the parameters outlined by Lewis are helpful in understanding the process of ritual formation put forth by the Tat Khalsa reformers within the context of the initiation rite. Clearly, in comparison to the highly standardized routine of initiation for males, female initiation, even among those of the reformed Singh Sabha mindset (the Amritsar and Lahore Singh Sabhas had formed an uneasy truce) was *not* uniform, precise, or explicit. The lack of prescribed routine for women's initiation into the Khalsa order becomes significant in the light of the highly acclaimed assertions of inherent equality of both men and women within the reformed world view that the Tat Khalsa was attempting to restore.

Lewis' clarification of the explicit separation between men and women in terms of ritual identity among the Gnau is particularly helpful in understanding this divergence in ritual behaviour among the Sikhs. Among the Gnau, children and women were not granted the equality or the responsibility that was accorded men. While Lewis maintains that there are a variety of influences shaping these gender differences, 'rites have a special place in creating it and providing impressive direction to male aspiration. By excluding others, making some knowledge and experience esoteric, they find a justification for their capacity to act in these matters and enhance the value of what they do' (1988: 167).[5] In essence, *control* of ritual knowledge and behaviour allowed for the creation of a tightly bonded brotherhood equipped to face the traditionally 'masculine' realities of war, disputes, and defense. Similarly, the continued divergence between male and female initiation in Sikh reform stemmed from a perceived need to control women's access to full-fledged and equal membership within the Khalsa order. For the militaristic, hypermasculine roots of the Sikh initiation rite were pervasive, and women had had no place within the order at its time of inception or during its subsequent development. The propensity to exclude them from the consummate 'brotherhood' continued well into the twentieth century.

Nonetheless, the reformers were aware of the incongruity between their interpretations and postulations of Sikh tenets and the practices and attitudes upholding the secondary ritual identity of women. Consequently, a committee was formed at the annual meeting of the Singh Sabha in Ferozepur in 1900 to come to a consensus on the matter of female initiation practices. A motion was passed that the form of initiation to be endorsed by the Tat Khalsa was to be identical for both women and men (see Dhillon 1995: 134). Thus, a carefully prescribed routine for women's initiation came to be ratified, at least for a small sector of the Sikh populace. Not surprisingly, the variance of female baptismal arrangements already well established came to be presented as indicative of the degenerate state of contemporary Sikhism. Increasingly, the use of a single-edged sword for women's initiation came to be viewed as a deviant development. At a meeting of the Punjab Historical Society in 1914, the tradition of different initiation practices for men and women was presented as a corrupt and *later* development. Nonetheless, despite the valiant efforts of these reformers, initiation for women, particularly by the double-edged sword, continued to be the exception rather than the norm. The *Khalsa Dharam Shastar*, an influential manual compiled under the auspices of the head of the Anandpur Soudhi Guru lineage, continued to insist that women were not entitled identical initiation practices because women were not warriors; the rite of khande di pahul was inaugurated to produce a warring race of men (Singh, S.R.N. 1908: 122–3). Pandit Sheo Narain (in *Khalsa Advocate*, 14 March) noted as late as 1914 that the practice of women's initiation by the double-edged sword was not widely observed. Barstow substantiates this claim in the 1928 edition of *Handbook on Sikhs* (pg. 228), where he specifically altered significant portions of the earlier edition to reflect the transformations that had taken place in Sikh society. He observed that in 'mingling the sugar and water for women, a one edged, and not a two edged dagger is used.' This situation did not bode well for the Tat Khalsa as the new guardians of the Sikh faith. Thus, when female initiations by the double-edged sword did take place, they were often of the mass variety and thus highly publicized. Not surprisingly, their occurrence was acclaimed as indicative of reform achievements in alleviating the status of Sikh women (*Khalsa Advocate*, 29 April, 15 August 1910).

By and large, however, the initiation of women into the Khalsa order was not deemed nearly as imperative as it was for men, even among the Tat Khalsa reformers. Harnam Kaur only received initiation a number of years after playing an important role in furthering Singh Sabha ideology. While she toiled for years for the Singh Sabha educational enterprise *without* having been initiated, it would have been inconceivable for her husband Bhai Thakat Singh not to have received pahul. By 1920, however, the situation had dramatically changed. While Singh Sabha educational institutions were still desperate for women teachers, by this time requirements for female applicants included proper initiation into the Khalsa order. Still, contrary to Harnam Kaur's experience, her biography unequivocally maintained that baptism by khande di pahul for women was imperative. Bhai Surat Singh insisted that the original and uncorrupted rite of initiation could be traced directly to Guru Gobind Singh (1909: 30–7). This position adeptly furthered the central Singh Sabha claim that Tat Khalsa reform initiatives were simply a *revival* of the basic tenets of equality integral to the Sikh tradition, that the practical manifestation of true Sikh doctrines had fallen into disuse given its contemporary state of debasement.

Bhai Vir Singh also addressed this issue through his heroine, Sundri. Only upon her 'proper' initiation was Sundri equipped to face the hardships awaiting her. Moreover, her gesture of devotion had the desired effect of mobilizing the entire community around her to loftier heights of purpose. According to Vir Singh, '[t]his was the purity and excellence of character which the Guru had taught to the Sikhs. That is the reason why the community, overcome by the love of the Guru was ready to sacrifice itself.' Sundri's life, and especially her initiation, led to her being pronounced as a holy goddess and held up as the role model for contemporary women to emulate. However, not content to merely proffer to his readers a novel vision of the effects of proper Sikh rituals, Bhai Vir Singh seized the opportunity to denounce all manner of custom, habit, and dress of his female contemporaries:

O Sikh maidens of today.... Just look at yourselves and find out for yourself if you are damaging the Sikh community or not! You have abandoned the *Amrit* and regarded the left-overs of robed Sadhus as part of Sikh religion.... You have given up the recitation of Sri Guru Granth Sahib and disgraced your intellect by wearing threads said to be sanctified by *mantras* (talismans). You have become the butt of ridicule by replacing clean and thick garments with thin and flashy dresses.... The true and unique Immortal God has been abandoned and you have taken the road to hell and persuaded your husbands and sons to follow the same foolish path. Just reflect for a moment on the calamities faced by Sundri.... Remove the confusion from your mind and become pure Sikh women (Singh, B.V. 1988: 99–100).

However, still not satisfied with the slow pace of disassociation between Sikh women and their Hindu counterparts, Tat Khalsa reformers continued their attempts to further extricate their females from the miscellany of identities that shaped Sikh women's existence. Within this context, reforms also began to address the patterns of female nomenclature that had traditionally served to distinguish Punjabi female co-religionists.

WHAT'S IN A NAME? CIRCUMSCRIBING SIKH FEMALE NOMENCLATURE

Early sources of the injunctions of Guru Gobind Singh for his newly founded order not only asserted that members of the Khalsa brotherhood were to be recognized by outward symbolism and garb, they also placed considerable emphasis on the naming practices to be followed within the Khalsa. Those installed into the brotherhood were to adopt the surname 'Singh' and were strictly prohibited from omitting this appellation (McLeod 1987: 35). Injunctions regarding Khalsa naming conventions focused exclusively on males, wholly neglecting naming specifications for Sikh women. Nonetheless, a tradition whose origin is highly obscure existed among a significant proportion of the Sikh populace, namely, the appellation 'Kaur' for women. As the term 'Singh', meaning lion, was adopted from the militant Rajputs, so too was Kaur. The term was a derivative of the Rajput term 'kanwar', customarily defined as 'prince' or 'bachelor' (see Turner 1966).[6] Guru Gobind Singh, highly conscious of his lineage, made a clear connection with the new order and Kshatriya combative obligations (Grewal and Bal 1987: 119). Things are not nearly as clear regarding Kaur among the Sikhs.

Early sources indicate that the name was given to both females and males in Punjab. The appellation appears in both the *Adi Granth* and the *Dasam Granth*, the former using it in its traditional sense of 'prince' (*Adi Granth*: 417), the latter referring to a woman's name during the time of Guru Gobind Singh (*Dasam Granth*: 1053).[7] Given the paucity of sources for Punjabi patterns of nomenclature during the early and late guru periods, it is difficult to move beyond a mere verification of its usage for both males and females. It must also be noted that women, apart from those playing a central role in the formation of the Sikh panth or those of the upper echelons of society, were seldom named in Sikh historical sources. Even among the guru lineages there is considerable confusion regarding women's names. Questions regarding the application and incentive for the naming practices among the early Sikhs can at best be speculative. It does appear that some variances in the usage of the name Kaur emerged during the seventeenth and nineteenth centuries between the Jats and Khatris of Punjab. 'Kaur' continued to be used by both males and females of the Khatri caste, but by the eighteenth century exclusively referred to females among the Jats. Ganesh Das' *Char Bagh-i-Panjab*, completed in 1849, made repeated references to a number of both Sikh and Hindu males with the name Kaur. The work is by and large focused on the Khatris of Punjab before the rule of the British. In a number of instances the name appears to be used as 'prince', or it appears as a second name within Udasi circles. Udasis, similar to the bulk of the Khatri population, refused to heed Guru Gobind's invitation to join the Khalsa brotherhood (Grewal and Banga 1975). Further, a central figure in the formation of the Khalsa order during the time of Guru Gobind Singh was Ram Kaur, a scribe and close associate of the guru. After his initiation he was renamed Gurbakhsh Singh. The records are also inconsistent with regard to Khatri females. For most Khatri Sikhs, at least among the upper echelons,

'Devi' or 'Devan', the name customarily given to Hindu females, continued to be utilized as the middle or last name. One of the wives of Guru Gobind Singh, also of the Khatri lineage, was Sahib Devan. On the other hand, the Khatri wife of Guru Gobind Singh's arch-rival was known as Punjab Kaur. The scant sources available give little indication of uniform practices in this regard. It is most likely that women for the most part were only given a single name.

The appropriation of highly specific Rajput distinctions such as 'Kanwar/Kaur' and 'Singh' can most likely be attributed to active attempts by specific segments of the Sikh population during the mid-to-late guru period to Rajputize their identity.[8] The process of Rajputization becomes intelligible given the elevation of the once lowly Jat to a hegemonic position within the social hierarchy of the Sikh panth, still stigmatized, however, within the wider social arena. Proverbs testify to the prevailing negative attitudes about them. Jats continued to be presented as crude and averse to education: 'What does a Jat know about dainties? He might as well be eating toad-stools'; 'A scythe has no sheath, a Jat has no learning'. They also attest to traditional attitudes of superiority held by the Jat: 'The Jat stood on his corn-heap and called out to the King's elephant drivers, "Hi there, what will you take for those little donkeys?"' (Risley 1915: 309–10). By the nineteenth and twentieth centuries, British assumptions of the 'manliness' of both the Rajputs and the Jats had accomplished a great deal; at least for the colonial masters, the heritage of the Jats and the Rajputs were inextricably intertwined. According to Ibbetson, whatever the original lineage of both groups 'the two now form a common stock, the distinction between the Jat and the Rajput being social rather than ethnic' (1993: 100–1). The common naming practices of the Jats and Rajputs presumably benefited colonial claims regarding this kinship.

Certainly the Jat populace had formed the bulk of the new order put in place by Guru Gobind Singh; Jat males en masse followed the injunction to take on the appellation 'Singh'. As already noted, Jats, far more than the highly established and traditionally respected Khatris, were in need of signifiers that connoted their rise in the social hierarchical patterns of the day. While Khatris were content to stay with the established customs of nomenclature, traditional biases against the inferior social position of the Jats were compelling incentives to consolidate their hegemonic position within Sikh and Punjabi society at large. The taking on of distinctive and highly esteemed Rajput names aided this process. In some cases, Rajputs, highly fastidious in preserving their esteemed lineage, retained their contempt toward the lowly Jats.

It is entirely plausible that with the consolidation of Rajput martial identity through the inauguration of the Khalsa, particularly with the adoption of 'Singh' for Jat males, the Rajput name Kanwar, and its Punjabi equivalent Kaur, was embraced as its natural ancillary for females. By the eighteenth century this was particularly the case among women of the newly established aristocracy, the leadership of the misldoms (confederacies) that were largely dominated by Jat leadership (Grewal 1990: 82–100). Numerous records indicate that women of Sikh royalty were invariably given two names, the second being Kaur (Latif 1994: 334). The usage of Kaur for Sikh princesses, given the term's implications of royalty, is highly understandable among the newly established Sikh nobility of Punjab. The naming practices of the elite however offer little insight into the patterns of nomenclature among the masses. While Kaur among the females of Sikh royalty was eventually embraced by the wider populace as well, it is highly conceivable that single names were more common than dual names for women before and after the eighteenth century. Earlier, this had been the case in Guru Gobind Singh's first two wives, Sundri and Jito, and for the majority of the women of the guru lineage. In the mid-nineteenth century, even among the elite of Punjab, many women had only single names.

Unfortunately, the earliest attempt made to elucidate the linguistic conventions of Punjab offers little guidance or insight in this regard. The first dictionary of the Punjabi language published in 1854 by the Lodhiana Mission retained the princely definition of 'kaur' and its alternate reference to a *male* child (Janver 1987: 109). Although evidence points to the signifier being utilized by both Sikh males and females throughout the eighteenth and early nineteenth centuries, this inaugural *Dictionary of the Punjabi Language* makes no reference to its usage by Sikhs in particular. Nor does it refer to specific cultural conventions of the term as an addendum for females. The dictionary of Bhai Maya Singh of 1895 also refers exclusively to its masculine and princely delineation (Singh, B.M. 1992). Singh's definition is indeed surprising, for by the late nineteenth century British accounts indicate that the usage of the appellation Kaur for males had ceased and it was henceforth exclusively a feminine signifier (Rose 1990: 551). Interestingly, while Kaur as a middle or last name for males ceased to be in use by the late nineteenth century, it continued to be employed spuriously as a *first* name. The famed compiler of the *Guru Shabad Ratan Prakash* a thesaurus of the *Adi Granth* published in 1923, underwent a name change from Puran Singh to Kaur Singh upon his initiation in 1906. He was later known as Akali Kaur Singh Nihang (see Singh, H. 1996: 463–4).

Needless to say, the scant sources available with regard to the appellation Kaur, as well as its wide though inconsistent application throughout Sikh history, make an analysis of the normative naming practices among Sikh females difficult. For even the increasingly authoritative *Prem Sumarg* offers little insight in this regard; it does, however, point to the variability of female naming patterns among the Sikhs. Completely omitting mention of Kaur, females after being initiated into the Khalsa order were instructed to add the epithet 'Devi' alongside their given name (Singh, R. 1965: 25). Given these obvious variances, certitude can only be replaced by speculation—at *best* until the beginning of the twentieth century, Kaur as a feminine epithet can only be understood as indicative of a diffuse *cultural* identity but as having no definitive *religious* signification. To return to Gilbert Lewis' delineation of ritual as prescribed behaviour, the designation Kaur had no standardized import in a ritualistic sense. The appellation Singh on the other hand was a specifically prescribed injunction and consequential to the rite of initiation; it was also central to the identity formation of Khalsa Sikhs at large. However, by the mid-nineteenth century the epithet 'Singhni' had become the linguistic complement to Singh (Janver 1987: 55–6). The term's linguistic correspondence must be stressed given the appellation's apparent lack of ritual signification. While for males the name Singh connoted initiation into the Khalsa, the position of women in the order remains obscure. This is particularly the case given the explicit mandate in earlier textual sources not to administer khande di pahul to the female sex.

The diversity of women's naming patterns continued well beyond the nineteenth century. Names of prominent women within the Singh Sabha fold who collected funds for the victims of the Kangra Valley earthquake attest to this variance. Of the ninety-nine names of women listed in the *Khalsa Advocate* article of 5 May 1905, less than half of the entries included the appellation Kaur. The majority was reported as having only one name; others were denoted as

Singhni; others had two names, excluding Kaur, including Dai or Devi. Lakshman Singh sheds some light on the naming patterns of women among the traditional religious orthodox and aristocratic echelons of the Sikhs. Names listed by him include Dai and Devi, particularly among the guru lineages; few women were known as Kaur. For instance, Lakshman Singh's grandmother was known as Gulab Devi; the grandfather's name was Sirdar Karam Singh (Singh, G. 1965: 9–12, 239). Their names attest to the fluidity of identity between Sikhs and Hindus in the late nineteenth and early twentieth centuries.

There were, however, distinct rumblings of a shift in the significance of female naming patterns among the Tat Khalsa reformers. The impetus for this change is not difficult to appreciate or understand. While Hindu and Muslim women of Punjab were securely distinguished by appellations distinct to their communities, Devi and Begum respectively, Sikh female identity remained indistinct and multifarious.

Lakshman Singh tells of an encounter that brings these distinctions to light. The incident revolved around the language issue in Punjabi schools; in this case, whether Sanskrit or Persian was to be taught. Bhagat Lakshman Singh was an avid promoter of Sanskrit and took it upon himself to convert the students to his cause. Addressing a Hindu boy, Lakshman Singh queried of him:

[w]ill you give up Persian and take up Sanskrit instead?' 'Why should I? I am not going to turn into a Brahman priest', was the reply. I then turned to a Musalman child, 'Kaka', repeated I, 'Will you take up Sanskrit in place of Persian?' 'Am I a Hindu?' was this child's reply. I again turned to the previous Hindu child and said, 'Are you a Musalman, my boy? Yes you are. You see you are learning a language of the Musalmans'. And, added I, 'Is your mother's name Bibi Jamalo or Begam Bano?' 'No, my mother's name is Bishen Devi' was the angry reply... (ibid.: 110–11).

Albeit barely discernible, opposition to the ambiguous nature of Sikh female nomenclature was also beginning to make an impression on the Sikh literary horizon. Bhai Vir Singh's novel, *Sundri*, brings what would appear to be an inconsequential issue to the fore. For Surasti's (Sundri's earlier name) initiation into the Khalsa fold by the amrit ceremony was accompanied by a change of name; henceforth she was to be known as Sunder *Kaur*, and popularly as Sundri (Singh, B.V. 1988: 26).

Another seemingly innocuous though important indicator of this shift can be traced to Bhai Kahn Singh Nabha's celebrated tract, *Ham Hindu Nahin* (We Are Not Hindus). According to Kahn Singh, Guru Gobind Singh pronounced himself the father and Sahib *Kaur*, not *Devan*, as the mother of the Khalsa (Nabha 1914 in McLeod 1990: 134–6). The notion of Sahib Devan as the mother of the Khalsa warrants explication. In an attempt to come to terms with the tenth guru's practice of polygamy, tradition notes that while Sahib Devan was offered to the guru in marriage, she was rejected by Gobind Singh on the grounds of his having relinquished family life. Her father, however, agreed to a life of service to the guru for his daughter without conjugal privileges; it was thus that a marriage took place between them. One day, as she was shampooing her husband, she conceded that as the guru's two previous wives had borne sons, she too desired sons. The guru replied, 'I will give thee a son who will abide for ever. I will put the whole Khalsa into thy lap' (Macauliffe 1990 Vol V: 143–4). It is thus that Sahib Devan is known as the mother of the Khalsa. Whether Sahib Devan actually remained a virgin or whether she was simply unable to bear children is open to conjecture. Certainly the tradition of the virgin mother of the Khalsa has remained dominant in Sikh historiography.

The context of Kahn Singh's change in nomenclature, from Sahib Devan to Sahib Kaur, is highly significant. For, according to the world view of the Tat Khalsa, Sikhs were not Hindus; Hindu names, particularly those associated with the inauguration of the Khalsa, necessitated transformation into a form acceptable to the increasingly defined ideology of the Tat Khalsa. This purging of Hinduized names can best be understood within the context of the larger issue of Singh Sabha reformers' attempts to distance themselves from the Hindu aspects within their own history. The earliest Sikh accounts, known as *gurbilas* literature, consistently maintained that Guru Gobind Singh not only paid homage to Goddess Devi, but that she also played a central role in the actual creation of the Khalsa. The gurbilas were similar to the janam-sakhis in that more than being an accurate statement of historical events, they clearly offered testimony to the beliefs and world views of their writers. Goddess Devi was elemental to this genre in the eighteenth and nineteenth centuries. The eighteenth century narrative, *Gurbilas Daswin Patshahi*, clearly notes that Kalika or Devi, was the mother of the new order (see Sukha Singh 1912, cited in Hans 1980: 427).[9]

Another important account is Sainapati's *Sri Gur Sobha*, the earliest example of gurbilas writings. Sahib Devan received no mention by Sainapati in connection with the creation of the Khalsa order. The author did, however, present the earliest perspective on the parentage of the Khalsa. For Sainapati, Guru Gobind Singh was *both* the father and the mother of the Khalsa (see Grewal 1982: 79–80).

By the mid-eighteenth century there was a definitive shift in the parenthood of the Khalsa; Ratan Singh Bhangu, commissioned by the British army to write a history of the Sikhs, sanctioned Mata Sahib Devan and Guru Gobind Singh as the mother and father of the Khalsa (Bhangu 1939: 40–2). The development of Mata Sahib Devan as the mother of the Khalsa, as opposed to Goddess Devi, was likely to have been influenced by Bhangu's attempt to establish the distinct nature of the Sikhs from the wider Hindu community for his British audience. The *Gurbilas Patshahi 10*, attributed to Koer Singh in the mid-eighteenth century, attests to Bhangu's tailoring of historiography; Koer Singh on the other hand, stayed within the traditional rendering of accounts by maintaining that the Devi played a central role in the development of the Khalsa. Moreover, the goddess is presented as responsible for its very creation (in Hans 1988: 267). Certainly, Devi as mata of the Khalsa would have made the distinction Bhangu was attempting to make highly untenable. It is likely that for similar reasons Devi had also disappeared at the time of the amrit preparation in *Prem Sumarg*.

This development culminated with the Singh Sabha reformers in the late nineteenth and early twentieth centuries: the goddess could have no place within the world view the Tat Khalsa was valiantly attempting to contour, particularly in the light of the Singh Sabha objectives to conclusively establish Sikh distinctiveness from the Hindu community. Earlier claims regarding Guru Gobind Singh's homage to the goddess were met with calls for pragmatism. '[W]ho out of the bedlam would ever believe that the Great Guru approached a goddess for help in founding a religion inculcating the worship of none else but God, and condemning that of even Durga whom the Guru is alleged to have addressed, adored and worshipped?' (*Khalsa Advocate*, 19 August 1916). Albeit inconsistently, attempts to establish distinct Sikh patterns of nomenclature for women continued. For instance, while Vir Singh clearly connected the appellation Kaur with his heroine's baptismal rite, he nonetheless maintained Sahib Devan's original name as the mother of the Khalsa

(Singh, B.V. 1988: 26). Needless to say, the shift from Sahib Devan to Sahib Kaur was by the end of the nineteenth and beginning of the twentieth century in its rudimentary stage and thus inconsistently endorsed. Interestingly, on this particular point there was no invoking of *Prem Sumarg*; it had called for Sikh women to take on the name Devi instead. The ability to pick and choose specific portions of 'authentic' Sikh sources remained a hallmark of the Singh Sabha movement, as they attempted to establish conclusive identity markers for Sikh women in the face of the widely varied historical sources at their disposal. By 1909, enthusiastic attempts to rewrite history, Sikh women's history in particular, accompanied this seemingly innocuous transformation of Sahib Devan's name and the eradication of Durga among Tat Khalsa writings. In fact, Singh Sabha claims of females' unobstructed inclusion within the order of the Khalsa necessitated novel versions of history. Max Arthur Macauliffe, the celebrated British historian, was particularly obliging in this regard. Bypassing all early sources, Macauliffe noted that the third wife of Guru Gobind Singh, Sahib Devan, was baptized by Guru Gobind Singh, and subsequently renamed Sahib Kaur (Macauliffe 1990 Vol. V: 143–4).[10]

Macauliffe had devoted fifteen years to his magnum opus, *The Sikh Religion*. His predecessor, Earnest Trumpp, who had been charged by the government with the enormous task of writing a categorical summary of Sikh history and theology, had come under a great deal of fire from within the Sikh community due to his interpretations of Sikh sacred scripture and religion. Macauliffe was determined to bypass the opprobrium of the Sikhs. Relying upon interpretations from prominent individuals within the Singh Sabha movement such as Bhai Khan Singh of Nabha, Macauliffe ensured that his writings were approved of by the new leaders of the Sikh community. Drafts of his work were submitted to a special committee established by the Khalsa Diwan of Amritsar. According to N. Gerald Barrier, the final product must thus be viewed as a series 'of compromises and a composite of documents' (1978: 176–7). Certainly the influence of Sikh reform initiatives were palpable, given an earlier assertion by Macauliffe that Guru Gobind Singh had *not* included women in his directives for initiation (1881: 162). Proponents of the Singh Sabha reform movement, insisting that women were initiated as early as 1750, objected to these observations. Persuaded by the reformers, Macauliffe rewrote this particular chapter of Sikh history. He also took great pains to refute sources claiming that Guru Gobind Singh had three wives (1990 Vol. V: 143–4); Sundri was declared to be an alternate name for Jito, and not the name of a third wife.[11] Sahib Devan, as already noted, was presented as the guru's wife in name only. Many reformed Sikhs had difficulty with the apparent polygamous marriage practices of the tenth guru. Yet two of the guru's wives wrote hukamnamas to assemblies of Sikhs in the early eighteenth century (Kaur, G. 1988: 109). They pertained specifically to offerings to be made for the community kitchen and fostering fraternal causes. Kesar Singh Chhibber, responsible for the earliest major writing of the eighteenth century after Sainapati's *Gur Sobha*, also referenced a fascinating dimension to the extant information available. Mata Sahib Devan, according to his *Bansavlinama*, was the guru of the Sikhs for twenty-five years after the death of Guru Gobind Singh (cited in Hans 1988: 285). Further, as already noted, a pivotal work of the mid-nineteenth century was Ratan Singh Bhangu's *Prachin Panth Prakash*, written between the time of Maharajah Ranjit Singh's death and British conquest of Punjab. Again, Bhangu is clear that Gobind Singh had more than one wife (1939: 1789–90).

The perceived need to adjust the number of the wives of Guru Gobind Singh is indicative of the systematic attempts made by the Singh Sabha reformers to purge spurious aspects of Sikh history not conducive to the highly refined Tat Khalsa mindset. It was thus important that the beau ideal of the Sikhs, Guru Gobind Singh, be represented as having only one wife. Nonetheless, reformers could not deny that polygamy existed within their history. Out-workings of this concession can be found within the contemporary and authoritative Sikh Code of Conduct, which stipulates that Sikhs *generally* are not to have more than one wife [italics mine] (see Dharam Parchar Committee 1994: 29).

REDEFINING THE SIKH CODE OF CONDUCT IN THE TWENTIETH CENTURY

Given the variety of claims, doctrines, and attitudes in the development of the Sikh tradition, a prominent group of Singh Sabha reformers met in 1910 to take issue with the existing Sikh codes of conduct stemming from the eighteenth and nineteenth centuries. The discrepant injunctions found within these codes were deemed as having been tainted by Hindu tradition. The objectives of this group of notables were primarily focused on eliminating the diversity of practices among the Sikhs by formulating an undefiled Sikh code that concurred with the reformed world view of the early twentieth century. As noted earlier, Baba Khem Singh Bedi had already produced such a code in the late nineteenth century; the *Sanskar Bagh*, highly influential among his large following, was held suspect by the Tat Khalsa. Determined to produce a more authentic rahit, this newly formed group also tackled the performance of life-cycle rituals, an aspect that earlier codes had neglected. These included birth, marriage, and death rituals. Later sources, namely, *Prem Sumarg* and *Sau Sakhian*, while touching on Sikh rites of passage, did little to expand on them. According to Oberoi, it is probable that the specific attention to these rites indicate their later date of composition (1988: 155).

The committee seeking amendments to the existing rahit initially met in 1910. The Chief Khalsa Diwan, determined to ensure wide-ranging consensus regarding the dictates within the newly-formed code known as the *Gurmat Prakas*, had issued a letter in October 1910 reporting that a draft of the document had been completed. It also outlined the plan of action to be taken with regard to the dissemination of the new rahit. Two thousand copies were to be printed and distributed at all the Singh Sabha headquarters, to the major Thakats, Diwans, and Gurdwaras, and to the various sects, including the Akalis, Nirankaris, Namdharis, and Nirmalas. Further, the draft was to be printed in the *Khalsa Samachar*, seeking suggestions from its readership. Yet it was not until 1915, after years of intense deliberation, that the manual was completed. Not surprisingly, the new code determined that both men and women were to be initiated into the Khalsa order by khande di pahul. Perhaps more significantly, the document did *not* attend to the increasingly persistent voices that were advocating a distinctive form of nomenclature for Sikh females; the *Gurmat Prakas* was silent about Kaur as an epithet for Sikh females (*Chief Khalsa Diwan* 1952: 11, 26, 28). Moreover, it evidently rejected the name Devi for Sikh women sanctioned by *Prem Sumarg*. Further, the mother of the Khalsa was designated as Sahib Devan, not Sahib Kaur. This was despite the fact that Kaur and Devan were utilized interchangeably in the writings of the day. This was the case in Khazan Singh's newly published *History and Philosophy of the Sikh Religion*; he was, however, silent with regard to Sahib Devan's initiation into the Khalsa order (1914: 165–6).

Notwithstanding the valiant efforts of the committee, consensus on the rahit was difficult to attain. The high hopes for the *Gurmat Prakas* to conclusively delineate Sikh rahit were ultimately dashed by the continuing controversy surrounding the document, on the one hand, and its ineffectuality among the populace, on the other. Evidently an agreement on proper rahit was not possible even among the tightly-knit fraternity of the Singh Sabha leadership. Thus, despite the hopes and efforts of these notables, *Gurmat Prakas* never gained widespread acceptance among the Sikh community. It would appear that the issue of female initiation was a major point of contention. As late as 1920, at another meeting of prominent Sikhs, the issue of women's initiation once again came to the fore. One of the official panj piare of this gathering continued to insist that women being the 'weaker' sex, were to receive initiation by a single-edged sword. At this point, however, a number of Sikh women rose up and insisted that the reforms that gave them equal membership within the Khalsa order were to stay in place (*The Akali*, 25 November 1920).

This impasse necessitated another attempt in 1931 to formulate another, more acceptable, Sikh rahit, this time under the auspices of the Shiromani Gurdwara Parbandhak Committee, or SGPC. In 1920, disillusioned by British politics and by the unceasing loyal obedience of the Chief Khalsa Diwan towards their British rulers, radical Sikhs, organized under the banner of the newly announced Central Sikh League, created the SGPC; its mandate was to move into a position of control of gurdwara and shrine management. This concentrated action was a direct resistance to the authority of the traditional orthodoxy among the Sikhs, especially towards the existing custodians of gurdwaras, the mahants. By and large, mahants were not members of the Khalsa order, many completely rejected the outward Khalsa symbols. Given Tat Khalsa endeavours to unify Sikh identity markers and practices, mahants had long proved a source of irritation and dismay for the reformers. Yet mahants were legally in positions of power due to their historic associations with the shrines they maintained. They were, however, increasingly denigrated as representing the worst of Hinduized Sikhism and as definite obstacles to Sikh interests. Ultimately, Tat

Khalsa reformers came to see the fruits of their intense labours against these custodians. In 1925, the Sikh Gurdwaras Act was legislated; with this Act, control of Sikh shrines was wrested away from the 'old' orthodoxy—mahants and Sanatan Sikhs who were represented by guru lineages—and placed under the jurisdiction of the 'new' orthodoxy. Leaders of the new orthodoxy, by the 1920s, were radicalized remnants of the Singh Sabha legacy.

It was within this context that attempts were made in 1931 to finally formulate a decisive rahit for Sikhs. The final result appeared in 1950 as the *Sikh Reht Maryada*. This time it was finally recognized as the definitive statement of conduct for Sikhs, and has remained so to this time. The contents of the *Maryada* had far-reaching effects, particularly with regard to Sikh female identity. What had during the early years of the twentieth century remained an ill-defined, disjunctive, and even cryptic endorsement of Sikh female nomenclature, had by this time been transformed to the level of *prescription* for Sikh females and fundamental to their very identity. Upon a child's birth, boys were required to be given the suffix Singh and girls the suffix Kaur. In the new code, the appellation Kaur as a specific Sikh *symbol*, was for the first time officially sanctioned. Mata Sahib *Kaur* too was by this time firmly entrenched in the historiography of the Sikhs as the spiritual mother of the Khalsa Panth.

This later delineation of specified Sikh appellations to be given *at the time of birth* is indeed remarkable given its originality, at least at the level of explicit rahit. In the thirty-five-year time period between *Gurmat Prakas* and *Sikh Reht Maryada*, Bhai Kahn Singh Nabha had published his monumental *Gurusabad Ratanakar Mahan Kosh*.[12] It definitively corresponded Kaur with female initiation into the Khalsa panth. Yet Kahn Singh's interpretation of the significance of the name at the time of initiation was rejected by 1950; the epithets Kaur and Singh henceforth came to be given at the time of birth instead.

As indicated earlier, the various applications of the signifier Kaur point to the heterogeneous nature of Sikhism in the nineteenth and twentieth centuries. They are also indicative of the varied and fluctuating needs of a rapidly developing Sikh community during the pivotal stages of its growth. The distinctions between Sikhs and Hindus, put in place through the process of reform spearheaded by the Singh Sabha movement, were widely accepted by the 1950s. By the mid-twentieth century, Kaur had become *the* signifier of Sikh female collective identity. As such the application thereof came to be transferred to an even more fundamental platform than that of baptism, namely, the naming ritual occurring just days after a child's birth. Public exhibitions of Sikh distinctiveness through overt signifiers applied at the time of initiation were no longer necessary; infants were quietly furnished with the now widely accepted Sikh forms of nomenclature in the confines of their homes. In comparison, in the early 1920s, the conversion of a Muslim woman to Sikhism was highly publicized; this was the case despite the fact that she had already been married for many years to her Sikh husband. However, at that point in time, her conversion necessarily included a name change. Upon being administered holy amrita she was given the name Kishan Kaur (cited in Singh, H. 1975: 323). Certainly this was the same point Bhai Vir Singh was making in his novel, *Sundri*.

Needless to say, Singh Sabha initiatives intent on injecting new definitions and applications to previously indistinct cultural practices, particularly as they pertained to Sikh womenfolk, were immensely successful. Nonetheless, and perhaps surprisingly, it was only by the 1950s that they came to be *officially* ratified. With the gradual authorization of specific Sikh naming practices for both males and females in the form of rahit, Sikh communal consciousness was inevitably heightened. By the mid-twentieth century, the 'performance of each of these ritual acts continually communicated, reaffirmed, and rehearsed' had become securely established within the Sikh ritual drama (Oberoi 1988: 156). Uniformity of practice had become the new watchword of ritual expression. Carrol Smith-Rosenberg's observations of the final stage of hegemonic ritual identity construction, though written within a different context, ring true in this case as well. She notes: 'Finally, however, the new order will establish its hegemony. The new wielders of power will move to suppress symbolic as well as literal disorder. The language of diversity will be muffled. We will be left with the sounds of silence' (1985: 164).

CONTEMPORARY SCHOLARS AND THE REWRITING OF HISTORY

As has been shown, extant historical sources are unanimously varied with regard to both women's initiation into the order of the Khalsa, as are applications of Kaur among the Sikhs. Nonetheless, contemporary assumptions allow for scant contention in this regard. Khushwant Singh, for example, in *A History of the Sikhs*, unequivocally notes that the surname Kaur is to be granted to Sikh women at the time of initiation (1991: 83).[13] W.H. McLeod, who has almost single-handedly transformed the academic study of Sikhism through his near-exhaustive scope of inquiry, has also failed to move beyond early twentieth-century assumptions in this regard. This is indeed remarkable, given McLeod's resounding insistence on the need for a systematic reorganization and rigorous analysis of all aspects of Sikh history. With regard to the critique at hand, McLeod, in addressing Chaupa Singh's injunction against the use of half-names for those of the Khalsa brotherhood, furthers the belief that the injunction encompassed women's naming practices as well; in essence he accords equal status to both Kaur and Singh (McLeod 1987: 237). Yet, the *Chaupa Singh Rahit-nama* gives no indication of distinct nomenclature for Sikh females. Here McLeod is fortuitously furthering a redaction of Sikh history that is tinged by the Singh Sabha tendency to reinterpret historical sources in order to fit the Tat Khalsa agenda.

Nikki Singh takes this contemporary re-visioning of Sikh history one step further when she analyses both the rite of initiation for women and the signifier Kaur from a professedly feminist perspective. Basing her insights wholly upon late Singh Sabha redactions of history, Nikki Singh maintains that the signifier Kaur, female initiation into the Khalsa, and military symbolism are in and of themselves explicit indicators of the inherent egalitarianism of the Sikh tradition. In her words (1993: 120, 245).

This baptism through steel was open to both men and women. Women were to wear the five emblems of the Khalsa, too. As men received the surname Singh, women received the surname Kaur, modified. Men and women no longer traced their lineage or occupation to the 'father.' As 'Singh' and 'Kaur,' both were equal partners in the new family.... When he [Guru Gobind Singh] created the Khalsahood, all men received the last name 'Singh' and women the name 'Kaur.' In this egalitarian structure, which the tenth Sikh prophet established, women were liberated from tracing their lineage to their father or adopting a husband's name after marriage.

Needless to say, in the light of the contradictions and immense variability within the tradition itself, Nikki Singh's certitude with regard to her interpretation denotes the longevity of Singh Sabha interpretations of Sikh history. Grewal and Bal's critique regarding the methods and means of traditional historical analysis among Sikh scholars, particularly with regard to the scant sources addressing the creation of the Khalsa, is highly applicable both to the issue of female baptism and the application of the appellation Kaur among Sikhs.

Most of the modern historians of Guru Gobind Singh have adopted the very simple method of selecting one and rejecting another detail from one of more of the chronicles. But once that selection is made the isolated point or passage is treated as literally true.... Now, it should be unwise on anyone's part to reject later tradition merely because it is much later to the events; and there is no doubt that traditions, as a valid form of evidence, can provide useful clues to past probabilities but later tradition cannot be accepted literally and it seldom leads to any certainties about the past (Grewal and Bal 1967: Appendix C).

If we turn to the positions taken by scholars addressing the inauguration of the Khalsa, initiation, and injunctions regarding nomenclature as they pertain to women, it becomes abundantly clear that this critique is remarkably pertinent. The concurrence of even the most meticulous of scholars in the furtherance of untenable, inaccurate, and variegated claims in this regard is indicative of the indifference surrounding Sikh scholarship with regard to a systematic study of women's history. In this regard, modern scholarship has inadvertently failed to move beyond Singh Sabha renditions of history, particularly the versions offered by Max Arthur Macauliffe, Kahn Singh of Nabha, and Bhai Vir Singh. This tendency has long been recognized in a generalized sense in the academic study of Sikhism. The editors of *Sikh History and Religion in the Twentieth Century* note with considerable astuteness that 'Singh Sabha scholars and writers were so successful in their attempt to reformulate the Sikh tradition that their general interpretation of the tradition acquired the status of implicit truth. That status it continues to hold to the present day.' They continue with the warning: 'It is essential that we recognize the actual nature and extent of this influence and conditioning, if we are to comprehend the historical development of the Sikh tradition' (O'Connell et al. 1988: 12). Indeed, while for the most part scholars have taken this counsel to heart, close scrutiny and rigorous analysis of sources with regard to historiography as it pertains to women has been virtually nonexistent. In short, scholars have done little to append to the contributions of the Singh Sabha reformers of the late nineteenth and early twentieth centuries. Historical questions regarding women within the Khalsa order have either been ignored or historians have simply furthered the highly biased outlook of the Singh Sabha reformers. For example, W. Owen Cole, in the popular 'Teach Yourself World Faiths' series, takes the feminized myth of the Khalsa inauguration one step further. He notes that after the panj piare were initiated, they in turn initiated both Guru Gobind Singh *and* his wife Mata Sahib Kaur. She was thus one of the initial participants at this central Sikh event (Cole 1994: 31). J.S. Grewal's recent book, arguably the most highly respected of contemporary volumes on Sikh history, is utterly silent with regard to the pivotal questions of women's inclusion in Sikh initiation rites; nor does it attend to Sikh female patterns of nomenclature in history (Grewal 1990).

The range of discrepant assumptions is indicative of the insignificance accorded not only to women's history, but also points to a pervasive unwillingness to engage in a careful analysis of the wider process of gender construction. Gender, understood as a construct, has significant consequences far beyond an awareness of the relationships between women and men. How and why the categories of male and female, subjective and collective, have actively been constructed, is crucial in coming to a more comprehensive understanding of the historical process. Analysis of the discursive structures in the formation of ritual identities from a gender perspective allows for a more complex understanding of the mechanisms of inclusion and exclusion, central to group identity formulation. Perhaps most importantly, the perspective of gender warrants an endorsement of historiography *beyond* the reiteration of rhetorical formulations, however imprecise, that served the purposes of a community in flux admirably well. More precisely, it allows for an understanding of how and why specific gender construction was fundamental to the very evolution of the Sikh community; this includes early configurations of identity, the process of Sikh adaptation to the colonial milieu, and the even more complex task of communal identity formation led by the Singh Sabha reformers.

NOTES

1. An earlier version of this chapter appears as 'What's in a Name? Circumscribing Sikh Female Nomenclature', Singh and Barrier, forthcoming by OUP.
2. For an analysis of the evolution of the rite of charan-amrit to that of charan di pahul, see McLeod 1987: 213.
3. I am grateful to W. H. McLeod for his observations, insights, and translation of pertinent segments of the *Prem Sumarg*.
4. Avtar Singh Vahiria was writing under the direct influence of his mentor, Khem Singh Bedi. The *Sanskar Bagh* was later transformed into the *Khalsa Dharam Sastra* and published in 1914. See Singh, N. 1990: 154.
5. Lewis' extensive fieldwork and ritual analysis is primarily based upon the myriad rites and observances among the Gnau in a West Sepik village, Papua New Guinea.
6. The name 'Kanwar' also refers to females in the present day.
   The contemporary usage of the appellation 'Kanwar' takes on the feminine form with the second 'a' vowel being long; it can be translated as princess, virgin, unmarried girl, or daughter. The second 'a' for the masculine form of 'Kanwar' is short and refers to 'prince' or 'son'. Dr Ann Gold also notes that 'Kanwar' is a common honorific middle name for Rajput women; women of non-Rajput castes, both high and low, continue to use 'Devi' as a middle name.
   Correspondence with Dr Ann Gold, December 1997.
7. I am grateful for the assistance of Satguru Jagjit Singh, the leader of the Namdhari Sikhs, who pointed out this particular usage of 'Kaur'. Private interview, Bhaini Sahib, Punjab 1997.
   An early example of 'Kaur' being utilized in the feminine was by Khatrani Rup Kaur who was avowedly responsible for the composition of the *Charitra*, the 'Wiles of Women'. See McLeod 1987: 169.
8. While Jats taking on aspects of Rajput identity characteristics has been a pivotal aspect of my own thought processes regarding the origins and development of the name 'Kaur', I am grateful to Jeevan Deol for the useful term 'rajputization' to better explicate this process. See his 'Rajputising the Guru? The Construction of Early Sikh Political Discourse', Paper presented at the South Asian Seminar, St. Anthony's College, Oxford, January 2000.
   Archana Varma's research among a low-caste Sikh group, the Mahton, indicates a similar process of 'rajputization' to enhance their

position. The Mahtons adopted the designation 'Rajput Mahta Sikhs'. She further notes that some Jat villagers of Bains followed upper-caste Rajputs in not practising karewa.

9. The *Gurbilas Daswin Patshahi* was written by Sukha Singh in 1797, at the height of Sikh rule in Punjab.

10. According to Macauliffe, a number of the guru mahals besides Guru Gobind Singh's third wife were also named 'Kaur', although it is difficult to ascertain whether these changes are indicative of the Singh Sabha's penchant to rewrite history. Ramo, the mother of Guru Angad, was apparently renamed Daya Kaur; Guru Ram Das' mother's name is given as Anup Devi though Macauliffe stipulates that she was known as Daya Kaur after her marriage. Another guru mahal associated with the appellation 'Kaur' was Krishan Kaur, wife of Guru Har Krishen.

11. Jito, the guru's first wife, was married to the guru in 1677; she was the mother of Jujhar Singh, Zorawar Singh, and Fateh Singh. Sundari, the mother of Ajit Singh, was the guru's second wife; they were married in 1684. Sahib Devan, his third wife, was wedded to the guru in 1700.

12. Kahn Singh Nabha's *Gurusabad Ratanakar Mahan Kosh* was first published in four volumes in 1931. A revised edition in a single volume was issued from Patiala in 1960 with subsequent reprints. It was known simply as *Mahan Kosh* and it is this volume that is cited here. See Nabha 1993: 352.

13. Although Singh is most widely known as a journalist, his influential two-volume *History* continues to be widely used by both academics and non-academics.

EIGHT

CONCLUSIONS

OVERVIEW

The preceding chapters have been conceptualized upon the notion that gender is a fluid construct, one that is open to the vicissitudes of circumstance and change. In essence, gender constructs are evolutionary, they emerge and develop with the shifting needs of the community within which they unfold. They are also susceptible to the forces surrounding them, be these political, economic, social, or cultural. The guru period of the Sikh community came to be transformed by its own needs and constituencies. It progressed from a tradition in the fifteenth century that stressed the interiority of devotion, to a community in the seventeenth century that stressed exterior distinction from the wider Hindu community. This evolution led to considerable changes in what it meant to be a Sikh woman and a Sikh man. A patriarchal value system was firmly established throughout the guru period, and by the end of the seventeenth century it had been transformed into an order that gave religious, symbolic, and ritual sanctioning to a specific gender hierarchy. With a primary focus on male Sikh identity, females were relegated to a secondary position; a 'theology of difference' based on gender was now firmly in place.

With the British Raj came well-defined conceptualizations of masculinity and femininity. Victorian assumptions about race, religion, gender, as well as economic and political designs, played an important role in the process of Sikh gender construction. But colonial rule did not take hold among the Sikhs without opposition. Reformatory groups among the Sikhs, such as the Namdharis, not only attempted to regenerate 'corrupted' Sikhism but also resisted the authority of the colonizers. Alternate visions of gender in the form of leadership and ritual space for women were significant features of Namdhari reforms.

By and large, however, the hypermasculine ethos pervading Sikh identity was singularly congruent with polarized British constructions of masculinity; this led to the 'politics of similarity' between the Raj and the Sikhs. The 'manly' Jat woman of rural Punjab, however, collided with the colonizers' notions of true femininity. Education programmes initiated by the British to uplift women from their condition were an attempt to amend their masculine character. Further, the winds of reform sweeping over colonial Punjab were conducive to British designs. Alighting upon the new keepers of tradition, Singh Sabha reformers, Victorian assumptions of gender came to be combined with traditional Sikh values.

Needless to say, reformist gender ideology during colonial times did not originate with the Sikhs. The Brahmo Samaj and Arya Samaj provided the yardsticks by which Singh Sabha reformers measured their success. Particularly with regard to Swami Dayanand, Sikh reformers, largely reacting to Arya Samaj visions of a purified gender ideology, fostered a contrasting and 'true' Sikh gender identity, especially with regard to Sikh womenfolk. Singh Sabha reformers consistently blamed the 'fallen' state of Sikhism on women's degenerate position; they also claimed that the true tenets of Sikhism were the foundations of the gender ideology they proposed. However, for the most part, the combined force of their response toward gender stemmed from the Arya Samaj *and* from Victorian assumptions. The result had far-reaching consequences, particularly in the case of Sikh educational institutions and ritual observances for Sikh women.

To return to Joan Wallach Scott's analysis of gender in the context of identity construction, that which is dominant requires the secondary for its very existence. The inauguration of the Khalsa led to a polarization of gender; the concentration on male identity demanded that women subsidize that equation by being the opposite and secondary aspect of that identity. Similarly, the 'civilized', dominant male construct of the Singh Sabha reform movement necessitated a 'civilized', educated, though secondary, female construct. The creation of the 'new' woman also demanded the removal of traditional ritual barriers that had led to her degenerate position. These attempts also included an extension of male control; reformers invaded and attempted to dismantle those arenas of popular religious traditions heretofore accepted as women's domain.

WOMEN IN THE SINGH SABHA MOVEMENT—AGENTS OF CHANGE
OR CASUALTIES OF REFORM?

While it was mainly male reformers that instigated reformatory
claims over the practices of females, this selective process of
feminine identity construction was also sanctioned by a select,
somewhat anomalous, and devoted group of females. Harnam Kaur
of the Ferozepur school was one such reformer. Although she was
known for her work in female education, her biography also
inculcated readers with proper Sikh female values that were indicative
of the reform agenda. Others included Bibi Livlin Kaur, Secretary of
the Bhujangan Diwan, Kairon, who was involved in fund raising for
the institution; collecting ornaments and money, she gathered women
together to travel as far as China and Burma to beg for funds for a
boarding house (*Khalsa Advocate*, 15 May 1909; 13 February 1911).
By 1914, Bibi Savitri Devi, the first woman speaker at the Sikh
Education Conference, called for loyalty to the Crown and extolled
the benefits of Sikh education and continued reform (Devi n.d.).

A number of female preachers (*updeshaks*) were also involved in
the dissemination of Sikh reform ideology. Significantly, many of them
were adherents of the various 'un-Sikh' sects maligned by the Singh
Sabha. Some female updeshaks were Udasis, the erstwhile bastion of
Sikh orthodoxy; this 'old order' was precisely the barrier to the new
and purified order visualized by the Tat Khalsa. Udasis advocated
education, celibacy, and asceticism, and refused to acknowledge the
symbolism and primacy of the Khalsa.[1] Given Udasi abilities to
expound on Sikh scripture, there were examples where an uneasy
truce was maintained between them and the Singh Sabha reformers.
Pandita Jiwan Mukta, a follower of Swami Chitgan Dev and head-
mistress of the Gurmat Kanya Pathshala in Jammu, toured,
preached, and collected funds for the school and the widows' home
attached to it. Given her efforts to promote female education, she
was warmly embraced in the reports of the day. Her swami, Chitgan
Dev, was also lauded by the reformers as a fine example for his
abiding interest in the education of Sikh girls and boys (*Khalsa
Advocate*, 4 August 1911). Shrimati Bibi Har Kour and Pandita Jiwan
Mukta were also recognized by the Tat Khalsa reformers; the latter
was lauded as a speaker at the All India Conference of Religions in
Allahabad in 1911. Nonetheless, her critics disparaged her presentation as 'makeshift'; Mukta had been given a last-minute invitation as

a conference presenter (*Khalsa Advocate*, 27 January, 24 March 1911). Soon thereafter, calls were made to tighten control over the activities of updeshaks. Another female preacher, Mai Ram Kaur, also had her detractors. She was soundly critiqued by one observer as being

utterly destitute at the tact of lecturing.... She cannot couch her bitter but sound advice in sugared language. She exposed to them their faults too bluntly. At first she elicited the applause of her audience, but her tedious lecture taxed their brains to such an extent that they grew weary and impatient.... Were she to learn a little more tolerance and knew how to quietly pocket insults when it is expedient to do so... she will prove a boon to the Panth (ibid., 14 September 1907).

Further, Lachhmi Devi, an Udasi outside of Singh Sabha circles, was a prolific poet-saint who published a monumental granth entitled *About Udasis, Bedhis, Sodhis, About Guru Nanak, About Jai Ram (Brother-in-law of Guru Nanak), About Lachhmi Das (Son of Guru Nanak) and many other tales and stories* (1916). Without doubt, Udasis tended to be the most educated and theologically trained among all Sikh factions. Singh Sabha reformers, however, maligned them as loafers who accepted the obeisance of their followers, did not follow true Sikh rahit, and were impure in their conduct and morals. Criticism of Udasis was of course further extended to those of the guru lineage. These individuals were maligned for allowing their followers to pay homage to them and for being addressed as 'gurus'. Another little-known poet named Pero, also called Mai Pero, 1833–73, was associated with the Gulab Dasi sect, a group largely based on Vedantist ideals and influenced by the Nirmalas (Shaiharyar 1997: 5–8). This was another Sikh ascetic group composed of well-educated Sanskrit scholars and teachers. The sect came to prominence with Ditt Singh, the celebrated Dalit Singh Sabha writer who was originally a Gulab Dasi follower; from the camp of Gulab Dasi, Ditt Singh moved to the Arya Samaj and finally to the Singh Sabha reform movement. Though there is little known about these women, they were in unique positions as writers, preachers, and teachers. Indeed, the 'new orthodoxy' maligned these various groups as being responsible for the degenerate state of Sikhism, claiming that, ultimately, these un-Sikh views and practices had led to the utter debasement of women. Ironically, it was precisely from within these associations that strong, determined, highly educated Sikh women emerged. While Tat Khalsa reformers hailed the simple education of girls as a high achievement, Udasi women had long been producing theological tomes! Eventually, even those women who had been grudgingly accepted because of their invaluable services came to be rejected by the Tat Khalsa. By 1920, apparently wearied by the 'bitter' tongue of female preachers, the newly appointed Shiromani Gurdwara Parbandhak Committee passed a motion that women updeshaks were no longer to continue their duties (Kaur, A. 1992: 25, Sahni 1922). Some, however, simply ignored the injunction and continued to tour the countryside and preach.

In looking to the women most active during the time of the Singh Sabha reform movement, one is faced with a number of perplexing contradictions. Without doubt a number of highly influential women were already active agents within the larger Sikh milieu, particularly within the Udasi establishment. They thus had little need of the uplifting endeavour that the male reformers were loudly proclaiming for the downtrodden of society, namely, women. Further, for those women *within* the parameters of the Singh Sabha movement, it is important to understand why they so vigorously promoted the male ideology that in actual fact constrained them and even diminished many choices they would otherwise have viewed as normative. Without doubt, they wished to be accepted within a system that professed as one of its foremost objectives women's reform. Adopting permissible ways and means of acting within that system must be understood as part of a coping strategy, a mode of conforming to the new standard of Sikh womanhood propounded by the Tat Khalsa. The Singh Sabha ideal also presented women with an opportunity to take part, however minimally, in the ongoing debate regarding the amelioration of women. Moreover, male criticism regarding the degenerate position of Sikhism and women's corresponding degradation was indeed making an impact on women. The education of females in terms of a proper Sikh learning came to be understood by *both* male and female agents of reform as the key to alleviating this fallen status of Sikh women.

It is indeed tempting to view the promotion of female education as a mere contrivance adopted by women as the most effective means to enhance their position. In Gail Minault's terms, it allowed for an active pursuance of 'the art of the possible' within the structures circumscribed by male leadership (1981: 9). However, the active promotion and, by implication, the ongoing dialogue within this discourse, *beyond* that of education, moved women into a more intricate position within the hegemonic discourse and its underlying stance toward religious authority. For the rhetoric posited by reform ideology vis-à-vis the inherent superiority of an unadulterated Sikhism was enticing, particularly the claims and promises of an elevated position for women. This in turn prompted an active engagement with and promotion of true Sikh ideology, albeit by a small group of educated women who usually stayed on the sidelines of the reform endeavour. Moreover, the stress on women's conceptual equality with men, propounded by Tat Khalsa reformers, provided women with the leverage needed to claim an extension of the space within which they normatively acted. They could also thus expect that their roles be substantiated, particularly within the realm of education. To be agents in the process of redefining tradition was an exciting and groundbreaking opportunity for women within the Sikh tradition. On the other hand, to blame and remonstrate against un-Sikh, and thus degenerate, customs was a convincing effort on the part of these women to come to terms with the degraded position of Sikh women at large.

Nonetheless, the reforms initiated by their male counterparts did indeed bring about significant changes in the lives of a number of women. With education came opportunities to further the larger reform endeavour through honorary teaching services. This offered women, *beyond* those of the orthodox religious establishment, novel occupational choices. Further, Sikh education conferences provided women with an opportunity to play a part in the unfolding drama of the Sikh social and political arena. These gatherings eventually allowed women to be spectators and even minor contributors to the significant decisions made by the principal players among the social and political elite. Perhaps most importantly, the ritual traditions that had barred women from becoming full-fledged members within the panth were slowly being eroded. The pivotal rite of initiation by khande di pahul, heretofore closed to women, allowed for a novel inclusion for females within the Khalsa order. The opportunity to take on substantial status and roles within the religious establishment was ultimately liberating for Sikh women. For, with attempts to displace un-Sikh elements during ritual or other ceremonial occasions came novel and highly significant roles for Sikh women; for example, in replacing professional musicians at ritual events, women occupied spaces that had earlier been barred to them. While these modifications were largely based on an augmented understanding of women's gratuitous *duty* to the cause of reform, they opened doors for women to become far more active in the religious establishment than ever before.

CIRCUMVENTING HEGEMONY—ALIGNMENT AND RESISTANCE

Nita Kumar has outlined four persistent modes for conceptualizing women in history. The first makes women 'the object of our gaze, by enlarging the scope of each particular discipline and including them in topics.' According to Kumar, this approach leads only to a further objectification of women. Another lens, through which to view women in history, presents them as actors and as subjects 'with the will, rationality and meaning to re-make the world'. In short, this mode gives women the prerogative of males. Needless to say, the actuality of women's history simply cannot sustain this view. A third approach focuses on the structures within which women exist, 'which seemingly control them without a chance for them to exercise agency, especially patriarchal, ideological, discursive structures.' The fourth mode outlined by Kumar looks at the 'hidden, subversive ways in which women exercise their agency even while outwardly part of a repressive normative order' (1994: 4). In coming to an understanding of Sikh women during the time of Singh Sabha reforms, it is impossible to speak only of the fourth approach, the one focusing on women's resistance, without also taking account of and giving credence to the force of male hegemonic ideology that circumvented these women's lives. According to Kumar,

We have subjects, in short, who act, as action is commonly understood, but it is more likely that we have subjects who at best 'merely' speak. In both cases, there is a larger structure that binds them—and is unquestionably dominant, powerful and controlling.... The jump we have to make is to envision how in both these, and other cases as well, there is an attempt to assert themselves within this structure of power, through the posing of alternative models, sometimes deceptive in their muteness. But in all cases there is partial alignment with these very dominant structures, so that autonomy is never complete, it is often ambiguous, and is probably not always desired (ibid.: 18).

In the case of the female Singh Sabha reformers, agency and subjectivity were so closely intertwined at times as to blur the boundaries between the seemingly opposite modes of being. A thorough understanding of the structures within which Tat Khalsa ideology developed thus allows for a discovery of women's acts of negotiation and even slight hints of resistance as opposed to less likely rebellion. According to James Scott, overt insubordination almost universally provokes an immediate and acrimonious response; the alternative, namely tactically chosen and circuitous forms of resistance, without contesting the formal definitions of hierarchy and power, may have more far-reaching results (1985: 33). In the case of Harnam Kaur, while maintaining that the ultimate duty of Sikh women was to provide happiness to their husbands, her belief in the inherent equality of girls and boys led to an active campaign for female education, despite persistent opposition from the education-wary populace. This included the establishment of a girls' boarding house at Ferozepur in the face of obdurate protest stemming from deeply held notions of family honour. The updeshak Ram Kaur, continued to preach in spite of faultfinding by her audience. Bibi Livlin Kaur travelled as far as China, Malaya, and Hong Kong to collect funds in the hallowed name of education. Women thus enlarged the framework offered by male reformers in the acquisition of individual and collective freedom. Women of the radical Bhasaur group too were stark embodiments of this new ethos; they continued to don turbans despite the censure of orthodox Sikh groups. By the 1920s women defiantly insisted that the reforms allowing for equal access through initiation rituals be upheld, in particular, the rite of khande di pahul, in spite of the overt efforts of powerful groups to place restrictions on women's full membership in the order.

James Scott's delineation of insubordination from the perspective of peasant culture, that which he calls the 'everyday forms of resistance', at times seemingly quiescent, often nuanced, though overtly persistent 'weapons of the weak', is helpful in this regard.

By reference to the culture that peasants fashion from their experience—their 'offstage' comments and conversation, their proverbs, folksongs, and history, legends, jokes, language, ritual, and religion—it should be possible to determine to what degree, and in what ways, peasants actually accept the social order propagated by elites.... Rejection of elite values, however, is seldom an across-the-board proposition, and only a close study of peasant values can define the major points of friction and correspondence (Scott 1985: 41).

Proverbs and popular maxims are alternately delineated by Scott (1990) as 'hidden transcripts' that are implicit in women's song. Though 'often veiled, but sometimes overt and public', words and actions were means by which 'women communicated their resistance to dominant North Indian characterizations of "women's nature... and of kinship relationships"' (Raheja and Gold 1994: 1–2). Thus, to the increasingly hegemonic Singh Sabha reform initiatives attempting to place restrictions on marriage celebrations, the populace retorted: 'To hell with Singh Sabha people, who prohibit singing and dancing.' As noted earlier, Singh Sabha ideology was also characterized by the wider population as 'Singh safa', likening the reform initiatives to plague epidemics.

Needless to say, these maxims are indicative of the estimation of the Tat Khalsa reformers by the wider populace. To understand their full significance, however, they need contextualizing. For the Sikh Jat who formed the bulk of the Sikh peasantry, what Robert Redfield calls the 'good life' included above all a strenuous work ethic, appeasement of the gods, and as a reward for their toils, hard drinking and spirited celebrations.[2] The reformers' attempts to solemnize festive occasions such as wedding festivities did not go unchallenged by their rural counterparts; neither did the peasantry give up on the calendrical festivities that served as signposts for the agricultural year. These times of revelry were an essential outlet for the frustrations and struggles of everyday existence. Moreover, the proclivity for excessive drinking, drawn-out festivities, and sexual exploits were part and parcel of deeply ingrained notions of manliness upheld by the Jat; the 'sturdy' Jat woman also found a respite from the often solitary, mainly servile, everyday drudgery of her life on these occasions. The 'effeminate' city dweller attempting to restrict and circumscribe these moments of celebratory diversion from the monotony of everyday life could only be derided and ultimately ignored.

WOMEN'S REFORM—LAYING THE FOUNDATION FOR A NEW ERA

Perhaps most importantly from the perspective of female agency, Tat Khalsa women became well versed in the art of mobilization. An insinuating booklet, depicted by members of the Tat Khalsa as insidious to the honour of Mata Ganga, the wife of Guru Arjan, united Sikh women in protest meetings; vehement objection to the booklet came to be expressed not only in women's meetings but also through letter-writing campaigns. The booklet by Raunaq Ram and Bishumbar Dutt, *Khalsa Panth ki Hakikat,* depicted Mata Ganga asking Bhai Buddha for *niyoga,* permitted by her husband. Niyoga was a form of conjugal relations prescribed by Swami Dayanand of the Arya Samaj, for those who were 'without control of their senses' and wished to have legitimate progeny. According to Dayanand, if 'the wife is pregnant or diseased, or if the husband has a chronic and incurable malady, what should the husband or the wife do if they are youthful and find themselves incapable to control their sexual appetites?' The restrictive guidelines for niyoga were minutely outlined by Dayanand. It was permissible for those widowed and, for instance, when one partner within a marriage was unfertile. It was also allowable when one partner was absent for over eight years, if he was tied up with preaching duties; six years, if he left in search of fame or learning; three years if he was absent for trade purposes. 'Similarly, if the husband is intolerably cruel, it is proper for the wife to desert him, have a niyoga and bear children as heirs to the married husband's property.' It was not, however, permissible for virgins and bachelors to practice niyoga. According to Dayanand,

Just as a marriage is performed by proclamation, so is niyoga. As marriage requires the sanction of the society and consent of the couple, so does niyoga. When man and woman want to perform niyoga, they ought to declare before the men and women of their families that they want to enter into niyoga relation for the sake of issues, that they will sever their connection when the purpose of niyoga is fulfilled, that they should be counted as sinners and be penalised by the society or the state if they do otherwise, that they will meet for intercourse only once a month and will abstain from intercourse for a year after the conception. (see Upadhyaya 1960: 165–76).

Not surprisingly, British sensibilities had little use for the practice. Farquhar protested that niyoga 'is simply sexual relationships without marriage. The details are too horrible to transcribe' (1924: 122). While niyoga as delineated by Dayanand was similar in most respects to the custom of karewa widely practiced by the Sikhs, the latter's connection to landed property and its protection from the whims of widows as opposed to the desire for progeny, made karewa far more acceptable to the rulers. Sikh women's objections to the pamphlet must be understood within this context.

Earlier, women's groups had joined the massive letter-writing crusade in support of the Anand Marriage Bill. Moreover, in support of British involvement in World War I, purdah meetings were called by women who contributing their sewing skills to the effort. According to Gail Pearson, the participation of women from within 'extended space' was essential to the process of universalisation of the nationalist movement. Closely tied to traditional male dominated structures, these women were familiar with the values of social reform and nationalism, but could also move 'from the traditional household to the rough and tumble of street politics in times of national crisis' (1981: 177). For the Sikhs who had hitherto remained outside of nationalist politics and had concentrated their efforts on Sikh loyalty to the Crown and to the solidification of Sikh identity, the ability to mobilize forces served both men and women well in the radically transformed and politicized milieu of the Sikhs in the 1920s. As noted earlier, the formation of the Central Sikh League, a political party formed in 1919, and the inauguration of the Shiromani Gurdwara Parbandhak Committee by the leaders of the league, also signalled the end of the Singh Sabha movement. What had for years been depicted as a religious reform endeavour, unabashedly loyal to the Crown, came to be replaced by an intense level of overt disaffection under a new banner of leadership. This was manifested in the political designs of the Central Sikh League and, subsequently, the Akali Dal. At this juncture the Akalis formally dedicated themselves to the cause of nationalism by passing a resolution supporting Gandhi's call for non-cooperation with the British. Sikh women, well versed in the watchwords of Singh Sabha reforms—self-denial, duty, honour—easily redirected that orientation from the arena of religious identity to the national front. A new era was thus ushered in; the participation of the Sikhs, both female and male, in India's nationalist struggle against the Raj had formally begun.

NOTES

1. Most caretakers, or *mahants*, of the major Sikh shrines claimed to be descendents of Udasi orders. See McLeod 1995: 214–215.
2. Redfield notes that the 'good life' refers to the 'integrated pattern of dominant attitudes' that represent the value-orientation of the peasantry. See Redfield 1960: 61–9.

Women and Women's Issues in Popular Sikh Literature, 1890–1920*

Heroism and Piety

Amar Singh, *Chhoti Nunh Ya Lachhmi*, Amritsar: Khalsa Agency, 1908.

Bhai Atma Singh, *Guru Hazar Hai*, Amritsar: Bhai Atma Singh, 1919.

Narinjan Kaur (Bibi), *Sur Bir Bhainan*, Kairon: Khalsa Bhujangan Conference, 1916.

Ram Kishan Singh (Bhai), *Sikh Istrian De Prasang*, Amritsar: Wazir Hind Press, 1914.

Sewa Das Pahiri, *Lilha Bhagtni Bhilni*, Amritsar: Chattar Singh, 1918.

Sohan Singh (Bhai), *Natak Rup Kaur*, Simla: Khalsa Youngmen's Association, 1916.

Teja Singh, *Rani Jhala Kaur*, Amritsar: Bhai Bahadur Singh, 1910.

Thakar Singh (Bhai), *Harpal Charitar*, Rangoon: Bhai Thakur Singh, 1912.

Vir Singh (Bhai), *Bijay Singh*, Amritsar: Wazir Hind Press, 1900.

————, *Rana Surat Singh*, Amritsar: Khalsa Tract Society, 1919.

————, *Srimati Sundriji De Dardnak Samachar*, Amritsar: Wazir Hind Press, 1898.

Martyrdom and Sacrifice

Bhagwan Singh (Arif), *Khalsa Deviyan Almaruf Singhaniyan De Sidq*, Bhalwal: Bhagwan Singh, 1914.

Ditt Singh (Gyani), *Shahidian*, Lahore: Baldev Singh, 1911.

————, *Singhanian, De Sadiq*, Lahore: Khalsa Press, 1898.

Partap Singh (Bhai), *Man Putar Di Shahidi*, Amritsar: Bhai Labh Singh, 1912.

---

* Adapted from Barrier 1970: 75–88.

Sohan Singh (Bhai), *Prasang Srimati Bibi Saran Kaur*, Amritsar: Bhai
Chattar Singh, 1919.

BENEFITS OF FEMALE EDUCATION

Haribhagan Singh (Sant), *Savitari Natik*, Amritsar: Sardar Dan Singh, n.d.
Mohan Singh Vaid (Bhai), *Subhag Kaur*, Tarn Taran: Bhai Mohan Singh
Vaid, 1912.
Parduman Singh (Bhai), *Anand Jhok*, Baddon (Hoshiarpur): Bhai
Parduman Singh, 1911.
Sunder Singh (Bhai), *Upkari Jiwan*, Amritsar: Sat Bivharak Agency, 1910.

DAILY INSTRUCTION BOOKLETS FOR WOMEN

Amar Singh (Bhai) , *Ghar Da Nirbah*, Amritsar: Khalsa Agency, 1905.
Bhagvanti, *Sidak De Bere Par*, Amritsar: Amar Press, n.d..
Jodh Singh (Bhai), *Bharosa*, Lahore: Sri Gurmat Press, 1906.
Wadhawa Singh (Sardar), *Granth Istri Updesh*, Amritsar: Sardar Wadhawa
Singh, 1900.

DIRECTIVES ON PROPER RITUALS AND KNOWLEDGE BEFITTING WOMEN

Amir Singh (Diwan), *Novel Prakash Kaur*, Amritsar: Diwan Amir Singh, 1915.
Dalel Singh, *Ak Nun Milni*, Hoshiarpur: Bhai Dalel Singh, 1909.
Dharm Dev (Pandit), *Istri Sudhar*, Lahore: Lala Mohan Lal, 1905.
Ganesh Singh (Sant), *Istri Amrit Nikhed*, Lahore: Sri Gurmat Press, 1902.
Gurmukh Singh (Bhai), *Gutt Hai Ke Sundaka?*, Ludhiana: Managing Com-
mittee, Sikh Kanya Pathshala, 1913.
Mohan Singh Vaid (Bhai), *Benati*, Tarn Taran: Bhai Mohan Singh Vaid, 1912.
Narain Singh (Bhai), *Khalsa Mat Istri Amrit Mandan*, Amritsar: Wazir
Hind Press, 1904.
Thakar Singh (Gyani), *Putri Nun Sikhya*, Amritsar: Gyani Thakur Singh,
1915.

SUITABLE FAMILY RELATIONSHIPS

Gurdit Singh (Kavi), *Jhagra Nunh Sauhara*, Lahore: Mohammad Abdal
Aziz, 1917.

Prohibitions against Women's 'Un-Sikh' Behaviour

Bela Singh (Bhai), *Singhni Parbodh*, Lahore: Bhai Bela Singh, 1917.
Ganda Singh (Bhai), *Manmattan Di Kartut*, Gujranwala: Bhai Ganda Singh, 1916.
Gurdit Singh (Bhai), *Bachchi Da Varlap*, Lyallpur: Bhai Gurdit Singh, 1915.
Jawahir Singh (Bhai), *Git Jawariye Di Istri Da Virlap*, Lyallpur: Bhai Jawahir Singh, 1913.
Mohan Singh Vaid (Bhai), *Abla Vilap*, Tarn Taran: Bhai Mohan Singh Vaid, 1918.
————, *Vidhva Vilap*, Amritsar: Wazir Hindu Press, 1918.

Loyalty to the British

Variam Singh (Kavishar), *Naukar Di Nar*, Amritsar: Sri Gurmat Press, 1918.

Anonymous Publications, Tracts, Pertaining to Women

Adhuri Vidya Jind Da Khun, Amritsar: Khalsa Tract Society, 1909.
Agyakar, Amritsar: Khalsa Tract Society, 1911.
An Mulli Tahlan, Amritsar: Khalsa Tract Society, 1900.
Atam Ghat, Amritsar: Khalsa Tract Society, 1900.
Bachche Palan Dian Mattan, Amritsar: Khalsa Tract Society, 1911.
Bhuyangan Pukar, Kairon: Singh Sabha, 1908.
Bhuyangan Virlap, Amritsar: Khalsa Bhuyangan Diwan, 1908.
Bibi Bhain, Amritsar: Khalsa Tract Society, 1900.
Eh Tan Garki Ai, Amritsar: Khalsa Tract Society, 1899.
Garib Kaur, Amritsar: Khalsa Tract Society, 1916.
Ghar Suar, Amritsar: Khalsa Tract Society, 1901.
Gharvich Suarg, Amritsar: Khalsa Tract Society, 1900.
Grahi Sikhya, Amritsar: Panjabi Prachar book Agency, 1910.
Hai Hai Bachchi Tun Kithon?, Amritsar: Khalsa Tract Society, 1897.
Heroism of Sikh Women; Martyrdom of a Sikh Youth; Bhai Har Pal; Bhai Madho, Amritsar: Khalsa Agency, 1906.
Hir Ware Shah De Phal, Amritsar: Khalsa Tract Society, 1898.
Ik Kanniyan De Dukhre, Amritsar: Khalsa Tract Society, 1899.
Istri Bharta, Amritsar: Khalsa Tract Society, 1900.

Istri Sambodh, Amritsar: Khalsa Tract Society, 1906.

Istrian Liye Amrit Di Lor, Amritsar: Khalsa Tract Society, 1898.

Kalhini Diurani, Amritsar: Khalsa Tract Society, n.d.

Karam Kaur, Amritsar: Khalsa Tract Society, 1918.

Nashang Kaur Kikur Laj Kaur, Ban Gai, Amritsar: Khalsa Tract Society, 1901.

Nisang Kaur, Amritsar: Khalsa Tract Society, 1906.

Pati Brit Dharam, Amritsar: Khalsa Tract Society, 1897.

Prem Patola, Amritsar: Khalsa Tract Society, 1904.

Rani Rup Kaur Te Tikka Manna Singh Ji Da Sangram, Arthat Jang Marauli, Amritsar: Khalsa Tract Society, 1903.

Sade Ghrandi Dasha, Amritsar: Khalsa Tract Society, 1911.

Saphal Gur Parb, Amritsar: Khalsa Tract Society, 1909.

Shrimati Golar Kaur, Amritsar: Khalsa Tract Society, 1910.

Shrimati Ranjit Kaur, Amritsar: Charan Singh, 1914.

Siape Da Siapa, Amritsar: Khalsa Tract Society, 1900.

Singhani Prabodh, Amritsar: Khalsa Tract Society, 1906.

Sudeshi Nunh Sarsari Nazar, Amritsar: Khalsa Tract Society, 1911.

Sukhwati Ke Chintamati Arthat Bal Biwah De Dukhre, Amritsar: Khalsa Tract Society, 1901.

Sundar Istri Te Sohna Mahal, Amritsar: Khalsa Tract Society, 1907.

Zaina Da Virlap, Amritsar: Khalsa Tract Society, 1913.

References and Selected Bibliography

Primary Sources Inclusive of the Early Twentieth Century:
Administrative, Army, Missionary, Education,
Reform Movements

A.D., *Until the Shadows Flee Away: The Story of C.E.Z.M.S. Work in India and Ceylon*, London: Church of England Zenana Missionary Society, n.d.

Bhai Amar Singh, *Anecdotes from Sikh History, No. 4: Stirring Stories of the Heroism of Sikh Women and the Martyrdom of a Sikh Youth*, Lahore: The Anglo-Sanskrit Press, 1906.

Baden-Powell, R.S.S., *Scouting for Boys: A Handbook for Instruction in Good Citizenship*, London: 1908.

Barstow, A.E., *Handbook on the Sikhs*, New Delhi: Uppal Publishing House, 1984. First published in 1899.

Beames, John, *Memoirs on the History, Folklore and Distribution of the Races of the Northwestern Provinces of India*, London: Trubner & Co., 1869.

Besant, Annie, *For India's Uplift*, Madras: G.A. Natesan, 1917.

Brown, John Care, *Indian Infanticide: Its Origin, Progress and Suppression*, London: W.H. Allen, 1857.

Campbell, George, *Memoirs of My Indian Career*, Vol. I, London: 1893.

Census Report of India, 1881, 1891, 1901, 1911, G.I.

Chhajju Singh Bawa, *The Ten Gurus and Their Teachings*, Lahore: Punjab Printing Works, 1903.

Court, Henry, *History of the Sikhs*, New Delhi: Nirmal Publishers & Distributors, 1989. First published in 1888.

Cunningham, J.D., *History of the Sikhs*, Delhi: Low Price Publications, 1990. First published in 1849.

Darling, Malcolm Lyall, *The Punjab Peasant in Prosperity and Debt*, London: OUP, 1928. First published in 1925.

Darling, Malcolm Lyall, *Wisdom and Waste in the Punjabi Village*, London: OUP, 1934.

Devi, Bibi Savitri, 'Sikh Education', A paper written for the Sikh Educational Conference, Jallundhar, Amritsar: The Educational Committee of the Chief Khalsa Diwan, n.d.

Dutta, R.C., *Pratap Singh: The Last of the Rajputs*, Allahabad, Kitabistan, 1943.

————, *A History of Civilization in Ancient India*, Delhi, Vishal Publishers, 1972 (first published 1888).

Falcon, R.W., *Handbook on Sikhs for the use of Regimental Officers*, Allahabad: Pioneer Press, 1896.

Farquhar, J.N., *Modern Religious Movements in India*, The Hartford-Lamson Lectures on the Religions of the World, London: The Macmillan Co., 1924.

Franklin, William, compiler, *Military Memoirs of Mr. George Thomas*, Calcutta: Hurkaru Press, 1803.

Garret, H.L.O., tr. and ed., *Punjab a Hundred Years Ago: As Described by V. Jacquemont (1831) and A. Soltykoff (1842)*, Patiala: Punjab Languages Department, 1971.

Gazetteer of the Punjab: Provincial Volume, 1888–9, Calcutta, Central Press Company Ltd., 1889.

Graham, J.A., *The Missionary Expansion of the Reformed Churches*, Edinburgh: R & R Clark Ltd., 1898.

Greenfield, M. Rose, *Five Years in Ludhiana on Work Amongst our Indian Sisters*, London: S.W. Partridge and Co., 1886.

Griffin, Lepel, *Ranjit Singh*, Oxford: Clarendon Press, 1892.

————, Charles Francis Massey, W.L. Conran, and H.D. Craig, *Chief and Families of Note in the Punjab*, Vol. 1, Lahore: Government Printing Press, 1940.

Guilford, E., *Non-Christian Religions. Sikhism*, Westminister: The Lay Reader Headquarters, 1915.

Heiler, Friedrich, *The Gospel of Sadhu Sunder Singh*, Olive Wyon, tr., London: George Allen and Unwin Ltd., 1927. First published in German under the title, *Sadhu Sundar Singh: Ein Apostel des Ostens und Westens* in 1926.

Henderson, A.E., *The Golden Gate of India: A Study of the Punjab Mission of the Presbyterian Church of New Zealand*, Dunedin: Foreign Missionary Committee, P.C.N.Z., 1922.

Ibbetson, Denzil, *Panjab Castes*, Delhi: Low Price Publications, 1993. First published in Lahore, 1916.

Innes, J.J. McLeod, *Sir Henry Lawrence: The Pacificator*, Oxford: Clarendon Press, 1898.

Kaur, Rajkumari Amrit, 'Woman in India', Congress Golden Jubilee Brochure No. 9, Swaraj Bhawan, Allahabad: All India Congress Committee, 1935.

_____, *Challenge to Women*, Allahabad: New Literature, 1946.

Khan, Sana Ullah, *A History of Education in the Punjab. Volume I, (Primary Education)*, Lahore: Rai Sahib M. Gulab Singh & Sons, 1932.

Singh, Khazan, *History and Philosophy of the Sikh Religion*, Part I, Lahore: Newal Kishore Press, 1914.

Lambeth, W.R., *Medical Missions: The Twofold Task*, New York: Student Volunteer Movement for Foreign Missions, 1920.

Latif, Syad Muhammad, *History of the Panjab. From the Remotest Antiquity to the Present Time*, New Delhi: Kalyani Publishers, 1994. First published in 1891.

Leitner, G.W., *History of Indigenous Education in the Panjab: Since Annexation and in 1882*, Patiala: Languages Department Punjab, 1971. First published in 1882.

Macauliffe, Max Arthur, *The Sikh Religion: It's Gurus, Sacred Writings and Authors*, 6 Vols, Delhi: Low Price Publications, 1990. First published in 1909.

MacMillan, Michael, *Tales of Indian Chivalry*, London: Blackie & Son Limited, n.d.

MacMunn, George, *The Martial Races of India*, London: Sampson Low, Marston & Co. Ltd., 1932.

Malcolm, John, *Sketch of the Sikhs*, London: John Murray,1812.

Mill, James, *The History of British India*, 2 Vols, New York: Chelsea House, 1968.

Narang, G.C., *Transformation of Sikhism*, Lahore: Tribune Press, 1912.

Oman, J. Campbell, *Cults, Customs and Superstitions of India*, London: T. Fisher Unwin, 1908.

_____, *The Mystics, Ascetics, and Saints of India*, Delhi: Oriental Publishers, 1973. First published in 1903.

Parry, R.E., *The Sikhs of the Punjab*, Drane's, 1921.

Pearse, Hugh, ed., *Soldier and Traveller: Memoirs of Alexander Gardner, Colonel of Artillery in the Service of Maharajah Ranjit Singh*, Patiala: Languages Department, 1970. First published in 1898.

Pollard, Edward B., *Women in all Ages in all Countries: Oriental Women*, Philadelphia: The Ruttenhouse Press, 1908.

Poole, John J., *Women's Influence in the East: As Shown in the Noble Lives of Past Queens and Princesses of India*, London: Elliot Stock, 1892.

Prinsep, Henry, *Origin of the Sikh Power in the Punjab. Political Life of Muha-Raja Runjeet Singh*, Calcutta: Military Orphan Press, 1834.

Ranade, Ramabai, *Himself, The Autobiography of a Hindu Lady*, New York: Longman, Green and Co., 1938.

Risley, Herbert, *The People of India*, W. Crooke, ed., London: Thacker & Co., 1915.

Rose, H.A., *A Glossary of the Tribes and Castes of the Punjab and North-West Frontier Province* (based on the Census Report for the Punjab, 1883), Vol. I, Patiala, Language Department, 1990 (first published 1883).

Sahibzade Bhagat Lakshman Singh, *Sat Sri Akal: The Sikh and His New Critics*, Tract No. 6, Mahilpur: The Sikh Tract Society, 1918.

Sahni, Ruchi Ram, *The Gurdwara Reform Movement and the Sikh Awakening*, Lahore: 1922.

Shah, Waris, *The Love of Hir and Ranjha*, Sant Singh Sekhon, tr., Ludhiana: Old Boys' Association, 1978.

Sohan Singh, *Truth and Bare Truth About the Sikh Kanya Maha Vidyala, Ferozepur*, Amritsar: Coronation Printing Works, 1915.

Steele, Flora Ann, *The Garden of Fidelity: Being the Autobiography of F.A. Steele, 1847–1929*, London: Macmillan and Co. Ltd., 1929.

Steinbach, Colonel, *The History of the Sikhs Together with a Concise Account of the Punjaub and Cashmere*, Calcutta: D'Rozario and Co., 1846.

Strachey, John, *India: Its Administration & Progress*, Fourth Edition, revised by Sir Thomas W. Holderness, London: Macmillan and Co. Ltd., 1911. First published in 1888.

Suri, Lala Sohan Lal, *Umdat-ut-Tawarkikh, Daftar IV, 1839–1845*, (Parts i–iii), an Outstanding Original Source of Punjab History, V.S. Suri, tr., Chandigarh: Punjab Itihas Prakashan, 1972.

Forty-eighth Annual Report of the Lodhiana Mission, Lodhiana: Lodhiana Mission Press, 1883.

The Imperial Gazetteer of India, Vol. XX, 1908.

Christian Literature Society, *The Advantages of Female Education*, Madras: The Christian Literature Society for India, 1892.

Talib, Gurubachan Singh, *Sri Guru Granth Sahib*, 4 Vols, Patiala: Punjabi University, 1987.

Talib, Gurubachan Singh, tr., *Sri Guru Granth Sahib*, 4 Vols, Patiala: Punjabi University, 1987.

Thorburn, S.S., *Musalmans and Moneylenders in the Punjab*, Delhi: Mittal Publications, 1983. First published in 1886.

Trumpp, Ernest, *Die Religion der Sikhs: Nach Den Quellen Dargestellt*, Leipzig: Otto Schultze, 1881.

————, *The Adi Granth or the Holy Scriptures of the Sikhs*, New Delhi: Munshiram Manoharlal, 1970. First published in 1877.

Upadhyaya, Ganga Prasad, tr., *The Light of Truth: English Translation of Swami Dayananda's Satyarth Prakasha*, Allahabad: The Kala Press, 1960. First published in 1875.

Vir Singh, *The Epic of Rana Surat Singh*, Gurbachan Singh Talib, tr., Chandigarh: Publication Bureau, Panjab University, 1986.

————, *Bijai Singh*, Devinder Singh Duggal, tr., Delhi: Bhai Vir Singh Sahitya Sadan, 1988.

————, *Satwant Kaur*, Ujagar Singh Bawa, tr., Delhi: Bhai Vir Singh Sahitya Sadan, 1988.

————, *Sundri*, Gobind Singh Mansukhani, tr., New Delhi: Bhai Vir Singh Sahitya Sadan, 1988.

PUNJABI AND OTHER SOURCES

Bhangu, Ratan Singh, *Prachin Panth Parkash*, Bhai Vir Singh, ed., Amritsar: Khalsa Samachar, 1939.

Chief Khalsa Diwan, *Gurmat Parkas*, Amritsar: Chief Khalsa Diwan, 1952. First published in 1915.

Dasam Granth, Vol. 1, Amritsar: Bhai Chatar Singh and Jeevan Singh Publishers, 1988.

Ganda Singh, ed., *Makhiz-I-Tawarikh-I-Sikhan*, Amritsar: Sikh History Society, 1949.

Jyotirudae, Lodhiana: Punjab Text Book Committee, Lodhianna Mission, 1882.

Kahn Singh Nabha, *Ham Hindu Nahin*, Amritsar: Khalsa Press 1914. First published in 1899.

Kirpal Singh, ed., *Janam-sakhi Parampara*, Patiala: Punjabi University Press, 1969.

Pritam Singh Kavi, *Istrian di Pahula* (The First Saviour of Women), Ludhiana: Bhani Sahib, 1979.

Randhir Singh, ed., *Prem Sumarg Granth*, Jalandhar: New Book Company, 1965. First published in 1953.

Shaiharyar, 'Punjabi di Pahili Shaira: Pero Preman', *Ajoke Shilalekh*, 1997.

Sagar, Lachhmi Devi Vidya, *Lachhmi Hulas Sagar*, Amritsar: Akhtar Hind Press, 1916.

Sodhi, Ram Narain Singh, *Khalsa Dharam Shastar*, Amritsar: Sri Gurmat Press, 1908.

Bhai Suraj Singh, *Sri Mata Bibi Harnam Kaur*, Amritsar: Wazir Hind Press, 1908.

Uttam Singh, *Khalsa Sanskara Pustaka*, Lahore: Arya Press, 1884.

SECONDARY SOURCES: BOOKS

Ahluwalia, M.M., *Kukas: The Freedom Fighters of the Panjab*, Delhi: Allied Publishers, 1965.

Alter, James P., *In the Doab and Rohilkhand: North Indian Christianity, 1815–1915*, Delhi: I.S.P.C.K., 1986.

Anand, Mulk Raj, *Folk Tales of Punjab*, Folk Tales of India Series, New Delhi: Sterling, 1978.

Parker, Andrew, Mary Russo, Doris Sommer, and Patricia Yaeger, eds, *Nationalisms & Sexualities*, New York: Routledge, 1992.

Arora, A.C., *British Policy towards the Punjab States, 1858–1905*, Jalandhar: Export India, 1982.

Ashta, Dharam Pal, *Poetry of the Dasam Granth*, New Delhi: Arun Prakashan, 1959.

Bajwa, Fauja Singh, *Kuka Movement*, Delhi: Motilal Banarsidass, 1965.

Bakhtin, Mikhail Mikhailovich, *Rabelais and His World*, H. Iswolsky, tr., Cambridge: MIT Press, 1968.

Bali, Yogendra, and Kalika Bali, *The Warriors in White: Glimpses of Kooka History*, Delhi: Har-Anand, 1995.

Ballhatchet, Kenneth, *Race, Sex and Class under the Raj: Imperial Attitudes and Policies and their Critics, 1793–1905*, London: Weidenfeld and Nicolson, 1980.

Banga, Indu, ed., *Five Punjabi Centuries: Polity, Economy, Society and Culture, c. 1500–1990*, Delhi: Manohar, 1997.

Barrier, N. G., *The Punjab Alienation of Land Bill of 1900*, Monograph and Occasional Papers Series, Number Two, North Carolina: Duke University, 1966.

———, *The Sikhs and their Literature: A Guide to Tracts, Books and Periodicals, 1849–1919*, Delhi: Manohar, 1970.

———, *The Census in British India: New Perspectives*, Delhi: Manohar, 1981.

Bedi, Sohinder Singh, *Folklore of Punjab*, Delhi: National Book Trust, 1971.

Bhagat Singh, *A History of Sikh Misals*, Patiala: Punjabi University, 1993.

Bhai Nahar Singh and Bhai Kirpal Singh, eds, *Rebels Against the British Rule (Guru Ram Singh and the Kuka Sikhs)*, Delhi: Atlantic Publishers, 1989.

Bhatia, Shyamala, *Social Change and Politics in Punjab, 1898–1910*, New Delhi: Enkay Publishers, 1987.

Borthwick, Meredith, *The Changing Role of Women in Bengal, 1849–1905*, Princeton: Princeton University Press, 1984.

Bose, Mandakranta, ed., *Visions of Virtue: Women in the Hindu Tradition*, Vancouver: M. Bose, 1996.

————, ed., *Faces of the Feminine in Ancient, Medieval and Modern India*, New York: OUP, 2000.

Brinda, *Maharani: The Story of an Indian Princess*, as told to Elaine Williams, New York: Henry Hold, 1954.

Butler, Judith P., *Gender Trouble: Feminism and the subversion of identity*, New York: Routledge, 1990.

Campbell, E.Y., *The Church in the Punjab: Some Aspects of its Life and Growth*, Nagpur: The National Christian Council in India, 1961.

Carroll, Berenice A., ed., *Liberating Women's History: Theoretical and Critical Essays*, Urbana: University of Illinois, 1976.

Chetan Singh, *Religion and Empire. Punjab in the seventeenth century*, Delhi: OUP, 1991.

Chowdhry, Prem, *The Veiled Women: Shifting Gender Equations in Rural Haryana, 1880–1990*, Delhi: OUP, 1994.

Cohen, Bernard S., *Colonialism and its Forms of Knowledge: The British in India*, Delhi: OUP, 1997.

Cole, W. Owen, *Teach Yourself Sikhism*, London: Hodder & Stoughton, 1994.

Singh, Darshan, *Western Perspective on the Sikh Religion*, Delhi: Sehgal, 1991.

de Bary, W. Theodore, *Sources of Indian Tradition*, New York: Columbia University Press, 1964.

de Beauvoir, Simone, *The Second Sex*, New York: Bantam, 1968.

de Lauretis, Theresa, ed., *Feminist Studies/Critical Studies*, Bloomington: Indiana University Press, 1986.

Domin, Dolores, *India in 1857–59: A Study in the Role of the Sikhs in the People's Uprising*, Berlin: Akademie-Verlag, 1977.

Dharam Parchar Committee, *The Sikh Reht Maryada* (The Code of Sikh Conduct and Conventions), Amritsar: SGPC, 1994.

Dhillon, B.S., *History and Study of the Jats, with reference to the Sikhs, Scythians, Alans, Sarmatians, Goths, and Jutes*, Gloucester: Beta Publishers, 1994.

Draper, Alfred, *Echoes of War: The Amritsar Massacre, Twilight of the Raj*, London: Buchan & Enright, 1985.

Falk, Nancy Auer and Rita M. Gross, eds, *Unspoken Worlds: Women's Religious Lives in Non-Western Cultures*, San Francisco: Harper & Row, 1980.

Fauja Singh, ed., *Historians and Historiography of the Sikhs*, New Delhi: Oriental Publishers, 1978.

Chief Khalsa Diwan, *Fifty Years of Service*, Amritsar: Wazir-i-Hind Press, 1952.

Forbes, Geraldine, *Women in Modern India*, Delhi: Cambridge University Press, 1996.

Foucault, Michel, *The History of Sexuality, Vol. I: An Introduction*, New York: Vintage, 1980.

Fox, Richard G., *Lions of the Punjab: Culture in the Making*, Delhi: Low Price Publications, 1990.

Fuchs, Stephen, *Godmen on the Warpath: A Study of Messianic Movements in India*, Delhi: Manoharlal Publishers, 1992.

Ganda Singh, ed., *Bhagat Lakshman Singh, Autobiography*, Calcutta: Sikh Cultural Centre, 1965.

_____, *Sikhism and Nirankari Movement*, Patiala: Guru Nanak Dev Mission, 1978.

_____, ed., *The Singh Sabha and other Reform Movements in the Punjab, 1850–1925*, The Panjab Past and Present, Patiala: Punjabi University, 1984.

Gerth, H.H. and C. Wright Mills, trs and eds, *From Max Weber: Essays in Sociology* New York: OUP, 1946.

Ghadially, Rehana, ed., *Women in Indian Society: A Reader*, New Delhi: Sage, 1988.

Ghose, J.C., ed., *The English Works of Raja Rammohan Roy*, Vol. 2, New Delhi: Cosmo, 1982.

Gilbert, Martin, *Servant of India, 1905–1910*, London, 1966.

Gill, M.K., *The Role and Status of Women in Sikhism*, Delhi: National Book Shop, 1995.

Göçek, Fatma Müge and Shiva Balaghi, eds, *Reconstructing Gender in the Middle East: Tradition, Identity, and Power*, New York: Columbia University Press, 1994.

Grewal, J.S., *From Guru Nanak to Maharajah Ranjit Singh*, Amritsar: Guru Nanak Dev University, 1972.

_____, ed., *Studies in Local and Regional History*, Amritsar: Guru Nanak University, 1974.

_____, *Guru Nanak in History*, Chandigarh: Panjab University, 1979.

Grewal, J.S., *The Sikhs of the Punjab*, Cambridge, Cambridge University Press, 1990.

_____, *Guru Nanak and Patriarchy*, Shimla, Indian Institute of Advanced Study, 1993.

_____, *Sikh Ideology, Polity and Social Order*, Delhi, Manohar, 1996.

_____, and S.S., Bal, *Guru Gobind Singh*, Chandigarh: Panjab University, 1967.

_____, and Indu Banga, trs and eds, *Early Nineteenth Century Panjab: From Ganesh Das'* 'Char Bagh-i-Panjab', Amritsar: Guru Nanak University, 1975.

Gross, Rita M., ed., *Beyond Androcentrism: New Essays on Women and Religion*, Montana: Scholars Press, 1977.

Guleria, J.S., ed., *Bhai Vir Singh: The Sixth River of Punjab*, Delhi: Bhai Vir Singh Sahitya Sadan, 1984.

Gupta, Hari Ram, *History of the Sikhs*, 6 Vols, New Delhi: Manoharlal Publishers, 1980.

Gurcharan Singh, *Studies in Punjab History and Culture*, New Delhi: Enkay Publishers, 1990.

Gustafson, W. Eric, Kenneth W. Jones, eds, *Sources on Punjab History*, Delhi: Manohar, 1975.

Habib, Irfan, *Essays in Indian History: Towards a Marxist Perception*, Delhi: Tulika, 1995.

Haddad, Yvonne Yazbeck and Ellison Banks Findly, eds, *Women, Religion, and Social Change*, Albany: SUNY Press,1985.

Hall, Donald E., ed., *Muscular Christianity: Embodying the Victorian Age*, Cambridge: University Press, 1994.

Hans, Surjit Singh, *A Reconstruction of Sikh History from Sikh Literature*, Jalandhar: ABS Publications, 1988.

Harbans Singh, *Bhai Vir Singh: A Short Biography*, Delhi: Bhai Vir Singh Sahitya Sadan, 1990.

_____, and N.G. Barrier, eds, *Punjab Past and Present: Essays in Honour of Dr. Ganda Singh*, Patiala: Punjabi University, 1996.

Hasrat, Bikrama Jit, *Life and Times of Ranjit Singh: A Saga of Benevolent Despotism*, Hoshiarpur: V.V. Resarch Institute, 1977.

Hawley, John Stratton, and Gurinder Singh Mann, eds, *Studying the Sikhs: Issues for North America*, Albany: SUNY Press, 1993.

Haynes, Douglas E., *Rhetoric and Ritual and Colonial India: The Shaping of a Public Culture in Surat City, 1852–1928*, Berkeley: UC Press, 1991.

Hess, Linda and Shukdev Singh, trs, *The Bijak of Kabir*, Delhi: Motilal Banarsidass, 1986.

Hobsbawm, Eric, and Terence Ranger, eds, *The Invention of Tradition*, Cambridge: Cambridge University Press, 1983.

Holm, Jean, with John Bowker, eds, *Women in Religion*, London: Pinter Publishers, 1994.

Howes, Ruth H., Michael R. Stevenson, eds, *Women and the Use of Military Force*, Boulder: Lynne Rienner Publishers, 1993.

Hyam, Ronald, *Empire and Sexuality: The British Experience*, Manchester: Manchester University Press, 1990.

Ingham, Kenneth, *Reformers in India, 1793–1833: An Account of the Work of Christian Missionaries on Behalf of Social Reform*, Cambridge: Cambridge University Press, 1956.

Isaksson, Eva, ed., *Women and the Military System*, London: Harvester-Wheatsheaf, 1988.

Jacquelin Singh, *Seasons*, Delhi: Penguin, 1991.

Jaswinder Singh, *Kukas of Note in the Punjab: Documents—1881*, Ludhiana: Namdhari Darbar, Bhaini Sahib, 1984.

_____, *Kuka Movement: Freedom Struggle in Punjab (Documents, 1880–1903 AD)*, Delhi: Atlantic Publishers, 1985.

Jolly, Surjit Kaur, *Sikh Revivalist Movements: The Nirankari and Namdhari Movements in Punjab in the Nineteenth Century—A Socio-Religious Study*, New Delhi: Gitanjali, 1988.

Jones, Kenneth W., *Arya Dharm: Hindu Consciousness in 19th-Century Punjab*, Delhi: Manohar, 1989.

_____, *Socio-Religious Reform Movements in British India*, Cambridge: Cambridge University Press, 1994.

Juergensmeyer, Mark, N.G. Barrier, eds, *Sikh Studies: Comparative Perspectives on a Changing Tradition*, Berkeley: Graduate Theological Union, 1979.

Kapur, Anup Chand, *The Punjab Crisis: An Analytical Study*, Delhi: S. Chand, 1985.

Kapur, Rajiv A., *Sikh Separatism: The Politics of Faith*, London: Allen and Unwin, 1986.

Kaur, Gurnam, ed., *Sikh Value System and Social Change*, Patiala: Punjabi University, 1995.

Kaur, Upinder Jit, *Sikh Religion and Economic Development*, Delhi: National Book Organization, 1990.

Kharak Singh, G.S. Mansukhani, and Jasbir Singh Mann, eds, *Fundamental Issues in Sikh Studies*, Chandigarh: Institute of Sikh Studies, 1992.

Khushwant Singh, *A History of the Sikhs*, 2 Vols, Delhi: OUP, 1991.

Kinsley, David, *Hindu Goddesses: Visions of the Divine Feminine in the Hindu Religious Tradition*, Berkeley: UC Press, 1986.

Kohli, Yash, ed., *The Women of Punjab*, Bombay: Chic Publications, 1983.

Kumar, Nita, ed., *Women as Subjects*, Charlottesville: University Press of Virginia, 1994.

Lateef, Shahida, *Muslim Women in India: Political and Private Realities— 1890s–1980s*, Delhi: Kali for Women, 1990.

Lawrence, Bruce B., *Defenders of God: The Fundamentalist Revolt Against the Modern Age*, San Francisco: Harper & Row, 1989.

Lewis, Gilbert, *Day of Shining Red: An Essay on Understanding Ritual*, Cambridge: Cambridge University Press, 1988.

Lewis, Oscar, *Village Life in Northern India: Studies in a Delhi Village*, New York: Vintage, 1965.

Liddle, Joanna, and Rama Joshi, *Daughters of Independence: Gender, Caste and Class in India*, Delhi: Kali for Women/Zed Books, 1986.

Lorber, Judith, and Susan A. Farrell, eds, *The Social Construction of Gender*, Newbury Park: Sage, 1991.

Lorenzen, David N., ed., *Bhakti Religion in North India: Community Identity and Political Action*, Albany: SUNY Press, 1995.

Macdonald, Sharon, Pat Holden, and Shirley Arderer, eds, *Images of Women in Peace and War: Cross-Cultural and Historical Perspectives*, London: Macmillan, 1987.

MacKenzie, John M., ed., *Popular Imperialism and the military—1850– 1950*, Manchester: Manchester University Press, 1992.

MacMillan, Margaret, *Women of the Raj*, New York: Thames & Hudson, 1988.

Malhotra, Anshu, *Gender, Caste and Religious Identities: Restructuring Class in Colonial Punjab*, Delhi: OUP, 2002.

Malik, Ikram Ali, *The History of the Punjab, 1799–1947*, Delhi: Neeraj Publishing, 1983.

Mangan, J.A., and James Walvin, eds, *Manliness and Morality: Middle-class Masculinity in Britain and America, 1800–1940*, Manchester: Manchester University Press, 1987.

Marenco, Ethne K., *The Transformation of Sikh Society*, New Delhi: Heritage Publishers, 1976.

Maskiell, Michelle, *Women Between Cultures: The Lives of Kinnaird College Alumnae in British India*, Syracuse: Foreign and Comparative Studies/South Asian Series, No. 9, 1984.

McFague, Sallie, *Metaphorical Theology: Models of God in Religious Language*, Philadelphia: Fortress Press, 1982.

McLeod, H., *Religion and Irreligion in Victorian England: How Secular Was the Working Class?*, Bangor: Headstart History, 1993.

McLeod, W.H., *The Evolution of the Sikh Community: Five Essays*, Oxford: Clarendon, 1976.

——, tr., *The B40 janam-sakhi*, Amritsar: Guru Nanak Dev University, 1980.

——, ed. and tr., *Textual Sources for the Study of Sikhism*, Chicago: University of Chicago, 1984.

——, *The Chaupa Singh Rahit-Nama*, Dunedin: University of Otago, 1987.

——, *The Sikhs. History, Religion, and Society*, New York: Columbia University Press, 1989.

——, *Who is a Sikh? The Problem of Sikh Identity*, Oxford: OUP, 1992.

——, *Historical Dictionary of Sikhism*, London: Scarecrow Press, Inc., 1995.

——, *Guru Nanak and the Sikh Religion*, Delhi: OUP, 1996.

——, *Sikhism*, London: Penguin, 1997.

McMullen, Clarence O., *Religious Beliefs and Practices of the Sikhs in Rural Punjab*, Delhi: Manohar, 1989.

Meijer, Maaike, and Jetty Schaap, eds, *Historiography of Women's Cultural Traditions*, Dordrecht: Foris, 1987.

Metcalf, Barbara Daly, *Islamic Revival in British India: Deoband, 1860–1900*, Princeton: Princeton University Press, 1982.

——, *Perfecting Women: Maulana Ashraf 'Ali Thanawi's Bihishti Zewar—A Partial Translation with Commentary*, Berkeley: UC Press, 1990.

Metcalf, Thomas R., *Ideologies of the Raj*, Delhi: Cambridge University Press, 1995.

Minault, Gail, ed., *The Extended Family: Women and Political Participation in India and Pakistan*, Delhi: Chanakya, 1981.

——, tr., *Voices of Silence: English Translation of Khwaja Altaf Hussain Hali's Majalis un-Nissa and Chup ki Dad*, Delhi: Chanakya, 1986.

Minh-ha, Trinh T., *Woman, Native, Other: Writing Postcoloniality and Feminism*, Indianapolis: Indiana University Press, 1989.

Mittal, S.C., *Freedom Movement in Punjab (1905–29)*, Delhi: Concept Publishers, 1977.

Mohanty, Chandra T., Ann Russo, and Lourdes Torres, eds, *Third World Women and the Politics of Feminism*, Bloomington: Indian University Press, 1991.

Mohinder Singh, ed., *Prof. Harbans Singh: Commemoration Volume*, Delhi: Prof. Harbans Singh Commemoration Committee, 1988.

Mohinder Singh, ed., *History and Culture of Panjab*, New Delhi, Atlantic, 1989.

Naggar, B.S., *Maharani Jind Kaur: The Mother-Queen of Maharajah Dalip Singh*, Delhi: P.K.B. Publications, 1975.

Narang, A.S., *Storm over the Sutlej: The Akali Politics*, Delhi: Gitanjali, 1983.

Nikki-Guninder Kaur Singh, *The Feminine Principle in the Sikh Vision of the Transcendent*, Cambridge: Cambridge University Press, 1993.

Novak, Michael, *Ascent of the Mountain, Flight of the Dove: An Invitation to Religious Studies*, New York: Harper and Row, 1971.

Nripinder Singh, *The Sikh Moral Tradition: Ethical Perceptions of the Sikhs in the Late Nineteenth/Early Twentieth Century*, Delhi: Manohar, 1990.

O'Connell, Joseph T., Milton Israel, and Willard G. Oxtaby, eds, *Sikh History and Religion in the Twentieth Century*, Toronto: University of Toronto, 1988.

Oberoi, Harjot, *The Construction of Religious Boundaries: Culture, Identity and Diversity in the Sikh Tradition*, Delhi: OUP, 1994.

Olson, Carl, ed., *The Book of the Goddess: Past and Present*, New York: Crossroads, 1983.

Parker, Andrew, Mary Russo, Doris Sommer, and Patricia Yaeger, eds, *Nationalisms & Sexualities*, New York: Routledge, 1992.

Singh, Pashaura, and N.G. Barrier, eds, *The Transmission of Sikh Heritage in the Diaspora*, Delhi: Manohar, 1996.

Pawar, Kiran, ed., *Women in Indian History: Social, Economic, Political and Cultural Perspectives*, Delhi: Vision & Venture, 1996. .

Radin, Paul, *Primitive Religion: Its Nature and Origin*, New York: Dover Publications, 1957.

Raheja, Gloria Goodwin and Ann Grodzins Gold, *Listen to the Heron's Words: Reimagining Gender and Kinship in North India*, Berkeley: UC Press, 1994.

Ray, Bharati, ed., *From the Seams of History: Essays on Indian Women*, Delhi: OUP, 1995.

Reagan, Charles E. and David Stewart, eds, *The Philosophy of Paul Ricoeur: An Anthology of His Work*, Boston: Beacon Press, 1978.

Redfield, Robert, *The Little Community* and *Peasant Society and Culture*, Chicago: University of Chicago, 1960.

Sandhu, Devinder Pal, *Studies in Indian Politics: Study of a Minority*, Delhi: Patriot Publishers, 1992.

Sangari, Kumkum, and Sudesh Vaid, eds, *Recasting Women: Essays in Colonial History*, New Jersey: Rutgers University Press, 1990.

Sawicki, Jana, *Disciplining Foucault: Feminism, Power, and the Body*, New York: Routledge, 1991.

Schimmel, Annemarie, *Mystical Dimensions of Islam*, Chapel Hill: University of North Carolina Press, 1975.

Schomer, Karine, and W.H. McLeod, eds, *The Sants: Studies in a Devotional Tradition in India*, Berkeley and Delhi: Berkeley Religious Studies and Motilal Banarsidass, 1987.

Scott, Joan Wallach, *Gender and the Politics of History*, New York: Columbia University Press, 1988.

Sharma, Arvind, ed., *Women in World Religions*, Albany: SUNY Press, 1987.

————, ed., *Religion and Women*, Albany: SUNY Press, 1994.

————, ed., *Today's Woman in World Religions*, Albany: SUNY Press, 1994.

Shattuck, Cybelle, *Hinduism*, New Jersey: Prentice Hall, 1999.

Bhai Nahar Singh and Bhai Kirpal Singh, eds, *Rebels against the British Rule (Guru Ram Singh and the Kuka Sikhs)*, New Delhi: Atlantic, 1989.

Fauja Singh, Guru Amar Das: Life and Teachings, New Delhi: Sterling Publishers, 1979.

Sinha, Mrinalini, *Colonial Masculinity: The 'Manly Englishman' and the 'Effeminate Bengali' in the Late Nineteenth Century*, Manchester: Manchester University Press, 1995.

Smith, Mark, *Religion in Industrial Society: Oldham and Saddleworth, 1740–1865*, Oxford: Clarendon Press, 1994.

Smith-Rosenberg, Carrol, *Disorderly Conduct: Visions of Gender in Victorian America*, New York: Alfred Knopf, 1985.

Stallybrass, Peter, and Allon White, *The Politics and Poetics of Transgression*, London: Methuen, 1986.

Stimpson, Catharine R., ed., *Women, History & Theory: The Essays of Joan Kelly*, Chicago: University of Chicago, 1984.

Talbot, Ian, *Punjab and the Raj—1849–1947*, Delhi: Manohar, 1988.

Talib, Gurubachan Singh and Attar Singh, eds, *Bhai Vir Singh: Life, Times & Works*, Chandigarh: Panjab University, 1973.

Tandon, Prakash, *Punjabi Century, 1857–1947*, Berkeley: UC Press, 1968.

Teja Singh, *Essays in Sikhism*, Lahore: Sikh University Press, 1944.

Tharu, Susie, and K. Lalita, eds, *Women Writing in India: 600 BC to the Present*, Vol. 1, New York: City University of New York, 1991.

Trautman, Thomas R., *Aryans and British India*, Berkeley: UC Press, 1997.

Turner, Victor W., *Dramas, Fields, and Metaphors: Symbolic Action in Human Society*, Ithaca, N.Y.: Cornell University Press, 1974.

Uberoi, Patricia, ed., *Social Reform, sexuality and the state*, Delhi: Sage, 1996.

Valenze, D.M., *Prophetic Sons and Daughters: Female Preaching and Popular Religion in Industrial England*, Princeton: Princeton University Press, 1985.

van den Dungen, P.H.M., *The Punjab Tradition: Influence and Authority in Nineteenth-Century India*, London: George Allen and Unwin Ltd., 1972.

Viswanathan, Gauri, *Masks of Conquest: Literary Study and British Rule in India*, New York: Columbia University Press, 1989.

Waheeduddin, Fakir Syed, *The Real Ranjit Singh*, Karachi: Lion Art Press, 1965.

Webster, John B., *The Christian Community and Change in Nineteenth Century North India*, Delhi: Macmillan, 1976.

————, *Nirankari Sikhs*, Delhi: Macmillan, 1979.

Wolffe, John, *The Protestant Crusade in Great Britain, 1829–1860*, Oxford: Clarendon Press, 1991.

————, ed., *Religion in Victorian Britain*, Manchester, Manchester University Press, 1997.

Wurgaft, Lewis D., *The Imperial Imagination: Magic and Myth in Kipling's India*, Connecticut: Wesleyan University Press, 1983.

ARTICLES AND CHAPTERS

Acker, Joan, 'Hierarchies, Jobs, Bodies: A Theory of Gendered Organizations', Judith Lorber and Susan A. Farrell, eds, *The Social Construction of Gender*, Newbury Park: Sage, 1991.

Ahuja, Jasbir Kaur, 'Mata Gujri—Consort and Mother', *The Sikh Review*, Vol. 41:5, No. 473, pp. 14–16, 1993.

Albrecht-Heide, Astrid, 'Women and War: Victims and Collaborators', Eva Isaksson, ed., *Women and the Military System*, London: Harvester-Wheatsheaf, 1988.

Alcoff, Linda, 'Feminist Politics and Foucault: The Limits to a Collaboration', Arleen B. Dallery, Charles E. Scott, with P. Holley Roberts, eds, *Crisis in Continental Philosophy*, Selected Studies in Phenomenology and Existential Philosophy, 16, Albany: SUNY Press, 1990.

Attar Singh, 'Political Change and Punjabi Literature in the Nineteenth Century', Indu Banga, ed., *Five Punjabi Centuries· Polity, Economy, Society and Culture, c. 1500–1990*, Delhi: Manohar, 1997.

Bagchi, A.K., 'De-industrialization in India in the Nineteenth Century: Some Theoretical Implications', *Journal of Development Studies*, vol. 12, pp. 135–64, 1975–1976.

Bagrian, Bhai Ashok Singh, 'Anand Karaj: A Model Wedding Sermon', *The Sikh Review*, Vol. 39:4, No. 448, pp. 25–9, 1991.

Bajaj, Satish K., 'Status of Women in the Pre-Modern Punjab', *Punjab History Conference*, Proceedings, Eighteenth Session, 1983.

Banerjee, Himadri, 'Maharani Jindan in Bengali Writings', *The Sikh Review*, Vol. 36, No. 415, pp. 32–7, 1988.

Banerjee, Sumanta, 'Marginalization of Women's Popular Culture in Nineteenth Century Bengal', K. Sangari and S. Vaid, eds, *Recasting Women: Essays in Indian Colonial History*, New Jersey: Rutgers University Press, 1997.

Banga, Indu, 'Socio-Religious Reform and Patriarchy', Kiran Pawar, ed., *Women in Indian History: Social, Economic, Political and Cultural Perspectives*, Delhi: Vision & Venture, 1996.

Barrier, N. Gerald 'Banned Literature in Punjab, 1907–1947', W. Eric Gustafson and Kenneth W. Jones, eds, *Sources on Punjab History*, Delhi: Manohar, 1975.

————, 'The Sikh Resurgence, 1844–1947', W. Eric Gustafson and Kenneth W. Jones, eds, *Sources on Punjab History*, Delhi: Manohar, 1975.

————, 'Trumpp and Macauliffe: Western Students of Sikh History and Religion', Fauja Singh, ed., *Historians and Historiography of the Sikhs*, Delhi: Oriental Publishers, 1978.

————, 'Sikh Politics and Religion: The Bhasaur Singh Sabha', Indu Banga, ed., *Five Punjabi Centuries: Polity, Economy, Society and Culture, c.1500–1990*, Delhi: Manohar, 1997.

Behar, Ruth, 'Gender, Identity, and Anthropology', Fatma Müge Göçek and Shiva Balaghi, eds, *Reconstructing Gender in the Middle East: Tradition, Identity, and Power*, New York: Columbia University Press, 1994.

Bhagat Singh, 'Giani Gian Singh', *Punjab History Conference*, Proceedings, Ninth Session, 1975.

Bhai Jodh Singh, 'Sri Guru Amar Das Ji', *The Punjab Past and Present*, Vol. 8, No. 2, pp. 251–99, 1979.

Boals, Kay, 'The Politics of Cultural Liberation: Male-Female Relations in Algeria', Berenice A. Carroll, ed., *Liberating Women's History: Theoretical and Critical Essays*, Urbana: University of Illinois, 1976.

Bosch, Mineke, 'Women's Culture in Women's History: Historical Notion or Feminist Vision?', Maaike Meijer and Jetty Schaap, eds, *Historiography of Women's Cultural Traditions*, Dordrecht: Foris Publications, 1987.

Bourdieu, Pierre, 'Social Space and Symbolic Power', *Sociological Theory*, Vol. 7, No. 1, Spring, pp. 14–25, 1989.

Brekus, Catherine A., 'Studying Women and Religion: Problems and Possibilities', *Criterion*, Vol. 32, No.3, pp. 24–8, 1993.

Brubaker, Richard L., 'The Untamed Goddesses of Village India', Carl Olson, ed., *The Book of the Goddess: Past and Present*, New York: Crossroads, 1983.

Caveeshar, Sardul Singh, 'The Sikh Kanya Mahavidyala Ferozepore', Ganda Singh, ed., *The Singh Sabha and other Reform Movements in the Punjab, 1850–1925: The Punjab Past and Present*, Patiala: Punjabi University, 1984. First published in 1937.

Chakravarty, Uma, 'The World of the Bhaktin in South Indian Traditions— The Body and Beyond', *Manushi*, No. 50, 51, 52, pp. 18–29, 1989.

———, 'Reconceptualising Gender: Phule, Brahmanism and Brahmanical Patriarchy', Kiran Pawar, ed., *Women in Indian History: Social, Economic, Political and Cultural Perspectives*, Delhi: Vision & Venture, 1996.

———, 'Whatever Happened to the Vedic *Dasi*? Orientalism, Nationalism, and a Script for the Past', K. Sangari and S. Vaid, eds, *Recasting Women: Essays in Indian Colonial History*, New Jersey: Rutgers University Press, 1997.

Chatterjee, Partha, 'Colonialism, Nationalism, and Colonized Women: The Contest in India', *American Ethnologist*, Vol. 16, No. 4, pp. 622–33, 1989.

———, 'The Nationalist Resolution of the Women's Question', K. Sangari and S. Vaid, eds, *Recasting Women: Essays in Colonial History*, New Jersey: Rutgers University Press, pp. 233–53, 1997.

Chhachhi, Amrita, 'The State, Religious Fundamentalism and Women: Trends in South Asia', *Economic and Political Weekly*, pp. 567–78, 1989.

Chowdhry, Prem, 'Popular Perceptions of Widow-Remarriage in Haryana: Past and Present', Bharati Ray, ed., *From the Seams of History: Essays on Indian Women*, Delhi, OUP, 1995.

———, 'Contesting Claims and Counter-Claims: Questions of the Inheritance and Sexuality of Widows in a Colonial State', Patricia Uberoi, ed., *Social reform, Sexuality and the State*, Delhi: Sage, 1996.

———, 'Customs in a Peasant Economy: Women in Colonial Haryana', K. Sangari and S. Vaid, eds, *Recasting Women: Essays in Indian Colonial History*, New Jersey: Rutgers University Press, 1997.

Christian, Barbara, 'The Race for Theory', *Cultural Critique*, No. 6, pp. 51–63, 1997.

Dewey, Clive, 'Images of the Village Community: A Study in Anglo-Indian Ideology', *Modern Asian Studies*, Vol. 6, pp. 291–328, 1972.

Dhillon, Gurdarshan Singh, 'Singh Sabha Movement and Social Change', Gurnam Kaur, ed., *Sikh Value System and Social Change*, Patiala: Punjabi University, 1995.

Dusenbery, Verne A., 'Of Singh Sabhas, Siri Singh Sahibs, and Sikh Scholars: Sikh Discourse from North America in the 1970s', N. Gerald Barrier and Verne A. Dusenbery, eds, *The Sikh Diaspora: Migration and the Experience Beyond Punjab*, Delhi: Chanakya, 1989.

Engels, Dagmar, 'The Limits of Gender Ideology: Bengali Women, the Colonial State, and the Private Sphere: 1890–1930', *Women's Studies International Forum*, Vol. 12, No. 4, pp. 425–37, 1989.

Esonwanne, Uzoma, 'Feminist Theory and the Discourse of Colonialism', Shirley Neuman and Glennis Stephenson, eds, *ReImagining Women: Representations of Women in Culture*, Toronto: UT Press, 1993.

Falk, Nancy, 'Introduction', Yvonne Yazbeck Haddad and Ellison Banks Findly, eds, *Women, Religion, and Social Change*, Albany: SUNY Press, 1985.

Fasick, Laura, 'Charles Kingsley's Scientific Treatment of Gender', Donald E. Hall, ed., *Muscular Christianity: Embodying the Victorian Age*, Cambridge: Cambridge University Press, 1994.

Fauja Singh, 'Guru Amar Das: Life and Thought', *The Punjab Past and Present*, Vol. 8, No. 2, pp. 300–33, 1979.

Fenech, Louis E., 'The Taunt in Popular Martyrologies', Pashaura Singh and N. Gerald Barrier, eds, *The Transmission of Sikh Heritage in the Diaspora*, Delhi: Manohar, 1996.

Fenn, Richard K., 'The Sociology of Religion: A Critical Survey', Tom Tottomore, Stefan Nowak, and Magdalena Sokolowska, eds, *Sociology: The State of the Art*, London: Sage, 1982.

Friedl, Erika, 'Notes from the Village: On the Ethnographic Construction of Women in Iran', Fatma Müge Göçek and Shiva Balaghi, eds, *Reconstructing Gender in the Middle East: Tradition, Identity, and Power*, New York: Columbia University Press, 1994.

Ganda Singh, 'Some Important Sources of Information on Maharajah Ranjit Singh's Period', *The Punjab Past and Present*, Vol. 15, No. 2, pp. 346–52, 1981.

————, 'Hair and Turban: Their Importance for the Sikhs,' *The Punjab Past and Present*, Vol. 16:1, No. 31, pp. 201–7, 1982.

Gilmartin, David, 'Kinship, Women and Politics in Twentieth-Century Punjab', Gail Minault, ed., *The Extended Family: Women and Political Participation in India and Pakistan*, Delhi: Chanakya, 1981.

Göçek, Fatma Müge and Shiva Balaghi, 'Reconstructing Gender in the Middle East Through Voice and Experience', Fatma Müge Göçek and Shiva Balaghi, eds, *Reconstructing Gender in the Middle East: Tradition, Identity, and Power*, New York: Columbia University Press, 1994.

Gopal, Madan, 'Legacy of Dyal Singh Majithia', *The Punjab Past and Present*, Vol. 26, No. 1, pp. 156–87, 1992.

Gordon, Ann D., Mari Jo Buhle, and Nancy Schrom Dye, 'The Problem of Women's History', Berenice A. Carroll, ed., *Liberating Women's History: Theoretical and Critical Essays*, Urbana: University of Illinois, 1976.

Gordon, Linda, 'What's New in Women's History', Sneja Gunew, ed., *A Reader in Feminist Knowledge*, London: Routledge, 1991.

Grewal, J.S., 'Khalsa of Guru Gobind Singh—A Problem in Historiography', *Punjab History Conference, Proceedings*, Second Session, 1966.

————, 'The Prem Sumarg: A Theory of Sikh Social Order', *Punjab History Conference*, Proceedings, First Session, 1968.

————, 'Dissent in Early Sikhism', *Punjab History Conference*, Proceedings, Fourteenth Session, 1980.

————, 'A gender perspective of Guru Nanak', Kiran Pawar, ed., *Women in Indian History: Social, Economic, Political and Cultural Perspectives*, Delhi: Vision & Venture, 1996.

————, 'The Prem Sumarg: A Theory of Sikh Social Order', Harbans Singh and N. Gerald Barrier, eds, *Punjab Past and Present: Essays in Honour of Dr Ganda Singh*, Patiala: Punjabi University, 1996.

Gross, Rita M., 'Androcentrism and Androgyny in the Methodology of History of Religions', Rita M. Gross, ed., *Beyond Androcentrism: New Essays on Women and Religion*, Montana: Scholars Press, 1977.

————, 'Studying Women and Religion: Conclusions Twenty-Five Years Later', Arvind Sharma, ed., *Today's Woman in World Religions*, Albany: SUNY Press, 1994.

Gulcharan Singh, 'Women's Lib in Sikh Scriptures & Sociology', *The Sikh Review*, Vol. 36, No. 411, pp. 38–43, 1988.

Gupta, Shiv Kumar, 'Arya Samaj: A Potent Factor in the National Movement for Raising Womanhood', *Punjab History Conference*, Proceedings, Twenty-fouth Session, 1991.

Gurbux Singh, 'Society in the Punjab under Ranjit Singh—Mufti Ali-Ud Din's Analysis', *Punjab History Conference*, Proceedings, Tenth Session, 1976.

Gurdarshan Singh, 'Origin and Development of the Singh Sabha Movement: Constitutional Aspects', Ganda Singh, ed., *The Singh Sabha and Other Socio-Religious Movements in the Punjab, 1850–1925, The Panjab Past and Present*, Patiala: Punjabi University, 1984.

Gurdarshan Singh, 'Chief Khalsa Diwan: Fifty Years of Service (1902–1951)', Ganda Singh, ed., *The Singh Sabha and other Socio-Religious Movements in the Punjab, 1850–1925—The Punjab Past and Present*, Patiala: Punjabi University, 1984.

———, 'The Singh Sabha Movement', Mohinder Singh, ed., *History and Culture of Panjab*, New Delhi: Atlantic, 1989.

Habib, Irfan, 'Jatts of Punjab and Sind', Harbans Singh and N. Gerald Barrier, eds, *Punjab Past and Present: Essays in Honour of Dr. Ganda Singh*, Patiala: Punjabi University, 1996.

Hans, Surjit, 'Jallianwala Bagh: The Construction of Nationalist Symbol', *Journal of Sikh Studies*, Vol. 18, pp. 1–17, 1993–4.

Hans, S.S., 'Prem Sumarg—A Modern Forgery', *Punjab History Conference*, Proceedings, Sixteenth Session, 1982.

Harbans Singh, 'The Bakapur Diwan and Babu Teja Singh of Bhasaur', *The Punjab Past and Present*, Vol. 9, No. 2, pp. 322–32, 1975.

———, 'Sikh faith and the Nirankaris: A historical perspective', *The Punjab Past and Present*, Vol. 13, No. 1, pp. 220–6, 1979.

———, 'Status of Women in Sikhism', Yash Kohli, ed., *The Women of Punjab*, Bombay: Chic Publications, 1983.

———, 'Origins of the Singh Sabha', Harbans Singh and N. Gerald Barrier, eds, *Panjab Past and Present: Essays in Honour of Dr. Ganda Singh*, Patiala: Punjabi University, 1996.

Jain, Sunil, 'Punjab's Response to Communal Representation', *Punjab History Conference*, Proceedings, Twentieth Session, 1986.

Jakobsh, Doris R., 'Gender Issues in Sikh Studies: Hermeneutics of Affirmation or Hermeneutics of Suspicion?', Pashaura Singh and N. Gerald Barrier, eds, *The Transmission of the Sikh Heritage in the Diaspora*, New Delhi: Manohar, 1996.

Jenkins, Mercilee and Cheris, Kramarae, 'A Thief in the House: Women and Language', Dale Spender, ed., *Men's Studies Modified: The Impact of Feminism on the Academic Disciplines*, Oxford: Pergamon, 1981.

Joginder Singh, 'The Illustrious Women of Punjab', in Yash Kohli, ed., *The Women of Punjab*, Bombay: Chic Publications, 1983.

———, 'The Sikhs and the Anti-British Agitation in the First Decade of Twentieth Century', *Punjab History Conference*, Proceedings, Twenty-fourth Session, 1991.

Jones, Kenneth W., '*Ham Hindu Nahin*: Arya-Sikh Relations, 1877–1905', *Journal of Asian Studies*, Vol. 32, No. 3, pp. 457–75, 1973.

———, 'Religious Identity and the Indian Census', N., Gerald Barrier, ed., *The Census in British India: New Perspectives*, Delhi: Manohar, 1981.

Jones, Kenneth W., 'Socio-Religious Movements and Changing Gender Relationships among Hindus of British India', James Warner Bjorkman, ed., *Fundamentalism Revivalists and Violence in South Asia*, Delhi: Manohar, 1988.

Juergensmeyer, Mark, 'Political Origins of a Punjabi Lower Caste Religion', Paul Wallace and Surendra Chopra, eds, *Political Dynamics and Crisis in Punjab*, Amritsar: Guru Nanak Dev University, 1988.

Kaur, Jasdip, 'An Egalitarian Faith', *The Sikh Review*, Vol. 41:7, No. 475, pp. 34–6, 1993.

Kaur, Kanwaljit, 'Sikh Women', Kharak Singh, G.S. Mansukhani, and Jasbir Singh Mann, eds, *Fundamental Issues in Sikh Studies*, Chandigarh: Institute of Sikh Studies, 1992.

Kaur, Mandajit, 'A Documentary Evidence on the Sikh Reaction at Trumpp's translation of the Adi Granth', *Punjab History Conference*, Proceedings, Fourteenth Session, 1980.

Kaur-Singh, Kanwaljit, 'Sikhism', Jean Holm with John Bowker, eds, *Women in Religion*, London: Pinter, 1994.

Khera, P.N., 'Social Life in the Sikh Kingdom', *The Punjab Past and Present*, Vol. 12, No. 2, pp. 45–65, 1979.

Khosla, G.S., 'The Dramatic Element in Bhai Vir Singh', Gurbachan Singh Talib and Attar Singh, eds, *Bhai Vir Singh: Life, Times & Works*, Chandigarh: Panjab University, 1973.

Kishwar, Madhu and Ruth Vanita, 'The Burning of Roop Kanwar', *Manushi*, No. 42–3, pp. 15–25, 1987.

Kishwar, Madhu, 'Nature of Women's Mobilization in Rural India. An Exploratory Essay', *Economic and Political Weekly*, No. 52, 53, pp. 2754–63, 1988.

Knight, F., '"Male and Female He Created Them": Men, Women and the Question of Gender', John Wolffe, ed., *Religion in Victorian Britain*, Manchester: Manchester University Press, 1997.

Kohli, S.S., 'Bhai Vir Singh's Novels', Gurbachan Singh Talib and Attar Singh, eds, *Bhai Vir Singh: Life, Times & Works*, Chandigarh: Panjab University, 1973.

Kosambi, Meera, 'Indian Responses to Christianity, Church and Colonialism. The Case of Pandita Ramabai', *Economic and Political Weekly*, October 24–31, pp. 61–71, 1992.

Kumar, Nita, 'Introduction', Nita Kumar, ed., *Women as Subjects: South Asian Histories*, Charlottesville: University Press of Virginia, 1994.

Kumar, Ravinder, 'Presidential Address: The Two Revolutions of the Punjab', *Punjab History Conference*, Proceedings, Tenth Session, 1976.

Kumar, Ravinder, 'On Gender Theory, The Social Sciences and "Relevant Modernity"', *Manushi*, No. 68, pp. 23–7, 1992.

Lalvani, Tasha, 'The Spirit of Sikh Women', *The Sikh Review*, Vol. 41:10, No. 478, pp. 6–12, 1993.

Lee, Harold, 'John and Henry Lawrence and the Origins of Paternalist Rule in the Punjab, 1846–1858', *International Journal of Punjab Studies*, Vol. 2, No. 1, 1995, pp. 65–88, 1995.

Lewis, Jane, 'Women, Lost and Found: The Impact of Feminism on History', Dale Spender, ed., *Men's Studies Modified: The Impact of Feminism on the Academic Disciplines*, Oxford: Pergamon, 1981.

Loehlin, C.H., 'Some Christian Leaders in the Punjab', *Punjab History Conference*, Proceedings, First Session, 1968.

Lorenzen, David, 'The Lives of Nirguni Saints', David N. Lorenzen, ed., *Bhakti Religion in North India: Community Identity and Political Action*, Albany: SUNY Press, 1995.

MacKenzie, John M., "Heroic Myths of Empire', John M. MacKenzie, ed., *Popular Imperialism and the Military. 1850–1950*, Manchester, Manchester University Press, 1992.

Mani, Lata, 'Contentious Traditions: The Debate on Sati in Colonial India', K. Sangari and S. Vaid, eds, *Recasting Women. Essays in Indian Colonial History*, New Jersey: Rutgers University Press, 1997.

Mansukhani, Gobind Singh, 'Human Equality in Sikhism', *The Sikh Review*, Vol. 39:7, No. 451, pp. 20–8, 1991.

Marriott, McKim, 'Little Communities in an Indigenous Civilization', McKim Marriott, ed., *Village India: Studies in the Little Community*, Chicago: University of Chicago, 1955.

McLeod, W.H., 'The Kukas: A Millenarian Sect of the Punjab', *The Punjab Past and Present*, Vol. 13, No. 1, pp. 164–87, 1979.

———, 'The Problem of the Panjabi Rahit-namas, S.N. Mukherjee, ed., *India: History and Thought: Essays in Honour of A.L. Basham*, Calcutta: Subarnarekha, 1982.

———, 'A Sikh Theology for Modern Times', Joseph O'Connell, Milton Israel, Willard G. Oxtaby, with W.H. McLeod and J.S. Grewal, eds, *Sikh History and Religion in the Twentieth Century*, Toronto: University of Toronto, Centre for South Asian Studies, 1988.

Mehervan Singh, 'Sikh Women: Equality and Spirituality. A Presentation at the Parliament of World's Religions', *The Sikh Review*, Vol. 41:12, No. 480, pp. 16–21, 1993.

Metcalf, Barbara D., 'Reading and Writing about Muslim Women in British

India', Zoya Hasan, ed., *Forging Identities. Gender, Communities and the State in India*, Boulder: Westview, 1994.

Metz, Johann Baptist, 'Prophetic Authority', J. Moltmann, H. W. Richardson, J.B. Metz, W. Oelmuller, and M.D. Bryant, eds, *Religion and Political Society*, New York: Harper & Row, 1974.

Minault, Gail, 'Introduction: The Extended Family as Metaphor and the Expansion of Women's Realm', Gail Minault, ed., *The Extended Family: Women and Political Participation in India and Pakistan*, Delhi: Chanakya, 1981.

———, 'Others Voices, Other Rooms: The View from the Zenana', Nita Kumar, ed., *Women as Subjects: South Asian Histories*, Charlottesville: University Press of Virginia, 1994.

Narenderpal Singh, 'Outstanding Women in Sikhism', Yash Kohli, ed., *The Women of Punjab*, Bombay: Chic Publications, 1983.

Nazer Singh, 'Notes on the Anjuman-Punjab, Aligarh Movement, Brahmo Samaj, Indian Association, Arya Samaj and Singh Sabha in the Context of Colonial Education in the Punjab, 1865–1885', *The Punjab Past and Present*, Vol. 26, No. 1, pp. 35–69, 1992.

Newton, Judith, 'History as Usual? Feminism and the "New Historicism"', *Cultural Critique*, Number 9, Spring, pp. 87–121, 1988.

Nikky Singh, 'Mother in the Guru Granth: A Literary Resource for the Emerging Global Society', *Khera: Journal of Religious Understanding*, Vol. 13, No. 1, pp. 1–17, 1993.

Singh Nikki-Guninder Kaur, 'True Significance of Guru Gobind Singh Recalling Durga', *The Sikh Review*, Vol. 37:7, No. 427, pp. 9–23, 1989.

———, 'Poetics as Hermeneutic Technique in Sikhism', Jeffrey R. Timm, ed., *Texts in Context: Traditional Hermeneutics in South Asia*, Albany: SUNY Press, 1992.

Oberoi, Harjot, 'From Ritual to Counter-Ritual: Rethinking the Hindu-Sikh Question, 1884–1915', Joseph T., O'Connell, Milton Israel, Willard G. Oxtaby, with W.H. McLeod, and J.S. Grewal, eds, *Sikh History and Religion in the Twentieth Century*, Toronto: University of Toronto, Centre for South Asian Studies, 1988.

———, 'Popular Saints, Goddesses, and Village Sacred Sites: Rereading Sikh Experience in the Nineteenth Century', *History of Religions*, Vol. 31, No. 4, pp. 363–84, 1992.

———, 'Brotherhood of the Pure: The Poetics and Politics of Cultural Transgression', *Modern Asian Studies*, Vol. 26, No. 1, pp. 157–97, 1992.

———, 'The Making of a Religious Paradox: Sikh, Khalsa, Sahajdhari as Modes of Early Sikh Identity', David N. Lorenzen, ed., *Bhakti Religion in North India: Community Identity and Political Action*, Albany: SUNY Press, 1995.

Ortner, Sherry B., and Harriet Whitehead, 'Introduction: Accounting for Sexual Meanings', Sherry B. Ortner and Harriet Whitehead, eds, *Sexual Meanings: The Cultural Construction of Gender and Sexuality*, Cambridge: Cambridge University Press, 1981.

Papanek, Hannah, 'The Ideal Woman and the Ideal Society: Control and Autonomy in the Construction of Identity', Valentine M. Moghadam, ed., *Identity Politics and Women. Cultural Reassertions and Feminisms in International Perspective*, Boulder: Westview, 1994.

Pearson, Gail, 'Nationalism, Universalization and the Extended Female Space in Bombay City', Gail Minault, ed., *The Extended Family: Women and Political Participation in India and Pakistan*, Delhi: Chanakya, 1981.

Petrie, D., 'Secret C.I.D. Memorandum on Some Recent Developments in Sikh Politics reprint in *The Punjab Past and Present*, Vol. 4, pp. 301–79.

Puri, Nina, 'The Nationalist Press in the Panjab, 1880–1900, Dayal Singh Majithia and the Tribune', Mohinder Singh, ed., *History and Culture of Panjab*, Delhi: Atlantic, 1989.

Radhakrishnan, R., 'Nationalism, Gender, and the Narrative of Identity', Andrew Parker, Mary Russo, Doris Sommer, and Patricia Yaeger, eds, *Nationalisms & Sexualities*, New York: Routledge, 1992.

Raheja, Gloria Goodwin, 'Women's Speech Genres, Kinship and Contradiction', Nita Kumar, ed., *Women as Subjects: South Asian Histories*, Charlottesville: University Press of Virginia, 1994.

Rai, Satya M., 'Agrarian Movement in the Punjab, 1906–09', *Punjab History Conference*, Proceedings, Eighth Session, 1973.

Ray, Bharati, 'The Freedom Movement and Feminist Consciousness in Bengal, 1905–1929', Bharati Ray, ed., *From the Seams of History: Essays on Indian Women*, Delhi: OUP, 1995.

Richards, Jeffrey, 'Popular Imperialism and the Image of the Army in Juvenile Literature', John M. MacKenzie, ed., *Popular Imperialism and the Military. 1850–1950*, Manchester: Manchester University Press, 1992.

Rogers, Susan Carol, 'Female Forms of Power and the Myth of Male Dominance', *American Ethnologist*, Vol. 2, No. 4, pp. 727–56, 1975.

Roy, Raja Rammohan, 'In Defense of Hindu Women', Theodore de Bary, *Sources of Indian Tradition*, New York: Columbia University Press, 1964.

Sainsara, Gurcharan Singh, 'A Sikh Heroine of the Ghadar Party—Gulab Kaur', *Journal of Sikh Studies*, Vol. 4, No. 2, pp. 93–8, 1977.

Sangari, Kumkum, 'Consent and Agency: Aspects of Feminist Historiography', Kiran Pawar, ed., *Women in Indian History: Social, Economic, Political and Cultural Perspectives*, Delhi: Vision & Venture, 1996.

Schomer, Karine, 'Kabir in the Guru Granth Sahib: An Exploratory Essay', Mark Juergensmeyer and N. Gerald Barrier, eds, *Sikh Studies: Comparative Perspectives on a Changing Tradition*, Berkeley: Graduate Theological Union, Berkeley Religious Studies Series, 1979.

_____, 'Introduction: The Sant Tradition in Perspective', Karine Schomer and W.H. McLeod, eds, *The Sants: Studies in a Devotional Tradition in India*, Berkeley and Delhi: Religions Studies Series and Motilal Banarasidass, 1987.

Shanker, Rajkumari, 'Women in Sikhism', Arvind Sharma, ed., *Religion and Women*, Albany: SUNY Press, 1994.

Sharma, R.K., 'The Unrest of 1907 in the Punjab', *Punjab History Conference*, Proceedings, Sixth Session, 1971.

Short, J., 'The Sikhs', *The Punjab Past and Present*, Vol. 15:2, No. 30, pp. 365–73, 1981.

Narenderpal Singh, 'Outstanding Women in Sikhism', Yash Kohli, ed., *The Women of Punjab*, Bombay: Chic Publications, 1983.

Singha, H.S., 'Sikh Educational Movement: Past and Present', Mohinder Singh, ed., *Prof. Harbans Singh: Commemoration Volume*, New Delhi: Prof. Harbans Singh Commemoration Committee, 1988.

Smith, Hilda, 'Feminism and the Methodology of Women's History', Berenice Carroll, ed., *Liberating Women's History: Theoretical and Critical Essays*, Urbana: University of Illinois Press, 1976.

Smith-Rosenberg, Carrol, 'Writing History: Language, Class, and Gender', Theresa de Lauretis, ed., *Feminist Studies/Critical Studies*, Theories of Contemporary Culture Series, Bloomington: Indiana University Press, 1986.

Springhall, John, 'Building Character in the British Boy: The Attempt to Extend Christian Manliness to Working Class Adolescents, 1880–1914', J.A. Mangan and James Walvin, eds, Manchester, Manchester University Press, 1987.

Suri, Surinder, 'Position of Women in Sikhism', Jyotsna Chatterji, ed., *The Authority of the Religions and the Status of Women*, Delhi: WCSRC–CISRS, 1989.

Talwar, K.S., 'The Anand Marriage Act', *The Punjab Past and Present*, Vol. 2, pp. 400–10, 1968.

Teja Singh, 'The Singh Sabha Movement', Ganda Singh, ed., *The Singh*

Sabha and Other Socio-Religious Movements in the Punjab, 1850–1925: The Panjab Past and Present, Patiala: Punjabi University, 1984.

Vig, I.K., 'Punjab: The Sword Arm of India During the Ancient Period', *Punjab History Conference*, Proceedings, Second Session, 1966.

Wadley, Susan S., 'Hindu Women's Family and Household Rituals in a North Indian Village', Nancy Auer Falk and Rita M. Gross, eds, *Unspoken Worlds: Women's Religious Lives in Non-Western Cultures*, San Francisco: Harper & Row, 1980.

Weber, Max, The Social Psychology & the World Religions', H.H. Gerth and C. Wright Mills, trs and eds, *From Max Weber: Essays in Sociology*, New York: OUP, 1946.

West, Candace and Don H. Zimmerman, 'Doing Gender', Judith Lorber and Susan A. Farrell, eds, *The Social Construction of Gender*, Newbury Park: Sage, 1991.

Whitehead, Judy, 'Modernizing the Motherhood Archetype: Public Health Models and the Child Marriage Restraint Act of 1929', Patricia Uberoi, ed., *Social Reform, Sexuality and the State*, Delhi: Sage, 1996.

Yadav, K.C., 'Presidential Address', *Punjab History Conference*, Proceedings, Twentieth Session, 1986.

Yadav, Kripal Chandra, 'British Policy Towards Sikhs, 1849–57', *Punjab History Conference*, Proceedings, Second Session, 1966.

Yang, Anand, 'The Many Faces of Sati in the Early Nineteenth Century', *Manushi*, No. 42–3, 1987.

Young, Katherine K., 'Hinduism', Arvind Sharma, ed., *Women in World Religions*, Albany: SUNY Press, 1987.

_____, 'Women in Hinduism', Arvind Sharma, ed., *Today's Woman in World Religions*, Albany: SUNY Press, 1994.

NEWSPAPERS, JOURNALS

Punjabi Bhain (1908–1930)
Khalsa Advocate (1903–1922).

DICTIONARIES

Bhai Maya Singh, *The Punjabi Dictionary*, Delhi: National Book Shop, 1992. First published in 1895.

Janver, L., ed., *Dictionary of the Punjabi Language*, Delhi: Nirmal, 1987. First published in 1854.

Nabha, Kahn Singh, *Mahan Kosh*, Patiala: Language Department, 1993. First published in 1930.

Turner, R.L., *A Comparative Dictionary of the Indo-Aryan Languages*, London: OUP, 1966.

Unpublished Theses

Dhillon, Gurdarshan Singh, 'Character and Impact of the Singh Sabha Movement on the History of the Punjab', unpublished PhD thesis, Patiala: Punjabi University, 1973.

Hans, Surjit Singh, 'Historical Analysis of Sikh Literature, AD 1500–1850', Unpublished PhD. thesis, Amritsar: Guru Nanak Dev University, 1980.

Kaur, Amarjit 'The Nascent Sikh Politics: 1919–1921', unpublished PhD thesis, Amritsar: Guru Nanak Dev University, 1992.

Kaur, Gurpreet, 'Historical Analysis of Sikh Rahitnamas', unpublished PhD dissertation, Amritsar: Guru Nanak Dev University, 1988.

Sidhu, Govinder Kaur, 'A Historical Study of the Development of Female Education in Punjab Since 1849', unpublished PhD thesis, Amritsar: Guru Nanak Dev University, 1985.

Varma, Archana, 'Status and Migration among the Punjabis of Paldi, British Columbia, and Paldi, Punjab', unpublished PhD dissertation, Burnaby: Simon Fraser University, 1994.

INDEX

Accommodation, principle of, 3,
12-16
Acker, Joan, 47
Adi Granth, 4, 11, 18, 25-6, 29, 34,
45, 47, 76, 92, 154, 220, 223
Ahluwalia, M.M., 88, 115
Aitchinson College, 93
Aiyanger, 25
Ajit Singh, 171-3
Akal Purakh concept, 60
Akali, The, 190, 209, 214, 230
Akali Dal, 248
Akalis, 111, 229
Akbar, 30
Akhbar-i-Anjuman-i-Punjab, 94
Algeria, role and status of women
in, 12-13
Algerian reformers, 12, 14
Alienation of Land Bill 1900,
124, 138
Aligarh movement, 94
All India Conference of Religions,
Allahabad, 240
Amar Das, Guru, 29-31, 33, 40,
76, 154, 179, 181
American Presbyterian Mission,
Ludhiana, 129
American Tract Society, 161
Amritsar Dharm Sabha, 4, 105-9,
117-18, 122, 202
Amritsar Singh Sabha, 91-3, 95,

97-8, 119, 130-2, 185,
214, 216
Amro, Bibi, 29
Anand, Mulk Raj, 139
Anand Marriage Act of 1909, 179,
190
Anand Marriage Bill, 179-94,
199, 248
Anand (marriage ceremony),
112, 122
Anandpur, battle of, 48
Angad, Guru, 29
Anglo-Sikh War 1845, 58, 87
Anjuman-i-Islamia, 148
Anjuman-i-Punjab, 89-90, 94
Arjan, Guru, 35-6, 247
Arjan Singh, Bawa, 95
Arora, A.C., 80
Arya Gazette, 180
Arya Messenger, 95
Arya Patrika, 95
Arya Samaj, 94-5, 98, 122 143-4,
147-9, 151, 153-60, 168,
172-4, 176, 180, 182, 184,
188, 239, 241, 247
Arya Samaj movement, 5, 119,
121-5
Aryan race, propagation of, 55,
67, 73, 120-21, 132
Ashta, Dharam Pal, 44-5
Askour, Rani, 79